ALSO BY

DAVID MCCULLOUGH

The Greater Journey

1776

John Adams

Truman

Brave Companions

Mornings on Horseback

The Path Between the Seas

The Great Bridge

The Johnstown Flood

THE
Wright Brothers

THE
Wright Brothers

The Dramatic Story
Behind the Legend

David McCullough

**SIMON &
SCHUSTER**

London · New York · Sydney · Toronto · New Delhi

A CBS COMPANY

First published in Great Britain by Simon & Schuster UK Ltd, 2015
A CBS COMPANY

Copyright © 2015 by David McCullough

1 3 5 7 9 10 8 6 4 2

Simon & Schuster UK Ltd
1st Floor
222 Gray's Inn Road
London WC1X 8HB

www.simonandschuster.co.uk

Simon & Schuster Australia, Sydney
Simon & Schuster India, New Delhi

A CIP catalogue copy for this book
is availablefrom the British Library.

ISBN: 978-1-4711-5036-4
eBook ISBN: 978-1-4711-5039-5

Interior design by Amy Hill

Front endpaper: The Wright Brothers confer beside their 1904 airplane at their
cow-pasture testing ground, Huffman Prairie, outside Dayton.
Back endpaper: Wilbur Wright flies past New York City on his October 4, 1909
flight up to the Hudson River and back, a spectacle like none ever
before and witnessed by more than a million people.
Both endpapers courtesy of Special Collections and Archives,
Wright State University

Printed and bound by CPI Group (UK) Ltd, Croydon, CR0 4YY

For Rosalee

No bird soars in a calm.

WILBUR WRIGHT

CONTENTS

THE
Wright Brothers

PROLOGUE

From ancient times and into the Middle Ages, man had dreamed of taking to the sky, of soaring into the blue like the birds. One savant in Spain in the year 875 is known to have covered himself with feathers in the attempt. Others devised wings of their own design and jumped from rooftops and towers—some to their deaths—in Constantinople, Nuremberg, Perugia. Learned monks conceived schemes on paper. And starting about 1490, Leonardo da Vinci made the most serious studies. He felt predestined to study flight, he said, and related a childhood memory of a kite flying down onto his cradle.

According to brothers Wilbur and Orville Wright of Dayton, Ohio, it began for them with a toy from France, a small helicopter brought home by their father, Bishop Milton Wright, a great believer in the educational value of toys. The creation of a French experimenter of the nineteenth century, Alphonse Pénaud, it was little more than a stick with twin propellers and twisted rubber bands, and probably cost 50 cents. "Look here, boys," said the Bishop, something concealed in his hands. When he let go it flew to the ceiling. They called it the "bat."

Orville's first teacher in grade school, Ida Palmer, would remember him at his desk tinkering with bits of wood. Asked what he was up to, he told her he was making a machine of a kind that he and his brother were going to fly someday.

Part I

Beginnings

If I were giving a young man advice as to how he might succeed in life, I would say to him, pick out a good father and mother, and begin life in Ohio.

WILBUR WRIGHT

I.

In as strong a photograph as any taken of the brothers together, they sit side by side on the back porch steps of the Wright family home on a small side street on the west end of Dayton, Ohio. The year was 1909, the peak of their fame. Wilbur was forty-two, Orville thirty-eight. Wilbur, with a long poker face, looks off to one side, as though his mind were on other things, which most likely it was. He is lean, almost gaunt, long of nose and chin, clean-shaven, and bald. He wears a plain dark suit and high-laced shoes, much in the manner of their preacher father.

Orville gazes straight at the camera, one leg crossed nonchalantly over the other. He is a bit stouter and younger-looking than his brother and has a touch more hair, in addition to a well-trimmed mustache. He wears a lighter-toned, noticeably better-tailored suit, snappy argyle socks, and wingtips. The argyles were about as far in the direction of frippery as any of the Wright men would ever go. Prominent, too, in the pose, appropriately, are the hands, the highly skilled hands that, by the time the picture was taken, had played a substantial part in bringing miraculous change to the world.

To judge by the expressions on their faces, they had little if any sense of humor, which was hardly the case. Neither liked having his picture taken. "Truth to tell," one reporter wrote, "the camera is no friend either to the brothers." But what is most uncharacteristic about the pose is that they sit doing nothing, something they almost never succumbed to.

As others in Dayton knew, the two were remarkably self-contained, ever industrious, and virtually inseparable. "Inseparable as twins," their father would say, and "indispensable" to each other.

They lived in the same house, worked together six days a week, ate their meals together, kept their money in a joint bank account, even "thought together," Wilbur said. Their eyes were the same gray-blue, though Orville's were less predominant and closer together. Their handwriting was quite alike—consistently straight and legible—and their voices so alike that someone hearing them from another room had trouble knowing which was doing the talking.

If Orville was always noticeably better dressed, Wilbur, at five feet ten, stood an inch or so taller and as would be said more often in France than Dayton, women found him somewhat mysterious and quite attractive.

Both loved music—Wilbur played the harmonica, Orville, the mandolin. At work they sometimes found themselves spontaneously whistling or humming the same tune at the same time. Both were strongly attached to home. Both liked to cook. Biscuits and candy were Orville's specialties. Wilbur took pride in his gravy, and for the Thanksgiving or Christmas turkey insisted on taking charge of the stuffing.

Like the father and their sister Katharine, the brothers had tremendous energy, and working hard every day but Sunday was a way of life, and if not on the job then at home on "improvements." Hard work was a conviction, and they were at their best and happiest working together on their own projects at the same waist-high bench, wearing shop aprons to protect their suits and ties.

Everything considered, they got along well, each aware of what the other brought to the task at hand, each long familiar with the other's particular nature, and always with the unspoken understanding that Wilbur, the older by four years, was the senior member of the partnership, the big brother.

Not that things always went smoothly. They could be highly demanding and critical of each other, disagree to the point of shouting "something terrible." At times, after an hour or more of heated argument, they would find themselves as far from agreement as when they started, except that each had changed to the other's original position.

As often said, neither ever chose to be anything other than himself, a quality that rated high in Ohio. Not only did they have no yearning for the limelight, they did their best to avoid it. And with the onset of fame, both remained notably modest.

Yet in a number of ways they were unidentical twins. There were differences, some obvious, others less so. Where Orville moved at a more or less normal pace, Wilbur was "tremendously active of movement," gesturing vigorously with his hands when making a point, walking always with a long, rapid stride. Wilbur was more serious by nature, more studious and reflective. His memory of what he had seen and heard, and so much that he read, was astonishing. "I have no memory at all," Orville was frank to say, "but he never forgets anything."

Such were Wilbur's powers of concentration that to some he seemed a little strange. He could cut himself off from everyone. "The strongest impression one gets of Wilbur Wright," an old schoolmate said, "is of a man who lives largely in a world of his own." Morning after morning, lost in thought, he would hurry out the door without his hat, only to reappear five minutes later to retrieve it.

Wilbur also, it was agreed, had "unusual presence," and remained imperturbable under almost any circumstance, "never rattled," his father was proud to say. He was an exceptional public speaker and lucid writer, which seemed out of context for someone so often silent, and though reluctant to speak in public, when he did his remarks were invariably articulate, to the point, and quite often memorable. In his professional correspondence, the innumerable proposals and reports he wrote, and in private correspondence no less, his vocabulary and use of language were of the highest order, due in large measure to standards long insisted upon by his father.

It had proven an ability of utmost importance to his and his brother's unprecedented accomplishments.

"Will seems to enjoy writing, so I leave all the literary part of our work to him," Orville would explain. In fact, Orville, too, greatly enjoyed writing, though in family correspondence primarily, and especially in letters to Katharine he did so with spirit and humor. That Wilbur, in the early stages of their enterprise, wrote nearly all letters concerning their interests in the first person, as if he were operating entirely on his own, seems not to have bothered Orville in the least.

Orville was the more gentle of the two. Though talkative and entertaining at home, often a tease, outside the house he was painfully shy, something inherited from their deceased mother, and refused to take any public role, leaving all that to Wilbur. But he was also the more cheerful, the more optimistic and naturally entrepreneurial, and his remarkable mechanical ingenuity figured importantly in all their projects.

Where Wilbur was little bothered by what others might be thinking or saying, Orville was extremely sensitive to criticism or mockery of any kind. Then, too, Orville had what were referred to within the family as his "peculiar spells," times when, overtired or feeling put-upon, he could turn uncharacteristically moody and irritable.

In public gatherings, it was invariably Wilbur who attracted the most attention, even if he had little to say. "By comparison," one observer wrote, "Mr. Orville Wright does not possess any pronouncedly distinctive personality. That is to say, your eye would not be drawn to him among a crowd of men in the fashion in which it would instinctively dwell on Mr. Wilbur."

Like their father, they were always perfect gentlemen, naturally courteous to all. They neither drank hard liquor nor smoked or gambled, and both remained, as their father liked to say, "independently" Republican. They were bachelors and by all signs intended to remain so. Orville liked to say it was up to Wilbur to marry first, he being the older. Wilbur professed to have no time yet for a wife. To others he seemed "woman-shy." As remembered one associate, Wilbur could "get awfully nervous" whenever young women were around.

What the two had in common above all was unity of purpose and unyielding determination. They had set themselves on a "mission."

They lived still at home with their father, an itinerant clergyman who was often away on church work, and their sister Katharine. Younger than Orville by three years, she was bright, personable, highly opinionated, the only college graduate in the family, and of the three still at home, much the most sociable. After finishing at Ohio's Oberlin College in 1898, she had returned to Dayton to teach Latin at the new Steele High School, where, Orville noted, she would flunk many of Dayton's future leaders. As she herself said of those she judged to be "notoriously bad" boys, "I nipped their smartness in the bud."

Neat and trim, with her gold-rimmed, pince-nez glasses, and dark hair tied back in a bun, she looked every bit the schoolteacher. "Of the sawed-off variety," as she said, she stood a bit over five feet, and all who knew her knew what a force she was. In a household of three men and one woman, she more than held her own. She was the most vivacious of the family, a tireless, all-season talker, and they all adored her for that. It was she who brought home her college friends and put on parties. Being the nearest in age, she and Orville were particularly close. They had the same birthday, August 19, and they had both been born there in the same house.

Bothered more by human failings than were her brothers, Katharine could turn "wrathy." Orville's practicing on the mandolin could set her off in grand fashion. "He sits around and picks that thing until I can hardly stay in the house," she complained to their father. "You have a good mind and a good heart," he would tell her. Still he worried. "I am especially anxious that you cultivate modest feminine manners and control your temper, for temper is a hard master."

To their friends they were Will, Orv, and Katie. Among themselves Wilbur was Ullam; Orville, Bubbo or Bubs; and Katharine, Sterchens, a variation of the German word *schwerchens*, meaning "little sister." Two brothers older than the three at home—Reuchlin and Lorin—were married and had families of their own. Reuchlin had moved to a farm in Kansas. Lorin, a bookkeeper, with his wife, Netta, and their four children, Milton, Ivonette, Leontine, and Horace, lived just around the corner from 7 Hawthorn Street. That both Lorin and Reuchlin had kept moving from job to job, trying to make ends meet for their families, appears to have given Wilbur and Orville further reason to remain single.

Their deceased mother, Susan Koerner Wright, had been born in Virginia, the daughter of a German wagon maker, and brought west as a child. Her children described her as highly intelligent, affectionate, and painfully shy. It was said that on her first visit to a grocery store after her marriage, when asked to whom the items should be delivered, she forgot her new name. But she was also cheerful and keen-witted, and to her family a "regular genius" in that she could make anything, and toys especially, even a sled, "as good as a store kind.

> She was the most understanding woman [wrote Katharine]. She recognized something unusual in Will and Orv, though she loved us all. She never would destroy one thing the boys were trying to make. Any little thing they left around in her way she picked up and put on a shelf in the kitchen.

The mechanical aptitude of "the boys," they all knew, came directly from their mother, quite as much as Orville's shyness. Her death, from tuberculosis in 1889, had been the worst blow the family had ever known.

Bishop Milton Wright was a devoted father abundantly supplied with strong opinions and words to the wise, a middle-sized, dignified figure with a full, gray patriarchal beard, but no mustache, who liked to comb his thin gray hair most carefully over the top of his bald head. As with Wilbur, his characteristic "grave countenance" was not necessarily the best way to judge his mood of the moment or how he viewed life.

He had been born in a log cabin in Indiana in 1828 and had grown up with frontier ways and values. Though little is known about his mother, Catherine, his father, Dan Wright, a farmer and Revolutionary War veteran, had been a hero in the boy's eyes. "He was grave in countenance, collected in his manners, hesitating in his speech, but very accurate," by Milton's account. He was an unyielding abstainer, which was rare on the frontier, a man of rectitude and purpose—all of which could have served as a description of Milton himself and Wilbur and Orville as well.

At age nineteen, Milton had joined the United Brethren Church in

Christ, a Protestant denomination. He preached his first sermon at twenty-two and was ordained at twenty-four. Though he took several courses in a small college run by the church, he was not a college graduate. Founded before the Civil War, the United Brethren Church was adamant about certain causes—the abolition of slavery, women's rights, and opposition to Freemasonry and its secretive ways—and so Milton Wright remained in his convictions, as all who knew him were aware.

His work as an itinerant preacher had taken him far and wide, by horseback and train, and he had seen as much of the country as almost anyone of his generation. Sailing from New York to Panama in 1857, he had crossed the isthmus by rail on his way to two years of teaching in a church school in Oregon.

He and Susan had been married in Fayette County, Indiana, close to the Ohio line, in 1859, and settled on a farm at Fairmont, Indiana, where their two oldest sons were born. In 1867, they moved to a five-room, frame farmhouse in Millville, Indiana, and it was there, on April 16, that Susan gave birth to Wilbur. (Both Wilbur and Orville were named for clergymen greatly admired by their father, Wilbur Fiske and Orville Dewey.)

A year later, the family moved to Hartsville, Indiana, and the year after that, 1869, to Dayton, where they bought the then new house on Hawthorn Street. The Reverend Milton Wright had been made editor of United Brethren's national weekly newspaper, *The Religious Telescope*, published in Dayton, and this had meant a major increase of his annual income, from $900 to $1,500.

In 1877, after Milton was elected a bishop and his duties with the church were increased still more, he and Susan leased the house and moved the family to Cedar Rapids, Iowa. Responsible now for the whole of the church's West Mississippi District, he would help plan and attend conferences from the Mississippi to the Rockies, traveling thousands of miles a year. In another four years, they moved still again, to Richmond, Indiana, where ten-year-old Orville began making kites for fun and for sale, and Wilbur started high school. Not until 1884 was the family able to return to Dayton to stay.

With a population of nearly forty thousand, Dayton had become Ohio's fifth largest city and was growing steadily. It had a new hospital, a new courthouse, and was up with the rest of the country in the use of electric streetlights. A grand new public library in the fashionable Romanesque style was under way. In another several years the new high school would be built, a turreted, five-story brick building that would have been the pride of any university campus. As was said in Dayton, these were buildings proclaiming "a devotion to something beyond mere material splendor."

Located on a broad, rolling floodplain in southwestern Ohio on the eastern bank of a great curve in the Miami River, fifty miles north of Cincinnati, Dayton had been settled by Revolutionary War veterans at the end of the eighteenth century and named for one of the original investors in the site, Jonathan Dayton, a veteran, a member of Congress from New Jersey, and a signer of the U.S. Constitution. Until the arrival of the railroads the town had been slow taking hold.

Once, in 1859, the front lawn of the old Greek Revival courthouse was the setting for a speech by Abraham Lincoln. Otherwise not a great deal of historic interest had taken place in Dayton. It was, however, spoken of proudly as a fine place to live, work, and raise a family, as indeed was all of Ohio. Was Ohio not the native state of three presidents thus far? And of Thomas Edison? Another of Dayton's notable sons, William Dean Howells, editor of *The Atlantic Monthly*, had written that the people of Ohio were the sort of idealists who had "the courage of their dreams."

> By this courage they have made the best of them come true, and it is well for them in their mainly matter-of-fact and practical character that they show themselves at times enthusiasts and even fanatics.

In a speech years later Wilbur would remark that if he were to give a young man advice on how to get ahead in life, he would say, "Pick out a good father and mother, and begin life in Ohio."

If, in 1884, a new railroad station was plainly in need and most of the streets in town were still unpaved, the prospects for future prosperity were brighter than ever. Most importantly, the National Cash Register Company had been founded and was thriving. In little time it would become the largest manufacturer of its kind in the world. Bishop Wright knew his life on the road would continue half the year or more. Nonetheless, there was never a question that Dayton was home.

———

An important part of the family's education in geography, not to say a continuing stimulant for their curiosity, was supplied by the Bishop in long letters written during his travels, often while on board a train. However far his travels, his love of his country and its splendors remained abundantly evident. Minneapolis and St. Paul were "cities of marvelous growth, in a wonderful wheat-producing country." He wrote with enthusiasm and amazement. So steep were the grades over the mountains west of Missoula that three locomotives were required, two in front, one behind, he reported to those at home. His world, and consequently theirs, kept growing. "Yesterday, I came down here, starting at 1:40 a.m.," he reported in a letter mailed from Biggs, California.

> You ought to have seen [the] Siskiyou mountains which we crossed yesterday on the cars. We rose pretty high, and to make grades, wound about for miles to get only a few. After a mile's run we would come back to 200 feet from where we were before, about 175 feet higher up. We [ran] through several tunnels, but none long, the last at the summit being the longest. It is the grandest scenery and highest rapid grade I ever went through.

From wide reading and observations of life, he had acquired what seemed an inexhaustible supply of advice on behavior, habits good and bad, things to beware of in life, goals to strive for. He lectured on dress, cleanliness, economy. At home he preached courage and good character— "good mettle," as he would say—worthy purpose and perseverance. Providing guidelines he understood to be part of a father's duty.

> It is assumed that young folks know best, and old folks are fogies. It may be so, but old folks may be as right about new fangles as young folks are about fogy ways.

Make business first, pleasure afterward, and that guarded.
All the money anyone needs is just enough to prevent one
from being a burden on others.

He made a point of treating the three of his children at home with
equal consideration and affection, praising each for his or her particular
talents or contributions to the family. But plainly his favorite was Wilbur,
"the apple of his eye," as Katharine said.

Wilbur had also been the cause of the greatest worry. In his youth
he had excelled in everything. He had been a star athlete—in football,
skating, and gymnastics especially—and outstanding as a student. In
his last full year of high school in Dayton, his grades were in the 90s in
everything—algebra, botany, chemistry, English composition, geology,
geometry, and Latin. There was talk of his going to Yale.

But all such plans ended when, playing hockey on a frozen lake beside
the Dayton Soldiers' Home, Wilbur was smashed in the face with a stick,
knocking out most of his upper front teeth.

What exactly happened is hard to determine, but to judge from the
little that is known, there is much more to the story. According to an entry
in Bishop Wright's diary written years afterward, in 1913, the "man who
threw the bat that struck Wilbur" became one of the most notorious mur-
derers in the history of Ohio, Oliver Crook Haugh, who, in 1906, was ex-
ecuted for the murders of his mother, father, and brother, and was believed
to have killed as many as a dozen others besides.

At the time of the hockey incident, Haugh lived just two blocks from
the Wrights. He was only fifteen, or three years younger than Wilbur, but
as big as a man and known as the neighborhood bully. As would be written
in the *Dayton Journal* following his execution, "Oliver never was without
the wish to inflict pain or at least discomfort on others."

Whether he "threw" the stick at Wilbur accidentally or intentionally
is impossible to determine. But it is known that he was then working in
a drugstore on West Third Street and that the druggist, in an effort to
relieve him of the pain of rotting teeth, was providing him with a popular
cure of the day, "Cocaine Toothache Drops." In little time young Haugh
became so dependent on drugs and alcohol, his behavior so out of control

that he had to be committed for several months to the Dayton Asylum for the Insane.

Wilbur undoubtedly knew him, but how well, or whether Haugh had some sort of score to settle with Wilbur, or was under the influence of drugs at the time of the incident, are all unknown. Except for Bishop Wright's brief diary mention, nothing on the subject is to be found anywhere in the Wright family correspondence or reminiscences. Nor is there much in the way of detail or firsthand description about the devastating after-effect of the accident on Wilbur. The whole episode seems to have been something the family wished to put behind them and remains a dark corner in Wilbur's life about which too little is known. But clearly it changed the course of his life.

For weeks he suffered excruciating pain in his face and jaw, then had to be fitted with false teeth. Serious digestive complications followed, then heart palpitations and spells of depression that seemed only to lengthen. Everybody grew more and more concerned. All talk of Yale ended. His ailing mother did what she could to care for him, but as her own health kept steadily deteriorating, he began looking after her.

"Such devotion of a son had rarely been equaled," wrote the Bishop, who would credit Wilbur with lengthening her life at least two years. In the morning she usually felt strong enough to come down, with some help, to the first floor, but at night Wilbur would have to carry her back upstairs.

Brother Lorin seems to have been the only one who disapproved. "What does Will do?" he wrote Katharine from Kansas, where he had gone to seek his fortune. "He ought to be doing something. Is he still cook and chambermaid?"

Wilbur remained a recluse, more or less homebound, for fully three years—three years when he began reading as never before.

———

The Wright house at 7 Hawthorn Street, the setting of so much of the family's life, was modest in size and appearance, and located in a comparably modest neighborhood. Like much of Dayton, Hawthorn Street remained unpaved until shortly after the turn of the century, and Number 7, with two linden trees and a stone hitching post in front, was a narrow, white frame structure very like others on the street, except for a decorative, wraparound front porch built by the brothers.

There were seven rooms, three downstairs, four up, all of them small, as was the lot. Only two feet separated the house from Number 5 next door on the north side. To get between the houses required one to turn and walk sideways.

The brothers were well into their twenties before there was running water or plumbing in the house. Weekly baths were accomplished sitting in a tub of hot water on the kitchen floor, with the curtains drawn. An open well and wooden pump, outhouse, and carriage shed were out back. There was no electricity. Meals were cooked on a wood stove. Heat and light were provided by natural gas. House and property had a total value of perhaps $1,800.

The front door opened from the porch into a small, formal front parlor, but most everyone came and went by a side door on the porch that opened into the sitting room. From there the front parlor was to the right, dining room and kitchen to the left. A narrow carpeted stairway led to the bedrooms above.

The first-floor furnishings were all of the inexpensive Victorian variety to be found in homes throughout Ohio, or for that matter nearly everywhere in the country at the time—the lace curtains at the windows in the front parlor, the upholstered wooden rockers and Gilbert clock on the mantelpiece that chimed every hour and half hour, the mirrored oak sideboard in the dining room. High ceilings and the modest scale and simplicity of the furnishings made the rooms considerably less cramped in feeling than they might have been.

The decor upstairs consisted of bare essentials only—beds, bureaus, chamber pots—with the exception of the bookcase and rolltop desk in the Bishop's cluttered bedroom at the front of the house overlooking the street. Wilbur slept in the room in the middle, Orville and Katharine in the two rooms at back. Since the gas fireplaces downstairs provided the only heat, bedroom doors upstairs had to be kept wide open during cold weather.

With the tracks of the Dayton Western and Union Railroad only blocks away, the sound of train whistles was part of the night in all seasons. The smell of coal smoke in the air was the smell of home.

The Wright family book collection, however, was neither modest nor commonplace. Bishop Wright, a lifelong lover of books, heartily championed the limitless value of reading.

Between formal education at school and informal education at home, it would seem he put more value on the latter. He was never overly concerned about his children's attendance at school. If one or the other of them chose to miss a day or two for some project or interest he thought worthy, it was all right. And certainly he ranked reading as worthy.

Those works he considered "very serious," on theology mostly, were in his bedroom, the rest, the majority, proudly in evidence in the sitting room in a tall, glass-fronted bookcase. There could be found the works of Dickens, Washington Irving, Hawthorne, Mark Twain, a complete set of the works of Sir Walter Scott, the poems of Virgil, Plutarch's *Lives*, Milton's *Paradise Lost*, Boswell's *Life of Johnson*, Gibbon's *Decline and Fall of the Roman Empire*, and Thucydides. There were books on natural history, American history, a six-volume history of France, travel, *The Instructive Speller*, Darwin's *On the Origin of Species*, plus two full sets of encyclopedias.

Everyone in the house read all the time. Katharine favored the novels of Sir Walter Scott; Orville, Hawthorne's *The House of the Seven Gables*, while Wilbur—and particularly during his homebound lacuna—read just about everything, but had a particular love of history.

In those interludes when the Bishop was at home, he insisted on time with his books or he could be found at the public library pursuing his love of genealogy. As one who so strongly believed in the importance of family, he could not know enough about those from whom he and his children were descended. He wanted to make them aware of that, too, just as he wanted them to have open and receptive minds and to think for themselves. As said, his was a mind that never slowed down. "He talked very freely to his children on all subjects," Orville would say, "except money making, a matter to which he gave little consideration."

Included among the ecclesiastical works on his bedroom shelves were the writings of "The Great Agnostic," Robert Ingersoll, whom the brothers and Katharine were encouraged to read. "Every mind should be true to itself—should think, investigate and conclude for itself," wrote Ingersoll. It was the influence of Ingersoll apparently that led the brothers to give up regular attendance at church, a change the Bishop seems to have accepted without protest.

Interestingly, for all the Bishop's dedication to church work, religion was scarcely ever mentioned in his letters to his children, or in what they wrote to him. No framed religious images or biblical quotations were part of the home decor, with the exception of a color print of Saint Dorothy, hanging to the left of the fireplace in the front parlor, but that was the part of the room where Orville customarily propped his mandolin against the wall, and she was the patron saint of music.

Years later, a friend told Orville that he and his brother would always stand as an example of how far Americans with no special advantages could advance in the world. "But it isn't true," Orville responded emphatically, "to say we had no special advantages . . . the greatest thing in our favor was growing up in a family where there was always much encouragement to intellectual curiosity."

II.

In early 1889, while still in high school, Orville started his own print shop in the carriage shed behind the house, and apparently with no objections from the Bishop. Interested in printing for some while, Orville had worked for two summers as an apprentice at a local print shop. He designed and built his own press using a discarded tombstone, a buggy spring, and scrap metal. "My father and brother seeing my determination to become a printer, managed after a while to get a small printing press for me," Orville later explained, and with the help of Wilbur, who was ready to resume life again, he began publishing a newspaper, the *West Side News*, devoted to the goings-on and interests of their part of Dayton on the west side of the river.

A first edition of four pages appeared on March 1 carrying the advertisements of seventeen local establishments, including F. P. Nipkin's drugstore, W. A. Lincoln's Dry Goods (offering "BIG BARGAINS"), Winder's Grocery, the Cleveland Laundry, and the H. Ruse Feed Store. Orville was listed as publisher. The subscription rate was 45 cents a year, or two weeks for 10 cents.

The editorial content for this and the editions that followed consisted mainly of one short article of general interest along with numerous bits and pieces of local news, these selected by Wilbur apparently. One could read of a freight car breaking down on the Wolf Creek bridge or that the Shakespearean reading by Professor C. L. Loos at the high school was widely appreciated by the large audience present, that the trunk factory of W. I. Denny had burned to the ground, or that George La Rue of South Hawthorn Street had presented his large collection of bird eggs to the public library. Or that Miss Carrie B. Osterday of West Third Street, and G. J. Nicholas and Tula Paisly Street were all sick with typhoid fever. Or that police officers O'Brien, Urmey, and Kitzelman had arrested Ed Kimmel and another boy for stealing chickens.

At the same time one could also find mention of the disastrous flood at Johnstown, Pennsylvania, or the completion of the Eiffel Tower in Paris.

Now and then the brothers would include items from other publications that they judged worthy of the readers' attention, such as one titled "Encourage Your Boy," reprinted from *Architect and Building News*.

> Do not wait for the boy to grow up before you begin to treat him as an equal. A proper amount of confidence, and words of encouragement and advice . . . give him to understand that you trust him in many ways, helps to make a man of him long before he is a man in either stature or years. . . .
>
> If a boy finds he can make a few articles with his hands, it tends to make him rely on himself. And the planning that is necessary for the execution of the work is a discipline and an education of great value to him.

By the end of April, with the paper showing some profit, Orville moved the business to a rented space on West Third Street, where the city's electric trolley ran, and Wilbur, now twenty-two, was prominently listed as editor.

A high school friend of Orville's, Paul Laurence Dunbar, who had been the class poet and the only black student in the school, became a contributor to the *West Side News*. Later, when Dunbar proposed doing a weekly paper for the black community, Orville and Wilbur printed it on credit, but it lasted only a short time.

At some point, Dunbar is said to have chalked on the shop wall this quatrain tribute:

> Orville Wright is out of sight
> In the printing business.
> No other mind is half so bright
> as his'n is.

In 1893, through the influence of Bishop Wright, a first collection of Dunbar's poems was published by the United Brethren Church, for which Dunbar himself paid the cost of $125. In another few years, having been discovered by the editor of *The Atlantic Monthly*, William Dean Howells, Dunbar had become a nationally acclaimed poet.

That July of 1889 the paper carried the obituary of Susan Koerner Wright. Which brother wrote it is unknown. Most likely it was a joint effort. She had died at home on July 4, at age fifty-eight, after an eight-year struggle with tuberculosis.

> She was of retiring disposition, very timid and averse to making any display in public, hence her true worth and highest qualities were most thoroughly appreciated by her family.

She was buried two days later at Woodland Cemetery, her whole family present. Never afterward was July 4 to be a day of celebration in the family. As the Bishop would write in another July to come: "The Fourth had its Chinese firecrackers . . . [and] Hawthorn Street furnished several displays, but No. 7 was not patriotic. Not a drum was heard, not a flag was [un]furled, and not a firecracker snapped there."

———

A year later, the brothers changed the name of their paper to *The Evening Item*, and the year following the *Item* ceased and they concentrated on making money as job printers.

The printing business had been Orville's idea from the start, and he enjoyed it most, working as hard as he could. But he seems to have found Wilbur's performance lacking. "We've been so busy for the past few weeks that we've had very little time to write," Orville reported to their father in the fall of 1892. "I've been making $2.00 to $3.25 a day in the office, but I have to divide it with Will so that when the week is over I don't have much left. Will's working on the press, at least he says he is, but I can see little signs of it from the appearance of things." At home, however, he reassured the Bishop, they were "getting along real well."

With Katharine away at college by this time, they had no choice but to get by domestically as best they could and in this they succeeded in good, even high spirits, to judge by a letter from Wilbur to Katharine.

> We have been living fine since you left. Orville cooks one week and I cook the next. Orville's week we have bread and butter and meat and gravy and coffee three times a day. My week I give him more variety. You see that by the end of his week there is a big lot of cold meat stored up, so the first half of my week we have bread and butter and "hash" and coffee, and the last half we have bread and butter and eggs and sweet potatoes and coffee. We don't fuss a bit about whose week it is to cook. Perhaps the reason is evident. If Mrs. Jack Sprat had undertaken to cook all fat, I guess Jack wouldn't have kicked on cooking every other week either.

About this time, too, they decided to proceed with major changes in the house, building the spacious wraparound porch. They installed new larger windows downstairs, shutters for the windows upstairs, doing all of it themselves.

Importantly, like much of the country, they had also taken up bicycling, and as Wilbur reported, they had lately headed off on a "run" to the south, down the Cincinnati Pike, stopping at the County Fair Grounds to pump around the track several times. From there they continued on to Miamisburg up and over numerous steep hills to see the famous prehistoric Adena Miamisburg Mound, largest of Ohio's famous conical-shaped reminders of a vanished Native American civilization dating back more than two thousand years. In all they covered thirty-one miles.

Bicycles had become the sensation of the time, a craze everywhere. (These were no longer the "high wheelers" of the 1870s and '80s, but the so-called "safety bicycles," with two wheels the same size.) The bicycle was proclaimed a boon to all mankind, a thing of beauty, good for the spirits, good for health and vitality, indeed one's whole outlook on life. Doctors enthusiastically approved. One Philadelphia physician, writing in *The American Journal of Obstetrics and Diseases of Women and Children*, concluded from his observations that "for physical exercise for both men and women, the bicycle is one of the greatest inventions of the nineteenth century."

Voices were raised in protest. Bicycles were proclaimed morally hazardous. Until now children and youth were unable to stray very far from home on foot. Now, one magazine warned, fifteen minutes could put them miles away. Because of bicycles, it was said, young people were not spending the time they should with books, and more seriously that suburban and country tours on bicycles were "not infrequently accompanied by seductions."

Such concerns had little effect. Everybody was riding bicycles, men, women, all ages and from all walks of life. Bicycling clubs sprouted on college campuses and in countless cities and towns, including Dayton. At Oberlin College, Katharine and a group of her fellow co-eds would pose for a memorable photograph with their new bicycles. Each looked highly pleased, but Katharine beamed with the biggest smile.

———

In the spring of 1893 Wilbur and Orville opened their own small bicycle business, the Wright Cycle Exchange, selling and repairing bicycles only a short walk from the house at 1005 West Third Street. In no time, such was business, they moved to larger quarters down the street to Number 1034 and renamed the enterprise the Wright Cycle Company.

Of the two brothers, Orville loved bicycles the most. As an admirer who knew him in later years would say, "Bring up the subject of the shapes of handlebars or types of pedals on early 'safety bicycles' and his whole face lights up."

Ever enterprising, incapable of remaining idle, the brothers now turned their off-hours to redoing the interior of 7 Hawthorn Street. They built a new gas fireplace and mantelpiece for the sitting room, redesigned and rebuilt the stairway, refinished all the trim, dressed up rooms with bright new wallpaper, ceilings included, laid new carpets, and with Katharine helping whenever she was home from college. Wilbur's particularly distinctive contribution was the decorative carving on a new cherry newel post at the foot of the stairs.

The work was just about finished in time for the arrival of spring in 1894. On Saturday, March 31, Bishop Wright recorded in his diary:

> Cloudy day, but moderate. At home. Orville and C[K]atharine arrange the house. First time for months, we had a room to sit in, all being torn up.

Business remained good, but with the opening of more bicycle shops in town, competition kept growing. When sales grew slack, Wilbur turned conspicuously restless, uncertain of what to make of his life. He had long thought he would like to be a teacher, "an honorable pursuit," but that required a college education. He had no knack for business, he decided. He felt ill suited for it and, as he explained to his father, was now weighing the "advisability" of taking a college course.

> I do not think I am specially fitted for success in any commercial pursuit even if I had proper personal and business influences to assist me. I might make a living, but I doubt whether I would ever do much more than this. Intellectual effort is a pleasure to me and I think I would [be] better fitted for reasonable success in some of the professions than in business.

In another letter, this to brother Lorin, Wilbur had still more to say. He was one who not only devoted much of his time to reading, but to thinking, and he had given a great deal of thought to the subject of business and reached a number of his own conclusions.

In business it is the aggressive man, who continually has his eye on his own interest, who succeeds [he wrote]. Business is merely a form of warfare in which each combatant strives to get the business away from his competitors and at the same time keep them from getting what he already has. No man has ever been successful in business who was not aggressive, self-assertive and even a little bit selfish perhaps. There is nothing reprehensible in an aggressive disposition, so long as it is not carried to excess, for such men make the world and its affairs move. . . . I entirely agree that the boys of the Wright family are all lacking in determination and push. That is the very reason that none of us have been or will be more than ordinary businessmen. We have all done reasonably well, better in fact than the average man perhaps, but not one of us has as yet made particular use of the talent in which he excels other men. That is why our success has been only moderate. We ought not to have been businessmen. . . .

There is always a danger that a person of this disposition will, if left to depend upon himself, retire into the first corner he falls into and remain there all his life struggling for bare existence (unless some earthquake throws him out into a more favorable location), where if put on the right path with proper special equipment, he would advance far. Many men are better fitted for improving chances offered them than in turning up the chances themselves.

But if not a "first corner" to fall into for the rest of life, what was "the right path"? As it was he felt trapped.

Bishop Wright offered to help with the cost of a college course. "I do not think a commercial life will suit you well," he wrote in agreement. Then sales at the Wright Cycle Company picked up again, to the point where they were selling about 150 bicycles a year, and Wilbur stayed with it.

In 1895, their third year in business, they moved to a corner building at 22 South Williams Street, with a showroom on the street level and space for a machine shop upstairs. There, on the second floor, the brothers began making their own model bicycles, available to order. The announcement of the new product read in part as follows:

> It will have large tubing, high frame, tool steel bearings, needle wire spokes, narrow tread and every feature of an up-to-date bicycle. Its weight will be about 20 pounds. We are very certain that no wheel on the market will run easier or wear longer than this one, and we will guarantee it in the most unqualified manner.

It sold for $60 to $65 and was called the Van Cleve, in honor of their great-great-grandmother on their father's side, who was the first white woman to settle in Dayton. With the Van Cleve in production, and available in all colors, a second, less-expensive model was introduced called the St. Clair, in tribute to the first governor of the old Northwest Territory, of which Ohio was part. Their income grew to the point where they were earning a handsome $2,000 to $3,000 per year.

"Van Cleves get there First," proclaimed one of their advertisements. And in the Van Cleve catalogue, the brothers declared:

> Through fair and liberal dealing we have built up a large and successful business, and we are proud to number among Van Cleve riders the best judges of bicycles and bicycle construction in the city. Without their assistance in spreading the fame and praise of the Van Cleve, we could not have hoped to have pressed it to its present high position in popular estimation. Through their testimonies the name Van Cleve has become the synonym of excellence in bicycle construction.

At home, the enjoyment of Lorin's children coming in and out grew only greater for both Wilbur and Orville. Their niece Ivonette would say of Orville in particular that he never seemed to tire of playing with them, and that if he ran out of games, he would make candy for them. Wilbur, too, would amuse them in equally wholehearted fashion, though not for long. "If we happened to be sitting on his lap, he would straighten out his long legs and we would slide off. That was a signal to us to find something else to do.

> When we were old enough to get toys, Uncle Orv and Uncle Will had a habit of playing with them until they were broken, then repair them so that they were better than when they were bought.

Perhaps it was because he was away so much of the time that Bishop Wright put such abiding emphasis on the importance of family life at 7 Hawthorn—"the home circle," as he said—and why it played so large a part in all of their lives however far those lives reached.

The Dream Takes Hold

I wish to avail myself of all that is already known. . . .

I.

As Katharine Wright said of her father, the habit of worry was strong in him. For as long as she and her brothers could remember, he had warned of the dire threat of contaminated water, and articles in the papers confirmed time after time that every case of typhoid fever was an instance of water poisoning.

In the late summer of 1896, twenty-five-year-old Orville was struck by the dreaded typhoid. For days he lay in a delirium, close to death, his fever at 105 degrees. The family doctor, Levi Spitler, who had nursed Susan Wright through her final illness, said little could be done. Wilbur and Katharine took turns keeping watch at the bedside. Bishop Wright, then on the road, wrote at once on hearing the news, dreadfully worried about Orville, but also Katharine and Wilbur. "Put him in the best room for air and comfort. Sponge him off gently and quickly. . . . Let no one use the well water at the store henceforth. Boil the water you all drink."

It was a month before Orville could sit up in bed, another two weeks before he could get out of bed, and during this time Wilbur had begun reading about the German glider enthusiast Otto Lilienthal who had recently been killed in an accident. Much that he read he read aloud to Orville.

A manufacturer of small steam engines and a mining engineer by training, Lilienthal had started gliding as early as 1869, and from the start he had been joined in his aviation experiments by a younger brother, which could only have given Wilbur and Orville a feeling of something in common.

He took his lessons from the birds, Lilienthal said, and he saw, as many "prominent investigators" had not, that the secret of "the art of flight" was to be found in the arched or vaulted wings of birds, by which they could ride the wind. He had no use for gas balloons as a means of flight, as they had nothing in common with the birds. "What we are seeking is the means of free motion in the air, in any direction." And only by flying oneself could one achieve "proper insight" into all that was involved. To do this, one had to be on "intimate" terms with the wind.

Over the years Lilienthal had designed and built more than a dozen different gliders, his *normal segel apparat* (sailing machines). One he particularly favored had wings shaped like the "fly-fans" to be seen at the tables of restaurants and men's clubs of the day, and a big vertical rudder shaped like a palm leaf. All but a few of these different models were monoplanes, the wings arched like a bird's and made of white muslin tightly stretched over a frame of willow. As pilot, he would hang by his arms below the wings. The setting for Lilienthal's flights, Wilbur learned, was a range of barren hills known as the Rhinow Mountains, a two-hour train ride north of Berlin.

A squarely built figure with red hair and a beard who dressed for his flights in knickers with heavily padded knees, Lilienthal would position himself on a steep slope, the wings held above his head. As one American eyewitness described the scene, he "stood like an athlete waiting for the starting pistol." Then he would run down the slope and into the wind. Hanging on as the wind lifted him from the ground, he would swing his body and legs this way or that—as his means of balancing and steering— glide as far as possible and land on his feet.

Lilienthal also had himself repeatedly photographed in action, something no gliding enthusiast had yet done. With advances in the technology of photography, the dry-plate camera had come into use. Reproduction of photographic half-tones had also been achieved, and thus unprecedented photographs of the daring "Flying Man" and his gliders appeared the world over. In the United States, his fame was greater than anywhere. A long article in the popular *McClure's Magazine*, illustrated with seven photographs of Lilienthal in flight, reached the largest audience of all.

In 1894 Lilienthal had crashed and lived to tell the tale. On August 9, 1896, flying a favorite "No. 11" glider, he crashed again, falling from an altitude of fifty feet. He died of a broken spine in a Berlin hospital the following day at age forty-eight.

"It must not remain our desire only to acquire the art of the bird," Lilienthal had written. "It is our duty not to rest until we have attained a perfect scientific conception of the problem of flight."

News of Lilienthal's death, Wilbur later wrote, aroused in him as nothing had an interest that had remained passive from childhood. His reading on the flight of birds became intense. On the shelves of the family library was an English translation of a famous illustrated volume, *Animal Mechanism*, written by a French physician, Etienne-Jules Marey, more than thirty years before. Birds were also an interest of Bishop Wright, hence the book's presence in the house, and Wilbur had already read it. Now he read it anew.

"Aerial locomotion has always excited the strongest curiosity among mankind," the author said by way of introduction.

> How frequently has the question been raised, whether man must always continue to envy the bird and the insect their wings; whether he, too, may not one day travel through the air, as he now sails across the ocean. Authorities in science have declared at different periods, as the result of lengthy calculations, that this is a chimerical dream, but how many intentions have we seen realized which have been pronounced impossible.

Marey's serious, largely technical study led Wilbur to read more of the kind, including such treatises as J. Bell Pettigrew's *Animal Locomotion; or Walking, Swimming, and Flying, with a Dissertation on Aeronautics.* For most readers the title alone would have been too daunting. For Wilbur the book was exactly what was needed.

> Those authors who regard artificial flight as impracticable [wrote Pettigrew] sagely remark that the land supports the quadruped and the water the fish. This is quite true, but it is equally true that the air supports the bird, and that the evolutions of the bird on the wing are quite as safe and infinitely more rapid and beautiful than the movements of either the quadruped on the land or the fish in the water.

But, the book stressed, "the way of 'an eagle in the air' must of necessity remain a mystery," until the structure and uses of wings were understood.

> Of all animal movements, flight is indisputably the finest. . . . The fact that a creature as heavy, bulk for bulk, as many solid substances, can by the unaided movements of its wings urge itself through the air with a speed little short of a cannonball, fills the mind with wonder.

Wilbur was to draw upon and quote Pettigrew for years. Like the inspiring lectures of a great professor, the book had opened his eyes and started him thinking in ways he never had.

Once fully recovered from his illness, Orville proceeded with the same reading list. They "read up on aeronautics as a physician would read his books," Bishop Wright would attest proudly.

———

Work at the bicycle shop went on with business better than ever. In 1897 the brothers moved the enterprise to a still larger and final location at

1127 West Third, which, like their previous business locations was only a few blocks from home. The building was a two-story, red-brick duplex, with the adjoining half occupied by Fetters & Shank, Undertakers and Embalmers. After considerable remodeling, the Wright Cycle Company had a front showroom, backed by a small office, and a machine shop to the rear with ample space for a drill press, metal lathe, and band saw, all powered by a gas engine, with room, too, for a workbench. Upstairs there was still more workspace.

Less than a year later, in the spring of 1898, Dayton suffered the worst flood in forty years. On the north side of town, two thousand people had to abandon their homes. For days it looked as if the West End, too, would be inundated. "We had a very narrow escape," Orville reported to his father. "By putting 500 men at work with teams they succeeded in building the levee high enough to keep the water out." Had the river risen another four inches, both 7 Hawthorn and the new shop would have been under three or four feet of water.

Years later, a hardware dealer in the neighborhood, Frank Hamberger, recalled how, at the time of the flood, he had been struggling to get started in his new business. Much of his stock consisted of nails stored in great quantity in the cellar and would have been ruined had the high water struck. When the Wright brothers heard of his troubles, he said, they came immediately, "pulled off their coats," and helped carry the kegs of nails out of the cellar, "without seeking or accepting remuneration."

Meantime, the automobile had made its appearance in the streets of Dayton in the form of a noisy homemade machine built by a friend of the Wrights named Cord Ruse, who occasionally helped out at the shop and with whom they enjoyed talking about all manner of mechanical problems and solutions. Orville was particularly interested in Ruse's automobile and thought perhaps he and Wilbur should build one of their own.

For Wilbur the idea had no appeal. He could not imagine, he said, how any contrivance that made such a racket and had so many things constantly going wrong with it could ever have a future. His mind was elsewhere.

II.

On Tuesday, May 30, 1899—Decoration Day, as it was then known—the weather in Dayton was unseasonably cool, the sky overcast, the Wright house uncommonly quiet. Wilbur was home alone. The Bishop and Katharine had gone to Woodland Cemetery to plant flowers at Susan Wright's grave. Orville was off somewhere else apparently.

Wilbur seated himself at Katharine's small, slant-top desk in the front parlor to write what would be one of the most important letters of his life. Indeed, given all it set in motion, it was one of the most important letters in history. Addressed to the Smithsonian Institution in Washington, it filled not quite two sheets of the Wright Cycle Company's pale blue stationery, all set down in Wilbur's notably clear hand.

"I have been interested in the problem of mechanical and human flight ever since as a boy I constructed a number of bats of various sizes after the style of Cayley's and Pénaud's machines," he began. (Sir George Cayley, a brilliant English baronet and aeronautical pioneer, had also devised a toy helicopter very like the one by Alphonse Pénaud given to the brothers by Bishop Wright.) "My observations since have only convinced me more firmly that human flight is possible and practicable. . . .

> I am about to begin a systematic study of the subject in preparation for practical work to which I expect to devote what time I can spare from my regular business. I wish to obtain such papers as the Smithsonian Institution has published on this subject, and if possible a list of other works in print in the English language.

Lest there be any doubts about him or the seriousness of his intentions, he added: "I am an enthusiast, but not a crank in the sense that I have some pet theories as to the proper construction of a flying machine."

From the list of books provided by the assistant secretary of the Smithsonian, Richard Rathbun, and with a generous supply of Smithsonian pamphlets on aviation forwarded to him, he and Orville both began studying in earnest.

Especially helpful were the writings of Octave Chanute, a celebrated French-born American civil engineer, builder of bridges and railroads, who had made gliders a specialty, and Samuel Pierpont Langley, an eminent astronomer and head, or secretary, of the Smithsonian. Formerly the director of the Allegheny Observatory in Pittsburgh and a professor of astronomy and physics at the Western University of Pennsylvania, Langley was one of the most respected scientists in the nation. His efforts in recent years, backed by substantial Smithsonian funding, had resulted in a strange-looking, steam-powered, pilotless "aerodrome," as he called it, with V-shaped wings in front and back that gave it the look of a monstrous dragonfly. Launched by catapult from the roof of a houseboat on the Potomac River in 1896, the year of Lilienthal's death, it flew more than half a mile before plunging into the water.

Along with Lilienthal, Chanute, and Langley, numbers of others among the most prominent engineers, scientists, and original thinkers of the nineteenth century had been working on the problem of controlled flight, including Sir George Cayley, Sir Hiram Maxim, inventor of the machine gun, Alexander Graham Bell, and Thomas Edison. None had succeeded. Hiram Maxim had reportedly spent $100,000 of his own money on a giant, steam-powered, pilotless flying machine only to see it crash in attempting to take off.

Meanwhile, the French government had spent a comparable sum on a steam-powered flying machine built by a French electrical engineer, Clément Ader, and with such dismal results that the whole project was abandoned, though not before Ader gave the name *avion*, for airplane, to the French language.

Along with the cost of experiments in flight, the risks of humiliating failure, injury, and, of course, death, there was the inevitable prospect of being mocked as a crank, a crackpot, and in many cases with good reason.

For more than fifty years, or long before the Wright brothers took up their part, would-be "conquerors of the air" and their strange or childish flying machines, as described in the press, had served as a continuous source of popular comic relief. In the 1850s, one French inventor's ingenious idea had consisted of a chair, a pair of wings attached to his back, and a huge umbrella. (Whether the umbrella was for "ascensional power" or shade was never explained.) In the 1870s, one Charles Dyer of Georgia came up with a flying device in the shape of a duck. In the 1890s, a *San Francisco Chronicle* roundup report on the subject described "the flying-machine crank" as one who, with advancing age, gets increasingly foolish to the point of "imbecility."

Among the more elaborate new ideas flooding the U.S. Patent Office for approval was a gigantic, fishlike machine called an "aerostat," with sheet aluminum body and fan-shaped tail. According to the *Washington Post*:

> The body is supported by a pair of wings that run its length, their inclination being controlled by a pilot wheel, so that the aerial vessel is able to rise or descend at will. It is propelled by a series of explosions in the rear, small pellets of nitroglycerine being fed automatically into a cup opening backward and discharged by electricity.

"It is a fact," the *Post* later categorically declared, "that man can't fly."

Of all that was reported or said by way of ridicule nothing evoked such widespread delight, or would be so long remembered and quoted, as a comic poem titled "Darius Green and his Flying Machine." Written by a popular New England author, J. T. Trowbridge, it had been a favorite for public readings and recitals at family gatherings the country over for more than thirty years.

Darius was a slow-witted farm boy who pondered: "The birds can fly and why can't I? Could blue-bird and phoebe, be smarter than we be?" In secret in the loft of a barn, he set to work

> . . . with thimble and thread
> And wax and hammer and buckles and screws,
> And all such things as geniuses use; —
> Two bats for patterns, curious fellows!
> A charcoal-pot and a pair of bellows;

. . . Some wire, and several old umbrellas;
A carriage-cover for tail and wings;
A piece of harness; and straps and strings . . .
These and a hundred other things.

When Darius leaped into the air in his creation from the barn loft, it was only to crash below in a heap of "tangled strings, broken braces and broken wings, shooting stars and various things," the moral of the story being, "Stick to your sphere."

In no way did any of this discourage or deter Wilbur and Orville Wright, any more than the fact that they had had no college education, no formal technical training, no experience working with anyone other than themselves, no friends in high places, no financial backers, no government subsidies, and little money of their own. Or the entirely real possibility that at some point, like Otto Lilienthal, they could be killed.

In an article in *Cosmopolitan* magazine several years before Lilienthal's death, Samuel Langley had emphasized that those willing to attempt flight ought to be granted the kind of attention and concern customarily bestowed on those who risk their lives for a useful purpose. It was a risk, however, from which both Langley and Octave Chanute had excused themselves, because of age.

All the same, and importantly, the times were alive with invention, technical innovations, new ideas of every kind. George Eastman had introduced the "Kodak" box camera; Isaac Merritt Singer, the first electric sewing machine; the Otis Company had installed the world's first elevator in a New York office building; the first safety razor, the first mousetrap, the first motor cars built in America—all in the dozen years since Orville started his print shop and Wilbur emerged from his spell of self-imposed isolation.

Then, too, there was the ever-present atmosphere of a city in which inventing and making things were central to the way of life. At about this time, just prior to the turn of the century, according to the U.S. Patent Office, Dayton ranked first in the country relative to population in the creation of new patents. The large factories and mills of Dayton kept growing larger, producing railroad cars, cash registers, sewing machines, and gun

barrels. (The Davis Sewing Machine Company, as one example, was turning out four hundred sewing machines a day in a factory fully a mile in
length.) In addition were the hundreds of small shops and workrooms
making horse collars, corsets, soap, shirts, brooms, carriage wheels, rakes,
saws, cardboard boxes, beer kegs, and overalls, not to say bicycles.

———

In his letter to the Smithsonian, Wilbur had made mention of his interest
in birds. To achieve human flight, he had written, was "only a question of
knowledge and skill in all acrobatic feats," and birds were "the most perfectly trained gymnasts in the world . . . specially well fitted for their work."

Among the material the Smithsonian provided him was an English
translation of a book titled *L'Empire de l'Air*, published in Paris in 1881.
It had been written by a French farmer, poet, and student of flight, Louis
Pierre Mouillard. Nothing Wilbur had yet read so affected him. He would
long consider it "one of the most remarkable pieces of aeronautical literature" ever published. For Wilbur, flight had become a "cause," and Mouillard, one of the great "missionaries" of the cause, "like a prophet crying in
the wilderness, exhorting the world to repent of its unbelief in the possibility of human flight."

At the start of his *Empire of the Air*, Mouillard gave fair warning that
one could be entirely overtaken by the thought that the problem of flight
could be solved by man. "When once this idea has invaded the brain, it
possesses it exclusively."

That said, Mouillard moved on to the miracle of flying creatures, writing with unabashed evangelical fervor.

> Oh, blind humanity! Open thine eyes and thou shalt see mil-
> lions of birds and myriads of insects cleaving the atmosphere.
> All these creatures are whirling through the air without the
> slightest float [support]; many of them are gliding therein,
> without losing height, hour after hour, on pulseless wings
> without fatigue; and after beholding this demonstration given
> by the source of all knowledge, thou wilt acknowledge that
> aviation is the path to be followed. . . .

By merely observing with close attention how the winged tribes perform their feats, by carefully reflecting on what we have seen, and, above all, by striving correctly to understand the *modus operandi* of what we do see, we are sure not to wander far from the path, which leads to eventual success.

It was only necessary to have "good eyes," and know how to keep in sight, with telescope or field glasses, a bird going at full speed, but still more "to know what to look at."

Wilbur had taken up bird-watching on a rugged stretch along the banks of the Miami River south of town called the Pinnacles. On Sundays he would ride off on his bicycle to spend considerable time there observing as Mouillard preached.

Mouillard had spent much of his life in Egypt and Algeria, where he came to love especially the great soaring vultures of Africa. He had observed them by the thousands, yet however often he saw one fly high overhead, he could not help following it with a feeling of wonderment.

He knows how to rise, how to float . . . to sail upon the wind without effort . . . he sails and spends no force . . . he uses the wind, instead of his muscles.

This, Mouillard said, was the way of flight that would "lead men to navigate the immensity of space."

III.

For Wilbur and Orville the dream had taken hold. The works of Lilienthal and Mouillard, the brothers would attest, had "infected us with their own unquenchable enthusiasm and transformed idle curiosity into the active zeal of workers."

They would design and build their own experimental glider-kite, drawing on much they had read, much they had observed about birds in flight, and, importantly, from considerable time thinking. They had made themselves familiar with the language of aeronautics, the terms used in explaining the numerous factors involved in attaining "equilibrium" or balance in flight, where balance was quite as crucial as in riding a bicycle. *Lift* came from air moving faster over the arched top of a wing, thereby making the pressure there less than that under the wing. *Pitch* was the lateral tilt of the flying machine, front and back, nose down, nose up. *Roll* applied to the rotation of the wing, up or down on one side or the other, like a boat rocking. *Yaw* applied to the direction of the flight, the turning of the plane pointing the nose left or right.

Equilibrium was the all-important factor, the brothers understood. The difficulty was not to get into the air but to stay there, and they concluded that Lilienthal's fatal problem had been an insufficient means of control—"his inability to properly balance his machine in the air," as Orville wrote. Swinging one's legs or shifting the weight of one's body about in midair were hardly enough.

Wilbur's observations of birds in flight had convinced him that birds used more "positive and energetic methods of regaining equilibrium" than that of a pilot trying to shift the center of gravity with his own body. It had occurred to him that a bird adjusted the tips of its wings so as to present the tip of one wing at a raised angle, the other at a lowered angle. Thus its balance was controlled by "utilizing dynamic reactions of the air instead of shifting weight."

The chief need was skill rather than machinery. It was impossible to fly without both knowledge *and* skill—of this Wilbur was already certain—and skill came only from experience—experience in the air. He calculated that in the five years Lilienthal had devoted to gliders and gliding, he spent a total of only five hours in actual flight. It was hardly enough and not how he and Orville would proceed.

On an evening at home, using a small cardboard box from which he had removed the ends, Wilbur put on a demonstration before Orville, Katharine, and a visiting Oberlin classmate, Harriet Silliman. He showed them how, by pressing the opposite corners of the box, top and bottom, the double wings of a biplane glider could be twisted or "warped," to present the wing surfaces to the air at different angles or elevations, the same as the birds did. Were one wing to meet the wind at a greater angle than the other, it would give greater lift on that side and so the glider would bank and turn.

With "wing warping," or "wing twisting," as it was sometimes referred to, Wilbur had already made an immensely important and altogether original advance toward their goal.

IV.

In the summer of 1899, in a room above the bicycle shop on West Third Street, the brothers began building their first aircraft, a flying kite made of split bamboo and paper with a wingspan of five feet. It was a biplane, with double wings, one over the other, the design Octave Chanute used for his gliders and that was believed to provide greater stability. The wings were joined in the fashion of a bridge truss, with vertical struts of pine and crisscrossing wires. Also included was an original system of cords whereby the operator on the ground, using sticks held in both hands, could control the wing warping.

In early August, Wilbur tested the model in an open field outside of town. Orville, for some reason, had been unable to attend. A few small boys were the only witnesses.

> According to Wilbur's account of the tests [Orville later wrote], the model . . . responded promptly to the warping of the surfaces . . . when he shifted the upper surface backward by the manipulation of the sticks attached to flying cords, the nose of the machine turned downward as was intended; but in diving downward it created a slack in the flying cords, so that he was not able to control further. The model made such a rapid dive to the ground that the small boys present fell on their faces to avoid being hit.

Nonetheless, the brothers felt the test had plainly demonstrated the efficiency of their system of control and that the time had come to begin work on a man-carrying glider.

In April of 1900 Wilbur turned thirty-three. Four months later, in August, Orville and Katharine turned twenty-nine and twenty-six. For her birthday, as Katharine was pleased to tell their father, "the boys" had given her a bust of Sir Walter Scott.

With the three of them working now, Katharine had decided to hire someone to come in by the day to help around the house. Carrie Kayler was fourteen years old and so small still that to reach the gaslight in the kitchen she had to stand on a chair. Orville loved to tease her about it until she was near tears and Wilbur would say, "I guess that's about enough, Orv."

"Mr. Orville would stop instantly," she would remember. "Mr. Orville always listened to Mr. Will, but *never* to anyone else." Carrie Kayler was to remain part of the family for nearly half a century.

On May 13, 1900, Wilbur wrote a letter to Octave Chanute—his first letter to the eminent engineer—asking for advice on a location where he might conduct flying experiments, somewhere without rain or inclement weather and, Wilbur said, where sufficient winds could be counted on, winds, say, of 15 miles per hour.

The only such sites he knew of, Chanute replied, were in California and Florida, but both were "deficient in sand hills" for soft landings. Wilbur might do better along the coasts of South Carolina or Georgia.

Wind was the essential, the brothers had already come to appreciate. And clearly, if ever they were to succeed with what they had set their minds to, they must learn—and learn from experience—the ways of the wind.

In answer to an inquiry Wilbur sent to the United States Weather Bureau in Washington about prevailing winds around the country, they were provided extensive records of monthly wind velocities at more than a hundred Weather Bureau stations, enough for them to take particular interest in a remote spot on the Outer Banks of North Carolina called Kitty Hawk, some seven hundred miles from Dayton. Until then, the farthest the brothers had been from home was a trip to Chicago for the Columbian Exposition of 1893. And though they had "roughed it" some on a few camping trips, it had been nothing like what could be expected on the North Carolina coast.

To be certain Kitty Hawk was the right choice, Wilbur wrote to the head of the Weather Bureau station there, who answered reassuringly about steady winds and sand beaches. As could be plainly seen by looking at a map, Kitty Hawk also offered all the isolation one might wish for to carry on experimental work in privacy.

Still further encouragement came when, on August 18, 1900, the former postmaster at Kitty Hawk, William J. Tate, sent a letter saying:

> Mr. J. J. Dosher of the Weather Bureau here has asked me to answer your letter to him, relative to the fitness of Kitty Hawk as a place to practice or experiment with a flying machine, etc.
>
> In answering I would say that you would find here nearly any type of ground you could wish; you could, for instance, get a stretch of sandy land one mile by five with a bare hill in center 80 feet high, not a tree or bush anywhere to break the evenness of the wind current. This in my opinion would be a fine place; our winds are always steady, generally from 10 to 20 miles velocity per hour.
>
> You can reach here from Elizabeth City, N.C. (35 miles from here) by boat . . . from Manteo 12 miles from here by mail boat every Mon., Wed., & Friday. We have telegraph communication & daily mails. Climate healthy, you could find good place to pitch tent & get board in private family provided there were not too many in your party; would advise you to come anytime from September 15 to October 15. Don't wait until November. The autumn generally gets a little rough by November.
>
> If you decide to try your machine here and come, I will take pleasure in doing all I can for your convenience and success and pleasure, and I assure you you will find a hospitable people when you come among us.

That decided the matter. Kitty Hawk it would be.

———

In the final weeks of August the brothers built a full-sized glider with two wings that they intended to reassemble and fly at Kitty Hawk, first as a kite, then, if all went well, fly themselves. Its wingspan was 18 feet. The total cost of all the necessary pieces and parts—ribs of ash, wires, cloth to cover the wings—was not more than $15. The only thing missing were long spruce spars for the glider, which had proven impossible to find in Dayton. But Wilbur felt confident they could be picked up on the East Coast.

All was packed up in crates for shipment east, along with the necessary tools and a tent. Wilbur was to go first and get things in order. For more gear and his clothing, he borrowed Katharine's trunk and suitcase. Not forgetting the example set by Otto Lilienthal, he also brought a box camera and tripod.

Katharine could hardly believe he was going where he said. "I never did hear of such an out-of-the-way place."

CHAPTER THREE

Where the Winds Blow

One ship drives east and another drives west
With the self-same winds that blow.
'Tis the set of the sails
And not the gales
Which tells us the way to go.

ELLA WHEELER WILCOX,
"WINDS OF FATE"

I.

The legendary Outer Banks, a narrow chain of sandbars and is-lands shielding the North Carolina coastline from the full force of the Atlantic Ocean, reach more than 175 miles from Norfolk, Virginia, south to Cape Lookout. In 1900 few lived there other than fishermen and their families, and those with the Life-Saving Service. No bridges as yet crossed from the mainland. One got to the Outer Banks by boat and about the only signs of civilization at Kitty Hawk were four Life-Saving Stations, one every six miles, and the Weather Bureau Station. There were no real roads. The one conspicuous structure on the skyline was a rambling summer hotel at Nags Head.

Wilbur reached Norfolk by train on September 7, 1900, roughly twenty-four hours after leaving Dayton, and checked in overnight at a hotel. The temperature in Norfolk the next day hit 100 degrees, and dressed in his customary dark suit, high collar, and necktie, he nearly collapsed.

He needed still to find the long spruce strips necessary for his "machine" and so set off to several lumberyards only to be told they had none. Settling for white pine, he gathered up everything and boarded a 4:30 train to Elizabeth City, sixty miles to the south, where the Pasquotank River flows to meet Albemarle Sound.

When, at Elizabeth City, he inquired about the best way to get over to Kitty Hawk, he received nothing but blank stares. No one he talked to seemed to know anything about the place or have the least idea how to get there.

It was another four days before he found a boatman on the waterfront, one Israel Perry, who said he had been born and raised at Kitty Hawk and agreed to take Wilbur across. Perry also had a friend to help him. Wilbur's heavy trunk and the pine strips would go over on the weekly freight boat.

To get to Perry's schooner required going by a small skiff much the worse for wear and leaking badly. When Wilbur asked if it was safe, Perry, to assure him, said, "Oh, it's safer than the big boat."

With constant bailing the whole three miles, they managed to reach the schooner, which was indeed in sadder shape. "The sails were rotten," wrote Wilbur, "the ropes badly worn and the rudder-post half rotted off, and the cabin so dirty and vermin-infested that I kept out of it from first to last."

The weather had been fine all day, but by the time they started out of the wide Pasquotank River and down the sound, it was nearly dark and the water much rougher than the light wind had led them to expect, as Israel Perry pointed out several times, clearly "a little uneasy." The voyage ahead was forty miles.

The wind shifted and grew increasingly stronger. The waves, now running quite high, "struck the boat from below with a heavy shock and threw it back about as fast as it went forward," Wilbur would write. He had had no experience with sailing, let alone rough water, but plainly the flat-bottom craft was woefully unsuited for such conditions.

In the strain of rolling and pitching, the boat sprang a leak, and with water crashing over the bow required still more bailing.

At 11 o'clock the wind had increased to a gale and the boat
was gradually being driven nearer and nearer the north shore,

but as an attempt to turn round would probably have resulted in an upset, there seemed nothing else to do but attempt to round the North River Light and take refuge behind the point.

The situation suddenly became more dramatic still.

> In a severe gust the foresail was blown loose from the boom and fluttered to leeward with a terrible roar. . . . By the time we had reached a position even with the end of the point, it became doubtful whether we would be able to round the light. . . . The suspense was ended by another roaring of the canvas as the mainsail also tore loose from the boom, and shook fiercely in the gale.

By now their only chance was to take in the mainsail, let the boat swing stern to the wind, and, under the jib only, make a straight run over the sandbar. This, as Wilbur wrote, was a highly dangerous maneuver in such a sea, but somehow Perry managed without capsizing.

He would not land on sandbars for a thousand dollars, Perry told Wilbur. So they lay at anchor in the North River the remainder of the night. Having no stomach for any food Perry might have below, Wilbur dipped into a jar of jelly Katharine had packed in his bag and stretched out on deck.

Setting the boat in order as best they could took half the next day. It was afternoon before they got under way again and not until nine that night were they anchored at Kitty Hawk, where again Wilbur slept on deck.

He finally went ashore the next morning, September 13, two days after leaving Elizabeth City.

———

He headed first to the home of William Tate, the former Kitty Hawk postmaster with whom he had corresponded.

In all, Kitty Hawk comprised perhaps fifty houses, nearly all the homes of fishermen, and Tate, too, made most of his living that way three months of the year, beginning in October when the fish were running. As he would later write, "The community of Kitty Hawk at that time was a hardy race, chiefly descendants of shipwrecked sailors whom storm and misfortune had cast upon the shores of the North Carolina coast." He himself was the son of a shipwrecked Scotsman. The life there, Tate stressed, was one of "double-barreled ISOLATION."

Houses had little in the way of furniture. Their bare floors were kept clean by scrubbing with white sand. Families raised most of what they ate in small vegetable gardens while the "men-folk" hunted all they could. Clothes were hand-sewn and most everyone got by with just two or three changes of clothes—"one for special occasions," it was said, "and then one on one day and one on the next." Mail came about three times a week. Children went to school about three months a year, and no one, it seemed, knew what a vacation was.

Tate and his wife, Addie, gave the visitor the warm greeting he had promised, and Wilbur, as Tate remembered, "proceeded to unfold a tale of hardship" about his trip from Elizabeth City. "He was a tenderfoot and of course had a tale of woe to tell.

> His graphic description of the rolling of the boat and his story that the muscles of his arms ached from holding on, were interesting, but when he said he had fasted for 48 hours that was a condition that called for a remedy at once. Therefore we soon had him seated to a good breakfast of fresh eggs, ham and coffee, and I assure you he did his duty by them.

When Wilbur asked if he might board there temporarily until his brother arrived, the Tates excused themselves to confer in the next room, but without closing the door. Hearing Addie say she was not sure their home would do for such a nicely dressed visitor, Wilbur stepped to the door to tell them he would be quite happy with whatever accommodations they could provide.

In a long letter to his father, Wilbur described the Tate home as an unpainted, two-story frame house with no plaster on the walls, "no carpets at all, very little furniture, no books or pictures." For Kitty Hawk, this was above the average.

A few men have saved a thousand dollars, but this is the saving of a long life. . . . I suppose a few of them see two hundred dollars a year. They are friendly and neighborly and I think there is rarely any real suffering among them.

Beside fishing, they tried to grow their own beans and corn. As there appeared to be nothing but sand, Wilbur thought it a wonder they could grow anything.

Until Orville's arrival, Wilbur worked at setting up camp on a good-sized hill half a mile from the Tate house, overlooking the water. That done, he began preparing their glider, most of his efforts taken up with a change in the wingspan from 18 to 17 feet, because of his failure to find the spruce spars needed and having to be satisfied with the pine substitutes that were two feet shorter. As a result the fabric for the wings—a beautiful white French sateen—had also to be cut back in size and resewn. To accomplish this he borrowed Addie Tate's sewing machine of the kind one pumped by foot.

In another letter to the Bishop, he tried to describe what the glider amounted to, stressing that it was to have no motor but depend on the wind only, that the central objective was to solve the problem of balance, and that he knew exactly what he was about, both in building the glider and what he expected to achieve with the tests to come. All this was remarkably clear and concise, and, as time would show, a stunning example of extraordinary prescience.

I have my machine nearly finished. It is not to have a motor and is not expected to fly in any true sense of the word. My idea is merely to experiment and practice with a view to solving the problem of equilibrium. I have plans which I hope to find much in advance of the methods tried by previous experimenters. When once a machine is under proper control under all conditions, the motor problem will be quickly solved. A failure of a motor will then mean simply a slow descent and safe landing instead of a disastrous fall.

Equilibrium—balance—was exactly what riding a bicycle required and of that he and Orville knew a great deal. Well aware of how his father worried about his safety, Wilbur stressed that he did not intend to rise many feet from the ground, and on the chance that he were "upset," there was nothing but soft sand on which to land. He was there to learn, not to take chances for thrills. "The man who wishes to keep at the problem long enough to really learn anything positively must not take dangerous risks. Carelessness and overconfidence are usually more dangerous than deliberately accepted risks."

As time would show, caution and close attention to all advance preparations were to be the rule for the brothers. They would take risks when necessary, but they were no daredevils out to perform stunts and they never would be.

Wilbur also assured his father he was taking "every precaution" about his drinking water.

As Bill Tate would later recall, the local people grew increasingly curious about the visitor and the "darn fool contraption" he was sewing, gluing, and tying together.

> In the meantime, it had been drawn out of him by adroit questioning that his brother would be down in a couple of weeks. They were going to live in a tent and were going to make some experiments with their contraption in the art of flying.

Outer Banks people were still pretty "set in their ways," Tate added. "We believed in a good God, a bad Devil, and a hot Hell, and more than anything else we believed that same God did not intend man should ever fly."

II.

Orville reached Elizabeth City on September 26, having traveled from Dayton without incident or inconvenience. The little delay he had reaching Kitty Hawk was only from lack of wind, and on arrival, again without any inconvenience, he found Wilbur had the "soaring machine" nearly ready.

With everything in place, it consisted of two fixed wings, one above the other, each measuring 5 by 17 feet. In addition it had warping controls and a movable, forward rudder—the "horizontal" rudder or elevator—of 12 square feet. There were no wheels for takeoffs or landings. Instead the machine had wooden skids, far better suited for sand.

The whole apparatus weighed slightly less than 50 pounds. With Wilbur aboard as "operator," it would total approximately 190 pounds. He would lie flat on his stomach, head first, in the middle of the lower wing and maintain fore-and-aft balance by means of the forward rudder.

Wind would be all-important and contrary to the old Irish wish— "May the wind be ever at your back"—a good wind had to be head-on. As would be said, for the Wrights the winds were never the enemy.

New to such experimental work as they were, the brothers had yet to realize the need for keeping records of all they did. But from their letters home, it appears the experiments began on October 3. "We've been having a fine time," Orville wrote to Katharine on October 14, "altogether we have had the machine out three different days, from 2 to 4 hours each time."

When, at the start of their experiments, a "terrific wind" was blowing at more than 30 miles an hour, "too strong and unsteady for us to attempt an ascent in it," they flew their machine like a kite, with lines hanging down to the ground by which they could work the steering apparatus. The greatest difficulty was keeping the glider at a height of no more than 20 feet or so. Even with an ideal wind of 15 to 20 miles an hour, the pull of the kite could be fierce. "It naturally wants to go higher and higher," Orville explained. "When it begins to get too high, we give it a pretty strong pull . . . to which it responds by making a terrific dart to the ground." If nothing had been broken, they sent it flying again and photographed it in the air.

Once, after they set the glider on the ground to make "adjustments," a sudden gust caught one corner and, "quicker than thought," threw it 20 feet, smashing it to pieces. Orville, who had been standing at a rear corner holding one of the upright spars, was yanked off his feet and landed in a heap 20 feet away, shaken but unharmed.

They photographed the wreckage, then dragged it all back to camp and talked of heading home. But after a night's sleep, they decided there was hope. Repairing the damage took three days.

As word of what they were up to continued to spread among the local populace, increasing numbers of them could be seen watching from a respectful distance. Bill Tate and several Tate family men and boys were also glad to lend a hand when needed.

The whole time Wilbur and Orville worked together side by side, no less than at home, with the exception of those days when the conditions seemed right to try a manned flight, and then it was Wilbur only who took to the air, if ever so briefly.

He would stand inside an opening in the lower wing, as Orville and Bill Tate stood ready at the wing tips. On signal, all three would take hold and start trotting forward, down the sand slope straight into the wind. Wilbur would hoist himself into position, stretch flat, and grasp the controls. Orville and Tate grabbed hold of the lines attached to the wing to keep the glider from sailing higher than wished.

———

Making themselves reasonably comfortable when not working took considerable time and effort. They had moved from the Tate home to Wilbur's good-sized tent with room enough for tools, supplies, and themselves. All was very different from back home, as Orville described for Katharine:

> The site of our tent was formerly a fertile valley, cultivated by some ancient Kitty Hawker. Now only a few rotten limbs, the topmost branches of trees that then grew in this valley, protrude from the sand. The sea has washed and the wind blown millions and millions of loads of sand up in heaps along the coast, completely covering houses and forest.

Except for an occasional meal with the Tates, they got by on their own rations and their own cooking. The water around teemed with fish—"you see dozens of them whenever you look down into the water"—and Kitty Hawk fishermen shipped tons of fish to Baltimore and other cities. But the

Bishop Milton Wright at age 60.

Susan Koerner Wright at age 27.

2

3

Reuchlin at age 11.

4

Lorin at age 9.

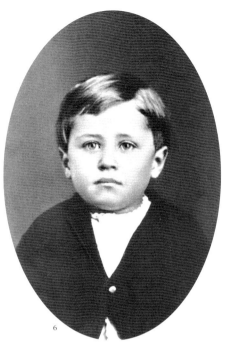

Wilbur at age 9.

Orville at age 4.

Katharine at age 4.

8

The Wright home at 7 Hawthorn Street, with porch and bicycle built by Wilbur and Orville.

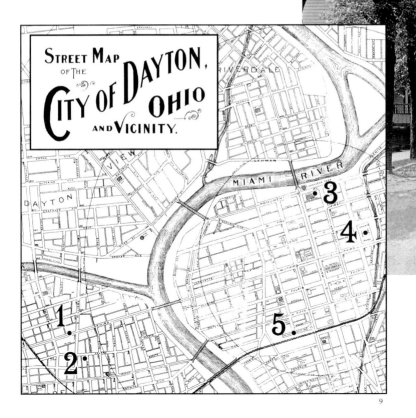

Tree-lined Hawthorn Street, the Wright home with porch at right.

Left: detail map of Dayton showing (1) Wright Cycle Shop at
1127 West Third Street, (2) Wright home, (3) Steele High School,
(4) Dayton Public Library, (5) Union Train Depot.

Orville's Dayton high school class of 1890. Orville is at center rear.
His friend the poet Paul Laurence Dunbar is at left rear.

Wilbur at age 17.

Photograph of Oliver Crook Haugh taken sometime before his execution in 1906.

13

Bishop Wright's diary entry of May 27, 1913, declaring the notorious murderer Oliver Crook Haugh to have been the one who, in boyhood, struck the blow with a hockey stick that changed the direction of Wilbur's life.

The Man Who Threw the Bat that Struck Wilbur at the Soldiers' Home.

Dr. Oliver Crook Haugh was electrocuted in Columbus, Ohio, November 4th 1906, just after midnight. He killed his father and mother and brother November 4th, 1905, and set fire to the house to conceal the crimes. When asked if he had anything to say, he simply shook his head. It is said, however, that he never admitted his guilt. Attempts have been made to connect him with the murder of several women who were mysteriously strangulated. Also, he was said to have been involved in the murder of Mary Twobey, who died at Lorian, Ohio; and Anna Patterson at Chicago. He was divorced from his wife, who had two children

WEST SIDE NEWS

Vol. I.   DAYTON, OHIO, MARCH 23, 1889.   **No. 3.**

West Side News.

PUBLISHED WEEKLY.

Orville Wright · · · Publisher.

TERMS:—One year, forty cents. Ten weeks, ten cents.

DAYTON, OHIO.

A French Detective.

We walked out together, and in the course of conversation we touched upon the way in which some persons can so disguise themselves as to hide their individuality from their most intimate the way to Versailles. When within ten minutes or so of our destination, my new friend took off his hat, pulled off a wig, got rid of a mustache, and to my utter amazement, sat revealed before me as my friend, the detective!

How he had managed to find out that I was going to Versailles —which I had no idea of myself when I left him—or how he had so effectually concealed his appearance, that I, sitting within three feet of him, had no idea he was the man I had left some four hours before, are problems which I can not solve. The detective himself only laughed when I ask-

HOLLINGER

IS THE

PHOTOGRAPHER.

Cor. Third and Jefferson.

To the Public.

Be it known, that I,

Thomas M. Hill,

have added to my Stock of Hardware

A TIN STORE.

Will keep all kinds of Tin, Copper, Granite and Sheet Iron Ware. Roofing, Gutter-

15

Front page of the weekly *West Side News,* the brothers' first joint enterprise.

Below: The Third Street Bridge over the Miami River, with the towered Steele High School on the right seen from Dayton's West Side. The multitude of rising smoke was taken as a proud mark of a city of enterprise.   16

The Wright Cycle shop at 1127 West Third Street. Showroom and backroom shop were on the left half of the building. The other half was occupied by an undertaker.

17

18

Wilbur working with a metal lathe.

Advertisement for the Wright brothers' popular, hand-built Van Cleve bicycle, named in honor of their great-great-grandmother on their father's side, who was the first white woman to settle in Dayton. The Van Cleve sold for $60 to $65 and was available in all colors.

Van Cleves get there First.

WRIGHT CYCLE CO.,
Manufacturers of
"Van Cleve" Bicycles,
1127 W. THIRD STREET, NEAR WILLIAMS.
REPAIRING, ENAMELING IN ALL COLORS, ETC.

19

20

Katharine (second on the right) and four of her
Oberlin College friends join in the bicycle craze.

4

grounds and ran around the track a
couple times, then started South and
began to climb the ~~to~~ "classic heights
of Runnimede". In the language of the lam-
ented A. Ward "They are a success" We climbed
and then we "clumb" and, ~~then~~ climbed again. To
rest ourselves we called it one name awhile
and then the other. The process was exactly alike
in both cases and looked a good deal like
this.   only I had to foreshorten
           the top of the hill when I came
           to the writing instead of continuing
it up about four feet past the ~~upper~~ north
east corner of the paper. Finally we got to
the top and thought that our troubles were
over but they were only begun for after riding
about half a mile the road began to "wobble"
up and down something after the following
fashion.

As Sir Boyle Roache would have said "just when we
had climbed to the highest of all possible hills we

21

Part of a humorous letter from Wilbur to Katharine describing the 31-mile
bicycle expedition he and Orville made to Miamisburg and back.

Katharine in her Oberlin graduation gown, 1898.

23

The only Wright to earn a college degree, Katharine returned home to teach Latin at Steele High School (above), where, as Orville later noted, she would flunk many of Dayton's future leaders.

24

Katharine (front right) and Orville (front left) pose at a party they gave at home in 1899. Her slant-top desk where Wilbur wrote his historic letter to the Smithsonian is at the right.

Lilienthal in flight with one of his creations. [25]

Otto Lilienthal, the German glider pioneer whose influence on the Wright brothers was immense. [26]

Samuel Pierpont Langley, prominent American scientist and head of the Smithsonian Institution, who believed mechanical flight was possible and that he had the solution.

27

28

Langley's costly and much ridiculed "aerodrome" ready for launching from atop a gigantic houseboat on the Potomac River.

Van Cleve
Bicycles
St. Clair

Wright Cycle Company

1127 West Third Street.

DAYTON. OHIO. May 30 1899.

The Smithsonian Institution.

Washington;

Dear Sirs;

I have been interested in the problem of mechanical and human flight ever since as a boy I constructed a number of bats of various sizes after the style of Cayley's and Penaud's machines. My observation since have only convinced me more firmly that human flight is possible and practicable. It is only a question of knowledge and skill just as in all acrobatic feats. Birds are the most perfectly trained ~~so~~ gymnasts in the world and are specially well fitted for their work, and it may be that man will never equal them, but no one who has watched a bird chasing an insect or another bird can doubt that feats are performed which require three or four times the effort required in ordinary flight. I believe that simple flight at least is possible to man and that the ~~comb~~ experiments and investigations of a large number of independent workers will result in the accumulation of information and knowledge and skill which will finally lead to accomplished flight.

The works on the subject to which I have had access

29

Page one of the letter Wilbur wrote to the Smithsonian
that started the Wrights on their pilgrimage.

only way the brothers could get fish was to catch it themselves. "It's just like in the north," Orville explained, "where our carpenters never have their houses completed, nor the painters their houses painted, the fisherman never has any fish."

Their self-reliance was put to the test. They lived mainly on local eggs, tomatoes, and hot biscuits, though these had to be made without milk, so "pitiable" were the local cows. The only things that thrived on the Outer Banks, Orville decided, were bedbugs, mosquitoes, and wood ticks. Wilbur longed especially for butter and coffee, corn bread and bacon.

On the other hand the scene from the tent door—the scene from almost any point—was spectacular, with great stretches of water and sand dunes and beach and a tremendous sky overhead, with cumulus clouds rising like castles, thrilling to behold against the blue. Long flat horizons reached far in the distance in every direction.

And then there was the wind, always the wind. It was not just that it blew nearly all the time, it was the same force that had sculpted the sand hills and great dunes of Kitty Hawk that shaped and kept shaping the whole surrounding landscape.

Far from home, on their own in a way they had never been, the brothers seemed to sense as they never had the adventure of life. Orville would later say that even with all the adversities they had to face, it was the happiest time they had ever known.

Birds on the wing, birds of every kind by the hundreds, filled the air—eagles, snow-white gannets, hawks, pigeons, turkey vultures, or buzzards as they were known on the Outer Banks, with wing spans of as much as six feet. Wilbur devoted hours to studying their movements in the wind, filling pages of his notebook, sometimes adding small drawings. The reality of what birds could do—the *miracle* of birds—remained a subject of continuing importance and fascination, and birdlife on the Outer Banks was beyond anything they had ever imagined, recalling lines from Mouillard's *Empire of the Air.*

> The vulture's needs are few, and his strength is moderate. And so what does he know? He knows how to rise, how to float aloft, to sweep the field with keen vision, to sail upon the wind

without effort . . . he sails and spends no force, he never hur-
ries, he uses the wind.

But how did the soaring bird use the wind, and wind only, to sail aloft
and bank and turn as it wished? Buzzards were masters of the art.

The dihedral angle, a shallow V-shape, of the wings was an advantage
only in still air, Wilbur wrote in his notebook.

The buzzard which uses the dihedral angle ⤵ finds
greater difficulty to maintain equilibrium in strong winds
than eagles and hawks which hold their wings level ⋀⋀

The hen hawk can rise faster than the buzzard and its
motion is steadier. It displays less effort in maintaining its
balance.

Hawks are better soarers than buzzards but more often
resort to flapping because they wish greater speed.

A damp day is favorable for soaring unless there is a high
wind.

No bird soars in a calm.

"All soarers, but especially the buzzard, seem to keep their fore-and-
aft balance more by shifting the center of resistance than by shifting the
center of lift," Wilbur wrote.

If a buzzard be soaring to leeward of the observer, at a distance
of a thousand feet . . . the cross section of its wings will be a
mere line when the bird is moving from the observer but when
it moves toward him the wings appear broad. This would in-
dicate that its wings are always inclined upward, which seems
contrary to reason.

A bird when soaring does not seem to alternately rise and
fall as some observers thought. Any rising or falling is irregu-
lar and seems to be disturbances of fore-and-aft equilibrium
produced by gusts. In light winds the birds seem to rise constantly without any downward turns.

For the local citizens the two brothers from Ohio were extremely hard to figure. One named John T. Daniels, known as "John T." to distinguish him from his father, who was also John Daniels, said later, "We couldn't help thinking they were just a pair of poor nuts. They'd stand on the beach for hours at a time just looking at the gulls flying, soaring, dipping." Gannets, the giant seabirds with a wingspread of five to six feet, seemed their particular interest.

> They would watch the gannets and imitate the movements of their wings with their arms and hands. They could imitate every movement of the wings of those gannets; we thought they were crazy, but we just had to admire the way they could move their arms this way and that and bend their elbows and wrist bones up and down and which way, just like the gannets.

"Learning the secret of flight from a bird," Orville would say, "was a good deal like learning the secret of magic from a magician."

For Katharine's benefit, he wrote also of a "very tame" mockingbird that lived in the one tree overhanging the tent and sang the whole day long. The sunsets, he told her, were the most beautiful he had ever seen, the clouds lighting up in all colors, the stars at night so bright he could read his watch by them.

They were now taking photographs of nearly everything—tent, views, sand, and water, even the mockingbird in the treetop, but primarily the glider in action.

Many nights the wind was such that they had to leap from bed to hold the tent down. "When we crawl out of the tent to fix things, the sand fairly blinds us," Orville wrote. "It blows across the ground in clouds." But they could not complain. "We came down here for wind and sand and we have got them." The night when one of Kitty Hawk's 45-mile-an-hour storms struck with a sound like thunder, there was no sleep. And the winds were cold. "We each have two blankets, but almost freeze every night," Orville wrote. "The wind blows in on my head, and I pull the blankets up over my head, when my feet freeze and I reverse the process. I keep this up all night and in the morning am hardly able to tell 'where I'm at.' "

Their daily sustenance had reached a new low:

> Well, part of the time we eat hot biscuits and eggs and toma-
> toes; part of the time eggs and part tomatoes. Just now we are
> out of gasoline and coffee. Therefore no hot drink or bread or
> crackers. The order sent off Tuesday has been delayed by the
> winds. Will is "most starved."

Nonetheless, as Katharine knew, they were having a splendid time, especially because of their work, but also in good measure because of the
"Kitty Hawkers," whose consistent friendliness and desire to be of help,
whose stories and ways of looking at life and expressing their opinions,
made an enormous difference. The brothers were now hearing, as they had
not before, words like "disremember" for "forget" and such expressions as
"I'll not be seeing you tomorrow," or smooth water described being "slick
calm." "Hoi toide" was "high tide."

A young Tommy Tate, the sixteen-year-old nephew of Bill Tate, informed Orville at one point that the richest man on Kitty Hawk was "Doc"
Cogswell, a "druggist" by profession. Orville inquired how much money
Doc had. "Why, his brother owes him fifteen thousand dollars!" Tommy
said, as though that settled the question.

Bill Tate's interest in what the Ohio men were trying to achieve and his
eagerness to be of help seemed only to grow. Needing to provide for his
family no less than ever, he put in two or three hours a day at his own work
in order to give the rest of his time to the brothers.

Others as well had come to see them as more than mere eccentrics.
Life on the Outer Banks was harsh. Making ends meet was a constant
struggle. Hard workers were greatly admired and in the words of John T.
Daniels, the Wrights were "two of the workingest boys" ever seen, "and
when they worked, *they worked.* . . . They had their whole heart and soul
in what they were doing."

———

By mid-October time was running short. Wilbur had been away from
Dayton for nearly six weeks and word had come from Katharine that she

had had to fire the young man Orville had left in charge of the bicycle shop in their absence. But the brothers still needed one sustained practice at manned flight.

With the help of Bill Tate, they dragged the glider four miles to Kill Devil Hills, a cluster of three prominent sand dunes that Tate, in his letter of August 18, had rightly described as having "not a tree or bush anywhere." The three hills, known as Big Hill, Little Hill, and West Hill, had heights of approximately 100 feet, 30 feet, and 60 feet respectively, but were also being constantly changed in height and shape by the winds.

The view from the top of Big Hill was spectacular in all directions. Three quarters of a mile to the east, beyond the beach, was the great sweep of the blue-green Atlantic; to the north stood a series of immense sand hills; to the south, a long fresh pond and dark woods; and to the west, "the view of views," with Roanoke Island and Roanoke Sound.

The day was clear, the wind just as wished. It was October 19, and after nearly four years of concentrated study and effort by the brothers, it proved a day of days.

Wilbur made one manned flight after another. How many is unknown, no count was kept. He did record, however, flights of 300 to 400 feet in length and speeds on landing of nearly 30 miles an hour.

Only Wilbur did the flying. But now, in contrast to his customary use of the first-person singular when describing how things were progressing, he switched to the first-person plural, as in the lengthy report he later wrote to Octave Chanute. "And although in appearance it was a dangerous practice, we found it perfectly safe and comfortable, except for the flying sand."

During his first days at Kitty Hawk, Wilbur had closed a letter to his father saying it would be no great disappointment to him were he to accomplish practically nothing there. He considered it "a pleasure trip." And certainly it was for both brothers—to be off on their own in a setting so entirely different from any they had ever known and doing what mattered to them above all. They had hoped to learn much of value there and they had, more even than expected. They felt they had found the way forward.

With characteristic understatement, Wilbur summarized by saying they were able to return home "without having our pet theories completely knocked in the head by the hard logic of experience, and our own brains dashed out in the bargain." He said nothing of the fact that for the first time he had experienced the thrill of flying.

They packed for home certain they would return. Their machine, having more than served its purpose, was left behind and Bill Tate was told the materials were his to use as he wished. From the undamaged portions of the sateen wing covering, Addie Tate was to sew dresses for their two daughters.

III.

Work at the bicycle shop and the routines of family life at home continued for Wilbur and Orville much as usual over the next eight months, but nothing so occupied their free time and thoughts as did preparations for a return to Kitty Hawk.

Plans for a new glider were under way, their concentration on the problems still to be solved. Writing again to Octave Chanute, Wilbur said the new glider would be built on the same general plan as the previous model, only larger and with "improved construction in its details." Exactly what those improvements might entail, he did not say, just as he did not say it would be the largest glider ever built until then. The further difference "in its details" was that the curve of the wings would be greater, based on measurements calculated by Otto Lilienthal.

When Chanute wrote to tell Wilbur he expected to be passing through Dayton sometime soon and would like to stop over, Wilbur said he and Orville welcomed the possibility of his visit, but explained that the bicycle business, being what it was in springtime, occupied their attention twelve to fourteen hours a day. However, they were "entirely free" on Sundays.

To have a man of Octave Chanute's standing come to call would be a high tribute. He was not only one of the world's leading authorities on aviation, and on gliders in particular, but enjoyed an international reputation as an engineer, builder of railroads and major bridges, including the Kansas City Bridge, the first span over the Missouri River. He arrived at 7 Hawthorn Street on June 26, a Wednesday not a Sunday, which seems not to have mattered. Bishop Wright, Wilbur, Orville, and Katharine were all on hand to welcome him as he came onto the front porch and into the house for lunch.

At age seventy, Chanute was short, stout, and dapper, with a lingering fringe of white hair about the ears, a mustache, and thin white goatee. He was both kindly in manner and extremely talkative. Katharine and young Carrie Kayler had worked hard on the preparations for the meal, but little notice seems to have been taken of it, so involved were the hosts and their guest with conversation.

The range and content of the discussion are not known, except that Chanute had brought a gift for the brothers, a portable French anemometer, by which they could accurately measure the speed of the wind, something of great value they had been unable to do before. Then, a few days after departing Dayton, Chanute wrote to suggest that two men with whom he worked join the brothers when they returned to Kitty Hawk the coming summer. Although the brothers did not necessarily agree with Chanute's philosophy that progress in science was always best served by everyone working openly together, they accepted Chanute's suggestion if only out of respect.

By mid-June they were far enough along with their new machine to move up their departure to early July, and, importantly, knowing that in their absence this time the bicycle shop would be in reliable hands.

Charles—Charlie—Taylor had been born on a farm in Illinois and arrived in Dayton in 1896, still in his twenties, looking for work as a mechanic. Employed first making farm machinery, he had soon set up his own machine shop, and from time to time helped out with the Wrights, making coaster brakes and other parts for their bicycles. Unlike the bachelor brothers, Charlie was married with two children, and he smoked cigars, one after another nearly all day. He also worked quite as hard as they and with skill rarely to be found.

Stopping by the bicycle shop one evening that June just to "gas," as he said, he was asked if he would like to work there full-time. "They offered me $18 a week," he later recalled. "That was pretty good money. . . . Besides, I liked the Wrights. . . . So far as I can figure out, Will and Orv hired me to worry about their bicycle business so they could concentrate on their flying studies and experiments. . . . And I must have satisfied them for they didn't hire anyone else for eight years."

Of all those who were to enter the lives of the brothers, few were to prove of such value and none was to so aggravate sister Katharine.

Wilbur and Orville left Dayton together on their second expedition to Kitty Hawk by train the evening of Sunday, July 7, 1901, and for the next several weeks were to experience conditions that made those they had known during their previous visit seem like mere inconveniences.

They arrived at Elizabeth City just after one of the worst hurricanes in memory, with winds recorded at 93 miles an hour. Two days passed before they were able to sail for Kitty Hawk.

After a night at the Tates', sharing the most uncomfortable bed either had ever endured, they set off for the foot of Kill Devil Hills and in an all-day drenching rain began setting up camp, a big part of which at that location required driving a pipe 10 to 12 feet into the ground to serve as a well, there being no source of fresh water within a mile.

It was Bill Tate who told them how to get "good water" and who arranged permission from the owners of the land at Kill Devil Hills to establish themselves there.

Because the new glider was to be so large, the shed or hangar for it had also to be good-sized. Orville would proudly describe what they built as a "grand institution with awnings at both ends, that is, with big doors hinged at the top, which we swing open and prop up." In little time, with pine boards shipped over from Elizabeth City, they built a long, solid shed, 16 by 25 feet and 6 feet in height, that would have been considered by many a substantial accomplishment in itself, and they did it in remarkably little time.

Then, just as they were about to start work on the glider, they were hit by misery of a kind and on a scale they had never experienced or even imagined.

Among long-standing summer visitors to Nags Head, the old wisdom was that the infamous Outer Banks "skeeters" struck en masse only once every ten or twelve years. On July 18, it suddenly became clear 1901 was one of those years. As Orville wrote, the mosquitoes appeared "in the form of a mighty cloud, almost darkening the sun." It was by far the worst experience of his life, he would tell Katharine. The agonies of typhoid fever were "as nothing" by comparison. There was no way of escaping the mosquitoes.

> The sand and grass and trees and hills and everything was fairly covered with them. They chewed us clear through our underwear and socks. Lumps began swelling up all over my body like hen's eggs. We attempted to escape by going to bed, which we did at a little after five o'clock. . . . We put our cots out under the awnings and wrapped up in our blankets with only our noses protruding from the folds, thus exposing the least possible surface to attack.

Until then the wind had been blowing at 20 miles an hour. Now it had dropped off entirely and the summer heat kept mounting.

> Our blankets then became unbearable. The perspiration would roll off of us in torrents. We would partly uncover and the mosquitoes would swoop down upon us in vast multitudes. We would make a few desperate and vain slaps, and again retire behind our blankets. Misery! Misery!

Morning brought little relief from the suffering. At first they tried working, but had to give up, so unrelenting was the onslaught. In preparation for the night ahead they built frames and mosquito nets for their cots, then moved the cots 20 to 30 feet from the tent, and crawled in under the nets and again under their blankets. None of this worked. Such was the torture of the night that followed, Orville vowed that come morning they would head for home.

By morning, however, their characteristic resolve returned. The demon mosquitoes had diminished appreciably and in the days to come grew fewer still. But the torment they had been through would never be forgotten.

As it happened, one of the two men Octave Chanute wished to have join the brothers in their experiments had arrived just as the mosquitoes struck and so shared in the miseries. He was Edward Huffaker of Chuckey City, Tennessee, a former employee of the Smithsonian Institution and author of a Smithsonian pamphlet, *On Soaring Flight*. Now a protégé of

Chanute, he had brought with him a disassembled glider of his own de-sign built at Chanute's expense. To Wilbur and Orville he seemed at first a welcome addition.

The second to join the group, young George Alexander Spratt from Coatesville, Pennsylvania, had little in the way of appropriate background for the work at hand. Chanute had described him as having medical train-ing that could prove valuable in case of an accident, but Spratt had aban-doned his medical ambitions after finishing medical school several years before. About all he could offer as reason for his participation was that flying had been the dream of his life, which was altogether true. He arrived in the last days of the mosquito siege.

The hangar-workshop at Kill Devil Hills was now to provide lodg-ing for four. As the chief cook, Orville arranged a corner kitchen with a gas stove fashioned out of a metal barrel and shelves lined with canned goods—Arm & Hammer baking soda, Chase & Sanborn coffee, Royal Purple Hand-Packed tomatoes, Gold Dust Green Gage plums. Fresh but-ter, eggs, bacon, and watermelon had to be carried on foot from Kitty Hawk.

Huffaker expressed amazement at the brothers' "mechanical facility" but was to prove increasingly irksome to them, lazy and indifferent about such daily necessities as washing dishes. He was also inclined to make use of the personal possessions of the others without bothering to ask permission. As tiresome as anything for the sons of Bishop Wright was to hear Huffaker go on about "character building," rather than hard work, being the great aim in life. The more they learned about the glider he had designed and planned to test but never did, the more they considered it a joke.

Spratt, by contrast, helped every way he could and was excellent company.

On July 27, with the glider at last ready, the experiments began. The day was clear, the wind at Kill Devil Hills, about 13 miles an hour. Besides Huffaker and Spratt, Bill Tate and his half-brother Dan were on hand to assist.

Wilbur was to do all the gliding. As they made ready for the first launch into the wind, Orville and Spratt positioned themselves at the corners. Expectations were high.

But no sooner was the machine up than it nosed straight into the ground only a few yards from where it started. Wilbur, it seemed, had positioned himself too far forward. In a second try, having shifted back a bit, he did no better. Finally, after several more failed attempts, he moved back nearly a foot from where he started and sailed off more than 100 yards.

To all present but Wilbur and Orville this flight seemed a huge success. To the brothers it was disappointing. The machine had not performed as expected, not, in fact, as well as the one of the year before. Wilbur had had to use the full power of the rudder to keep from plowing into the ground or rising so high as to lose headway. Something was "radically wrong."

In a glide later the same day, the machine kept rising higher and higher till it lost all headway, exactly "the fix" that had plunged Otto Lilienthal to his death. Responding to a shout from Orville, Wilbur turned the rudder to its full extent and only then did the glider settle slowly to the ground, maintaining a horizontal position almost perfectly, and landing with no damage or injury.

Wilbur went again. And again. Several times the same experience was repeated and with the same result. On one glide the machine even began to drift backward.

"The adjustments of the machine are away off," Orville explained to Katharine. The curvature, or "camber," of the wings, from the leading edges to the rear, was too great and had to be changed. It was this that concerned them the most, the ideal camber, or curve, of the wing from its leading to its trailing edge, being that which gave the wing the most lift against the pull of gravity. What was so troubling was that the ratio they had gone by was exactly what Lilienthal had recommended, about 1 to 12, whereas for their glider of the year before, Machine No. 1, the brothers had used a ratio of 1 to 22.

They stopped gliding for several days to rebuild—flatten—the wings back to a camber close to what it had been in 1900, and with fine results.

Photographs were taken of Wilbur soaring through the air exactly as wished. He himself would write, "The machine with its new curvature never failed to respond promptly to even small movements of the rudder.

> The operator could cause it to almost skim the ground, following the undulations of its surface, or he could cause it to sail out almost on a level with the starting point, and passing high above the foot of the hill, gradually settle down to the ground.

Further, he had no trouble landing quite smoothly at speeds of 20 miles an hour or more.

Work on the wings had filled the first week of August, during which Octave Chanute arrived on the scene. His protégé Huffaker had only praise for the Wrights. As Wilbur had said earlier in a letter to Bishop Wright, "Mr. Huffaker remarked that he would not be surprised to see history made here in the next six weeks.

> Our opinion is not so flattering. He is astonished at our mechanical facility, and as he has attributed his own failures to the lack of this, he thinks the problem solved when these difficulties . . . are overcome, while we expect to find further difficulties of a theoretic nature which must be met by new mechanical designs.

Chanute, too, was greatly impressed by what he saw. He recorded little at the time, however, and apparently had few questions, as different as his own methods had been over the years. For all the time and study he had devoted to the science of gliding, he himself had never physically ventured into the air.

The successful tests flown with the reconstructed wings took place on August 8. The following day Wilbur was back at the controls and in the air once more. But again there were problems, this time of a different and even more troubling kind.

Their wing-warping system of which the brothers were so proud was not responding as expected, and they could not understand why. When the left wing dipped low, while skimming close to the ground for landing, Wilbur had pulled hard on the elevator to no effect. It was like trying to open a barn door in a strong wind. Then suddenly the glider plunged into the sand, throwing him forward through the elevator and leaving him a bruised eye and nose and painful ribs.

Octave Chanute left Kitty Hawk two days later, convinced the Wrights had made more progress and with a larger glider than anyone thus far, and urged them to keep on with their work.

In the days following, it rained without letup, and to add to his miseries Wilbur contracted a cold. George Spratt departed, then Edward Huffaker, but not before helping himself to one of Wilbur's blankets.

On August 20, Wilbur and Orville, too, said their goodbyes to the Tates and others and were on their way home.

———

What they talked about on the train heading back to Ohio was neither recorded at the time nor discussed in any detail afterward. Yet it is clear from a few of their later comments that they were as down in spirit about their work as they had ever been, and especially Wilbur.

It was not just that their machine had performed so poorly, or that so much still remained to be solved, but that so many of the long-established, supposedly reliable calculations and tables prepared by the likes of Lilienthal, Langley, and Chanute—data the brothers had taken as gospel—had proven to be wrong and could no longer be trusted. Clearly those esteemed authorities had been guessing, "groping in the dark." The accepted tables were, in a word, "worthless."

According to what Orville was to write years later, Wilbur was at such a low point he declared that "not in a thousand years would man ever fly." Once home, however, according to Katharine, they talked mainly of how disagreeable Edward Huffaker had been.

CHAPTER FOUR

Unyielding Resolve

We had to go ahead and discover everything ourselves.

ORVILLE WRIGHT

I.

The pall of discouragement disappeared in a matter of days, replaced with a surge of characteristic resolve. They would make a fresh start. Wilbur's gloom on the train was only momentary. As Orville said, "He was at work the following day and it seemed to me was more hopeful and determined than ever."

"We knew that it would take considerable time and funds to obtain data of our own," Orville later recounted, "but there was some spirit that carried us through . . ."

The "boys" were working every night on their "scientific" investigations, Katharine reported to their father. "We don't hear anything but flying machine . . . from morning till night."

Not incidental to the sustaining of spirit were the glass-plate negatives of the photographs taken at Kitty Hawk, which the brothers developed in a darkroom set up in the carriage shed out back. There, Wilbur would write, he and Orville had moments of "as thrilling interest as any in the field, when the image begins to appear on the plate and it is yet an open question whether we have a picture of a flying machine, or merely a patch of open sky."

At the end of August came an invitation from Octave Chanute for Wilbur to address the Western Society of Engineers in Chicago on the subject of gliding experiments. It was his first request to speak in public, and he was extremely reluctant to accept, feeling the date set, September 18, left too little time to prepare anything of substance. But Katharine "nagged" him into going. That Wilbur might prove a poor speaker seems never to have entered her thoughts.

Only days later, in the first week of September, came the shocking news that President William McKinley had been shot by an insane anarchist named Leon Czolgosz, while attending the Pan-American Exposition at Buffalo, New York. For days he was at death's door. "McKINLEY IS DYING," read the large headline across the front page of the *Dayton Free Press* on September 13. The following morning, he was dead, and that same day at Buffalo, young Theodore Roosevelt took the oath of office as the twenty-sixth president of the United States.

William McKinley had been "Ohio's own." Born in Ohio, he had served through the Civil War in the 23rd Ohio Volunteer Regiment, married an Ohio girl, served long as an Ohio congressman and for two terms as the governor of Ohio. In Dayton, the day of his death, thousands of people filled the streets downtown. The scene was like nothing in the city's history. Fire bells tolled. The courthouse and other public buildings were quickly and heavily draped in black.

The Wright brothers, it appears, kept working as hard as ever at the shop, possibly as a way of coping with the tragedy. For Wilbur there was the added pressure of preparing his lecture. The morning he boarded the train for Chicago, September 18, Dayton was still shrouded in black, as McKinley was not to be buried for another two days.

Orville and Katharine having decided that Wilbur's wardrobe was insufficient for so important a public debut, he went off, as Katharine recorded, "arrayed in Orv's shirt, collars, cuffs, cuff-links, and overcoat." Never had he looked "so 'swell.' "

How he felt was another matter. Octave Chanute had written to inquire whether he would mind if the meeting of the society was designated "Ladies' Night." Wilbur had replied it was not for him to decide. "I will already be as badly scared as it is possible for a man to be." Asked by

Katharine and Orville whether his talk would be scientific or witty, he said, "Pathetic."

Arriving in Chicago, he went directly to Chanute's three-story brownstone on Huron Street to dine with Chanute prior to the speech and was relieved to find his host as cordial as ever and the kind of man whose top-floor, private study was so chock-full of models of flying machines and stuffed birds he could hardly get into it himself.

The gathering of some fifty society members and their wives convened at the Monadnock Building at eight o'clock. In his brief introduction Chanute spoke of the advances made in aerial navigation by "two gentlemen from Dayton, Ohio" bold enough to attempt things neither he nor Otto Lilienthal had dared try.

The speech Wilbur delivered—modestly titled "Some Aeronautical Experiments"—would be quoted again and again for years to come. Published first in the society's journal, it appeared in full or part in *The Engineering Magazine, Scientific American,* the magazine *Flying,* and the *Annual Report* of the Smithsonian Institution. In the words of a latter-day aeronautics specialist at the Library of Congress, the speech was "the Book of Genesis of the twentieth-century Bible of Aeronautics."

It was authentic Wilbur Wright, straightforward and clear. What was needed above all for success with a flying machine, he said, was the ability to ride with the wind, to balance and steer in the air. To explain how a bird could soar through the air would take much of the evening, he said. Instead he took a sheet of paper, and, holding it parallel to the floor, let it drop. It would not "settle steadily down as a staid, sensible piece of paper ought to do, but it insists on contravening every recognized rule of decorum, turning over and darting hither and thither in the most erratic manner, much after the style of an untrained horse." This was the kind of horse, he said, that men had to learn to manage in order to fly, and there were two ways:

> One is to get on him and learn by actual practice how each
> motion and trick may be best met; the other is to sit on a fence
> and watch the beast a while, and then retire to the house and
> at leisure figure out the best way of overcoming his jumps and

kicks. The latter system is the safest, but the former, on the whole, turns out the larger proportion of good riders.

If one were looking for perfect safety, he said, one would do well to sit on the fence and watch the birds. "But if you really wish to learn, you must mount a machine and become acquainted with its tricks by actual trial."

He praised the work of both Lilienthal and Chanute. "Lilienthal not only thought, but acted. . . . He demonstrated the feasibility of actual practice in the air, without which success is impossible." Noting that Lilienthal, over a period of five years, had spent no more than five hours in actual gliding, he said the wonder was not that he had done so little, but that he had accomplished so much. What if a bicycle rider tried to ride through a crowded city after only five hours' practice, spread out in bits of ten seconds over a period of five years?

He praised the biplane developed by Chanute as a "very great structural advance" and told how, with a few changes, he and Orville had built and tested their own double-deck glider in Outer Banks winds of up to 27 miles per hour.

Much that followed in the published version of the speech was highly technical and included mathematical equations and diagrams of wing curvatures. ("Do not be afraid of making it too technical," Chanute had urged.) How critical Wilbur had been about the unreliable data compiled by Lilienthal and Chanute when addressing the Chicago gathering is unknown, since no stenographic record was made of the actual speech. But in the published version he pulled back considerably out of respect for Chanute. Of Lilienthal's tables, he went only so far to say Lilienthal might have been "somewhat in error."

If Chanute took issue with anything Wilbur said, or was in any way offended, he never let on. In a letter written after he finished proofreading the speech before publication, Chanute called it "a devilish good paper which will be extensively quoted."

That Wilbur returned to Dayton from Chicago even more grateful for Chanute's friendship and counsel can be seen in the increased volume of their correspondence. Over the next three months, until the end of the year, Wilbur would write to Chanute more than twelve times, or once a week on average. Some of the letters ran as long as seven to nine pages, and Chanute invariably replied without delay.

Meanwhile, an article in the September issue of the popular *McClure's Magazine* written by Simon Newcomb, a distinguished astronomer and professor at Johns Hopkins University, dismissed the dream of flight as no more than a myth. And were such a machine devised, he asked, what useful purpose could it possibly serve? "The first successful flyer will be the handiwork of a watchmaker, and will carry nothing heavier than an insect."

———

With their former trust in the calculations of Lilienthal and Chanute shattered, the brothers set out that autumn of 1901 to crack the code of aeronautics themselves. It was a brave decision and a crucial turning point.

Of primary importance was to find a way to achieve accurate measurements of the "lift" and "drag" of a wing's surface, and the ingenuity, as well as patience, they brought to their experiments were like nothing done by anyone until then. For three months, working in one of the upstairs rooms at the bicycle shop, they concentrated nearly all of their time on these "investigations" and with stunning results.

They devised and built a small-scale wind tunnel—a wooden box 6 feet long and 16 inches square, with one end open and a fan mounted at the other end, and this powered, since the shop had no electricity, by an extremely noisy gasoline engine. The box stood on four legs about waist high.

Although a wind tunnel had been used by an English experimenter, Francis Herbert Wenham, as early as the 1870s, and by several others since, including Hiram Maxim, their tests were nothing like those of the brothers, who proceeded entirely on their own and in their own way.

For testing apparatus inside the box, they used old hacksaw blades cut to different sizes with tin shears and hammered into a variety of shapes and thicknesses—some flat, some concave and convex, or square or oblong, and each about six inches square and one-thirty-second of an inch thick—these strung on bicycle spoke wires.

Though such apparatus did not look like much, it was to prove of immense value. For nearly two months the brothers tested some thirty-eight wing surfaces, setting the "balances" or "airfoils"—the different-shaped hacksaw blades—at angles from 0 to 45 degrees in winds up to 27 miles per hour. It was a slow, tedious process, but as Orville wrote, "those metal models told us how to build."

Octave Chanute was astonished by what Wilbur had to report. "It is perfectly marvelous to me how quickly you get results with your testing machine," he wrote. "You are evidently better equipped to test the endless variety of curved surfaces than anybody has ever been." When Wilbur apologized for writing to him at such length, Chanute assured him his letters were always too brief.

The work was unlike anything the brothers had ever undertaken and the most demanding of their time and powers of concentration. They were often at it past midnight. As said later in the *Aeronautical Journal* of the Aeronautical Society of Great Britain, "Never in the history of the world had men studied the problem with such scientific skill nor with such undaunted courage."

In December came another voice of scientific authority denouncing, as Simon Newcomb had, the dream of flight as a total sham, the article appearing in the greatly respected *North American Review,* and written by no less than the chief engineer of the United States Navy, Rear Admiral George Melville. "A calm survey of certain natural phenomena leads the engineer to pronounce all confident prophecies for future success as wholly unwarranted, if not absurd. Where, even to this hour, are we to look for the germ of the successful flying machine? Where is the preparation today?"

By late December, their experiments finished and feeling the pressure of economic necessity, the brothers turned to the production of the next season's bicycles. As Charlie Taylor liked to stress, they had to keep the business going to pay for the experiments. Octave Chanute wrote to say how greatly he regretted their decision.

For some time Chanute had been offering to provide financial help to the brothers, which they greatly appreciated but were unwilling to accept. "Practically all the expense of our aeronautical experiments lies in the time consumed and we do not wish to increase the temptation to neglect our regular business for it," Wilbur wrote to him.

What if some rich man were to provide $10,000 a year, Chanute asked, adding that he happened to know Andrew Carnegie. "Would you like for me to write to him?" Again Wilbur tactfully declined. Besides, he added, it seemed likely Carnegie was "too hardheaded a Scotchman to become interested in such a visionary pursuit as flying."

As he and Orville had no need to say, they knew full well the importance of what they had achieved with their "laboratory work." They had done it together on their own, paying their own way, as they did everything, and they intended to keep going on their own.

Not for another several months, until the spring of 1902, were they able to begin building a new glider based on all they had learned from the wind tunnel tests, for even with the help of Charlie Taylor, production and sales of their bicycles still demanded a great part of their time and attention.

Word of what they were up to seems also to have been getting around in some circles and apparently with their approval if not at their own instigation. For on January 25, 1902, a short, unsigned notice appeared in the *Dayton Daily News* stating for the first time in any publication that two local "aeronautical experts" had demonstrated "to an absolute certainty that many of the theories heretofore advanced in flying machine circles may be cast to the four winds.

> These gentlemen are Wilbur and Orville Wright, cycle dealers and makers, who have experimented with marked success in [North] Carolina and who at present bid fair to revolutionize the work of experts in making tests of aerial navigation. . . .
>
> It would be fitting that Dayton should afford experiments which may lead to a complete solution to aerial navigation.

This notice, carefully clipped from the paper by the brothers, or perhaps Katharine, would figure prominently at the beginning of a first scrapbook documenting their efforts.

II.

A t the same time the family was facing a highly unpleasant situation involving Bishop Wright that put severe strain on them all, and Wilbur in particular. It was a burden he accepted without complaint, even as it required giving up days, eventually weeks of his time.

The trouble had first taken root some fifteen years before, in the 1880s, when two contentious factions within the United Brethren Church struggled for control. The issue was mainly the church's traditional anti-Masonic stance, one side holding firm to that position, the other arguing for acceptance of Freemasonry and its secret ways as one of the realities of the times and, not incidentally, as a clear means to increase church membership and revenues.

Those in favor of welcoming Masons to church membership were the so-called Liberals. Those opposed, the Radicals, were led by Milton Wright, never one afraid to speak out for what he believed, who, even then, had called on Wilbur to help write articles and editorials in response to attacks by the opposition.

But the Liberals prevailed. The Bishop lost his fight. His role in the church was reduced to virtually nothing. Undaunted, he continued with his travels as an itinerant preacher and in 1889, the year of Susan Wright's death, he set about establishing a new church to be known as the Old Constitution Church.

Time passed. Then, in 1901, an investigation initiated by Bishop Wright found the official in charge of publications for the Old Constitution Brethren, the Reverend Millard Keiter, had been making use of church money for his personal expenses, to the amount of nearly $7,000.

In February 1902, the Bishop asked Wilbur to examine the church account books, and from his review Wilbur concluded the Reverend Keiter had indeed helped himself to church funds to pay for his own insurance premiums, personal clothing, and part of the construction cost of his home. But when the church's board of trustees met to review the charges against Keiter, it was decided, despite the evidence, that any discrepancies had resulted from carelessness, not fraud.

"My chief regret," Wilbur wrote to his father, "is that the strain and worry which you have borne for fifteen years past shows no sign of being removed. . . . It would seem however that the fight only increases in intensity." Wilbur also had no doubt that the fight must go on.

> The question of whether officials shall rob the church and trustees deceive the church for fear of injuring collections, must be settled now for all time. In the long run nothing can be gained financially by deceit. To cheat the people by lying reports is more dishonest than Keiter's stealing, and so far as church interests are concerned, the penalty will be greater.

In mid-March, Wilbur took the train to Huntington, Indiana, for further examination of the publishing house records and returned home two days later to assure his father that Keiter's books and papers were "very crooked."

With strong encouragement from Wilbur, the Bishop decided to do something on his own. He and Wilbur spent a full day preparing "an exposé of Keiter's defalcations," as the Bishop wrote in his diary, and the day after, Orville finished typewriting the final tract.

Without waiting for approval from his church, the Bishop accused Keiter of criminal conduct. Keiter was brought to trial, but not convicted. Sentiment within the church began to turn against the Bishop for having overplayed his hand. Old friends, he told Katharine, spoke of him behind his back as an "egotist." Then in May, Millard Keiter filed formal charges against the Bishop, accusing him of libel.

Wilbur described the situation as "absolutely inconceivable, incomprehensible, and incredible." He had not stopped examining Keiter's books and was, as he wrote, "finding new instances of his stealing every few days." Worn down and filled with worry, his father had trouble sleeping.

The charges and countercharges continued on into summer. On August 15, Wilbur issued a tract in defense of his father.

> When my father and myself came to examine the charges [against the Bishop] carefully, we at once saw that the whole

thing was a mere sham. The charges were so trivial as to be laughable. . . .

Although Mr. Keiter and his followers are on general principles opposed to investigations and trials, nevertheless they saw some advantages in instituting a pretended prosecution against Bishop Wright. . . .

The institution of even a bogus case would afford opportunity for the wide circulation of reports that Bishop Wright's own character was under a cloud.

That day in a letter to his father, who was back on the road again, Wilbur wrote to assure him "things are moving nicely" and not to worry. Katharine followed with another letter to tell him Wilbur and Orville were so convinced things would turn out right that they were talking of leaving for Kitty Hawk the following week and that she thought it past time they got away for a while. "Will is thin and nervous and so is Orv. They will be all right when they get down to the sand where the salt breezes blow. . . . They think that life at Kitty Hawk cures all ills."

By late August, the brothers had reached the final stage in building their new glider—stitching yards of white Bride-of-the-West muslin for the wing covering—which they carried on in the backyard at 7 Hawthorn Street, and so inspiring much talk and speculation in the neighborhood. "Some say the boys just go camping and they make their own tents," said one neighbor. "Others say they are trying to fly. I don't believe they're that foolish."

"Will spins the sewing machine around by the hour," wrote Katharine, "while Orv squats around marking the places to sew."

On August 26 with everything needed for Machine No. 3 packed and crated for shipment, the brothers departed on their third expedition to Kitty Hawk, leaving it to Katharine and Charlie Taylor to carry on with the bicycle store.

She was particularly pleased to see Wilbur off—it was the best thing in the world for him to go away, Katharine told her father. "He _was_ completely unnerved. When he gets a thing on his mind, he thinks of it continually."

She also wanted her father to know she was in the fight with him every bit as much as the brothers. "We'll never stop fighting now, Pop, until we've shown those rascals up."

Soon she had more to contend with. Charlie Taylor, as she informed the brothers, was making her "too weary for words." The man claimed to know everything about everything. "I despise to be at the mercy of the hired man." Thankfully the school year had begun, her classes had resumed, and she was now making an unprecedented $25 a week.

———

Things would indeed turn out right for the Bishop in the end. Two years later, at a church conference in Grand Rapids, Michigan, in 1904, he would be completely exonerated by a two-thirds majority. Writing to a niece a few years later, the Bishop said of Millard Keiter, "His former friends have become convinced of his unworthy character, and he has gone to Tennessee as a timberland speculator."

In all, the continuing worry and frustrations involved in defending the Bishop's honor, the countless hours consumed, had brought the family closer together than ever, resolved to be ever wary of those of "unworthy character."

III.

She would just have to get used to some of Charlie Taylor's peculiarities, Orville told Katharine in his first letter to her since reaching Kitty Hawk, then went on to say the weather there was fine, that he and Wilbur had been assembling the machine and were nearly ready to start testing. He imagined, he said, that by the time she received the letter she would be back at school teaching again, and he asked her to send a list of her "victims." "I like to see someone else catch it besides us."

By the second week of September word from Kitty Hawk grew more extensive, as both brothers took time to fill her in with news of the kind she most liked to hear, no more trouble from the mosquitoes and that they were sprucing up their quarters at Kill Devil Hills with such "royal luxuries" as white oilcloth on the dining table and burlap upholstery on the dining chairs. Orville's letters, which delighted Katharine especially, refute any idea that he had no gift for writing and express how much he did not want "little sister" to feel left out.

Most enjoyable to her was a rendition from Orville of an all-out pursuit of an uncommonly resourceful mouse that kept prowling about the kitchen and thereby provided the only excitement of the moment.

"He met with a rather warm reception the other night when he undertook to promenade on Will's bed," Orville began, "[and] got tossed a good deal . . . in a blanket, until finally he escaped.

> We found him snugly wrapped up in our carpet this afternoon. We had a merry chase all about the building, inside and out. The large cracks in the floor making it easy for him to get in or out in a hurry when necessary. But as there were two of us, one with a stick and one with a gun, one above and one below the floor, his chances of escape were beginning to look rather shaky. Finally, he nestled up in a corner below the floor to take time to get a breath, when I blazed away at him with the gun. The mark of the bullet is in the corner right back of where he stood, nevertheless the little beastie turned around and calmly walked away and I in my astonishment just stood there and watched him go.

The standard of living at Kitty Hawk had been greatly enhanced. Damage done to the camp by storms in their absence had required immediate attention, but they also saw to considerably more. The kitchen was "immensely improved," and they slept now in new, more comfortable beds rigged up in the rafters. They hammered up battens to seal off the cracks between the boards the whole length and width of the building. They had sunk a deeper well that produced better water. Best of all, they had devised a bicycle that ran far better over sand than they could have hoped for, so a round-trip to Kitty Hawk now took only one hour, instead of three on foot.

Little if any of what the brothers did went unnoticed by the local residents, who by now, as John T. Daniels said, had "learned to love 'em," and in no small part because they "could do anything they put their hands to.

> They built their own camp; they took an old carbide can and made a stove of it; they took a bicycle and geared the thing up so that they could ride it on the sand. They did their own cooking and washing and they were good cooks too.

"There are other improvements too numerous to mention, and no Huffaker and no mosquitoes," Wilbur reported to George Spratt, who was to join them again.

This time, too, Orville was keeping far better day-to-day diary records of just how hard they were working.

> *Monday, September 8.* Finally began work on machine. . . . Completed frame of upper surface [wing] ready for ribs.

> *Tuesday, September 9.* Worked 8 hours on machine. Fastened ribs to frame and put on cloth.

> *Wednesday, September 10.* Worked about 5½ hours each, tacking and sewing on cloth. . . . Surface complete except part of covering to rear spar.

> *Thursday, September 11.* Completed covering of rear spar. Erected poles for testing angles at various velocities of wind. . . . Began work on lower surface in afternoon. Spliced spars, and fastened on end bows, ready for attaching ribs.

> *Friday, September 12.* Worked eight hours each on machine. Put on ribs and cloth. Took upper surface on Big [Kill Devil] Hill a little before noon. Find that much better results are found by walking the machine.

> *Saturday, September 13.* Finished lower surface. . . .

> *Monday, September 15.* Worked 10 hours each. . . .

With each wing, or "surface," measuring 32 by 5 feet this time, and a total wingspan therefore of 320 square feet, it was by far the largest glider yet built and, as Wilbur also told George Spratt, "an immense improvement over last year's machine."

———

On September 19, they took it to a small hill and began flying it first as a kite and with "very satisfactory" results. After moving to Kill Devil Hills they made nearly fifty glides in three days—including manned flights—but cautiously. Even the longest flights were not much over 200 feet.

Orville, too, was now gliding for the first time, and proudly so. Then only days later, he suddenly lost control and crashed. Luckily, he got out "without a bruise or a scratch," but it was a clear reminder of just how dangerous it all was, and how suddenly things could go wrong.

> My brother [wrote Wilbur to Octave Chanute], after too brief practice with the use of the front rudder, tried to add the use of the wing-twisting [wing-warping] arrangement also, with the result that, while he was correcting a slight rise in one wing, he completely forgot to attend to the front rudder, and the machine reared up and rose some twenty-five feet and sidled off and struck the ground. . . . We hope to have repairs made in a few days.

Close to the end of September brother Lorin Wright walked into camp for an unexpected visit, and George Spratt appeared soon after. At the same time came a rare lull in the wind lasting several days.

With all tests postponed, Lorin and Spratt went fishing, while Wilbur and Orville kept busy as usual, Wilbur also taking time to write an exuberant letter to his father to report how extremely well things were going. "We are in splendid health and having a fine time." And yes, they were being "very careful." Beyond that, he was proud to report, their new machine was a "very great improvement over anything anyone has built. . . . Everything is so much more satisfactory that we now believe that the flying problem is really nearing its solution."

The letter was dated October 2. That night, as Orville later told the story, discussion in camp on aeronautical theory went on at such length that he indulged himself in more coffee than usual. Unable to sleep, he lay awake thinking about ways to achieve an even better system of control when suddenly he had an idea: the rear rudder, instead of being in a fixed position, should be hinged—movable.

In the morning at breakfast, he proposed the change, but not before giving Lorin a wink, a signal to watch Wilbur for one of his customary critical responses. Wilbur, as George Spratt once told Octave Chanute, was "always ready to oppose an idea expressed by anybody," ready to "jump into an argument with both sleeves rolled up." And as Wilbur himself would explain to Spratt, he believed in "a good scrap." It brought out "new ways of looking at things," helped "round off the corners." It was characteristic of all his family, Wilbur said, to be able to see the weak points of anything. This was not always a "desirable quality," he added, "as it makes us too conservative for successful business men, and limits our friendships to a very limited circle."

This time, however, after a moment when no one spoke, Wilbur declared he liked the idea, then surprised Orville even more: Why not simplify the pilot's job by connecting control of the rudder with those of the wing warping?

Work began on the change that same day.

Rather than a fixed rudder of 2-foot vertical fins, as it had been until now, the glider hereafter would have a single movable rudder 5 feet high, and the operator, stretched on his stomach, would operate both the rudder and the warping of the wings by means of a new wooden "hip cradle." Thus no hands were needed, only movement of the hips, not coincidentally like the use of the hips in maneuvering a bicycle.

Two days later, the camp grew more crowded still. Octave Chanute and another of his associates, Augustus Herring, arrived, making six now at meals and even closer-packed sleeping accommodations aloft in the rafters. Further, they had brought a triplane hang glider of their own design they wished to test, which consumed far more time and attention than the brothers wished and proved a total failure. After Herring failed several times to get the cumbersome three-wing machine off the ground, Wilbur and Orville each gave it a try and did no better.

Chanute and Herring stayed a week. But Chanute, for all his disappointment in his own glider, understood the importance of what the brothers had achieved, and on his way back to Chicago, during a stopover in Washington, made a point of calling on Samuel Langley to report what he had seen at Kitty Hawk.

As head of the Smithsonian, Langley occupied a spacious office in the institution's turreted "Castle" on the Mall. He and Chanute were close in age, Langley, sixty-eight, Chanute, seventy-two, more than thirty years older than the Wrights. They were two personages of high reputation and accomplishment, and with their white beards looked every bit the savants they were.

But where Chanute espoused an open exchange of knowledge and ideas among those involved in the quest for flight, Langley maintained extreme secrecy about his efforts. Every aspect of his heavily financed Smithsonian experiments remained confidential. In sharp contrast to the affable Chanute, Langley, a thorough Boston Brahmin, had what his friends kindly termed a "shell of hauteur."

Since the launching of his pilotless, steam-powered aerodrome in 1896, Langley and his Smithsonian "team" had been at work on a far larger, and again well-financed, version of the same machine, except that this would be powered by a gasoline engine and carry a single operator. Almost no one, other than those directly involved, knew anything about it, just as Langley wished.

Until now Langley had paid little or no attention to the Wrights and their efforts, but hearing all Chanute had to report, he was suddenly quite interested and wrote at once to the brothers to say he would like to come to Kitty Hawk to see for himself. Wilbur and Orville politely declined, but for what reason is unknown.

———

Lorin, too, soon made his exit, and on October 17, with the help of Spratt, the brothers moved the remodeled glider to Kill Devil Hills to resume testing. The weather by now had turned cold enough that a fire had to be kept burning all night. Rations were down to little more than canned beans. None of this seemed to matter.

When Spratt's turn came to depart, the brothers were on their own again, and as so often before, with help only from the faithful Bill Tate. In ten days of practice they made more glides than in all the preceding weeks, and increased their record for distance to more than 600 feet. Altogether in two months on the Outer Banks they had made nearly a thousand glides and resolved the last major control problem.

They were elated and would gladly have stayed another several weeks had Bill Tate not long since committed himself to taking charge of a boat and crew at the opening of the fishing season.

They broke camp at first light on October 28 in a cold, driving rain and walked the four miles to Kitty Hawk to start the journey home and in a frame of mind far different from what it had been at their departure the year before. All the time and effort given to the wind tunnel tests, the work designing and building their third machine, and the latest modifications made at Kill Devil Hills had proven entirely successful. They knew exactly the importance of what they had accomplished. They knew they had solved the problem of flight and more. They had acquired the knowledge and the skill to fly. They could soar, they could float, they could dive and rise, circle and glide and land, all with assurance.

Now they had only to build a motor.

Part II

CHAPTER FIVE

December 17, 1903

When we got up a wind of between 20 and 25 miles was blowing from the north. We got the machine out early and put up the signal for the men at the station.

ORVILLE WRIGHT'S DIARY,
DECEMBER 17, 1903

I.

With the arrival of the New Year 1903, the outlook in Dayton was more promising than ever. The local population had reached nearly 100,000 and according to the *Evening News*, an equal number were now finding their way there to do business. It was no town for a pessimist, said the paper, "but if there is any hope for him, here he may breathe the glorious air of prosperity and imbibe the spirit of optimism and be cured."

To Americans throughout most of the country, the future was full of promise. A New Year's Day editorial in the *Chicago Tribune* said one would have to be of "dull comprehension" not to realize things were better than they had ever been and would be "better still when new science and new methods, and new educations have done their perfect work." The tempo of popular tunes was appropriately upbeat. Pianists north and south were playing ragtime, people singing and dancing to hits like "Bill Bailey, Won't You Please Come Home?" and "In the Good Old Summer Time."

Employment was up nearly everywhere. In the state of New York practically the entire labor force was working. Wages were rising, the national wealth increasing. Instead of a national debt, there was a surplus of $45 million. In Washington one sensed "a new velocity" under the leadership of Theodore Roosevelt. The country was about to take on the building of the Panama Canal, picking up where the French had failed. No new year had "ever brought the people of the United States a more encouraging outlook," said the *Albuquerque Journal-Democrat*. Further, as noted in numerous editorials, Sunday sermons, and at many a family dinner table, the world was at peace.

One of the few puzzling questions to be considered, said the *Philadelphia Inquirer*, was why, so far, after so much attention had been paid to "aerial navigation," had there been so few results?

———

It was shortly before the New Year when the Wright brothers sent out letters to manufacturers of automobile engines in seven states asking if they could supply an off-the-shelf engine light enough in weight but with sufficient power for their purposes. There was only one response, and in that case the motor was much too heavy. So again they had some original work to do and they had had no experience building engines.

In time to come the brothers would be widely portrayed as a couple of clever, hometown bicycle mechanics who managed to succeed where so many others had failed because of their good old-fashioned American knack for solving seemingly impossible mechanical problems. This was true only in part.

For Charlie Taylor, however, the description applied almost perfectly, except that he was more than a clever mechanic, he was a brilliant mechanic and for the brothers a godsend. If sister Katharine found Charlie's claim to know all the answers unbearable, Wilbur and Orville never lost sight of his ability and enormous value to their efforts. And he himself well understood how far beyond him they were in so many ways. As he later said, boasting about them, "Those two sure knew their physics. I guess that's why they always knew what they were doing and hardly ever guessed at anything." As for building the engine:

> While the boys were handy with tools, they had never done much machine-work and anyway they were busy on the air frame. It was up to me. . . . We didn't make any drawings. One of us would sketch out the part we were talking about on a piece of scratch paper and I'd spike the sketch over my bench.

His only prior experience with a gasoline engine had been trying to repair one in an automobile a few years before. But that January, working in the back shop with the same metal lathe and drill press used for building bicycles, he went to work and six weeks later had it finished.

The motor had four cylinders with a 4-inch bore and a 4-inch stroke. It was intended to deliver 8 horsepower and weigh no more than 200 pounds, to carry a total of 675 pounds, the estimated combined weight of the flying machine and an operator. As it turned out, the motor Charlie built weighed only 152 pounds, for the reason that the engine block was of cast aluminum provided by the up-and-coming Aluminum Company of America based in Pittsburgh. Other materials came from Dayton manufacturers and suppliers, but the work of boring out the aluminum for the independent cylinders and making the cast iron piston rings was all done by one man with a drooping walrus mustache working in the back room at the bicycle shop.

> The fuel system was simple [he would later explain]. A one gallon fuel tank was [to be] suspended from a wing strut, and the gasoline fed by gravity down a tube to the engine. . . . There was no carburetor. . . . The fuel was fed into a shallow chamber in the manifold. Raw gas blended with air in this chamber, which was next to the cylinders and heated up rather quickly, thus helping to vaporize the mixture. The engine was started by priming each cylinder with a few drops of raw gas.

Compared to later engines all was amazingly simple and crude. The ignition was of the "make-and-break type" in Charlie's expression, probably meaning that if broken it could be quickly fixed. There were no spark plugs.

The spark was made by the opening and closing of two contact points inside the combustion chamber. These were operated by shafts and cams geared to the main camshaft. The ignition switch was an ordinary single-throw knife switch we bought at a hardware store.

The "little gas motor," as Bishop Wright called it, was finished by mid-February, and when started up in the shop the first time the racket and clouds of smoke were nearly unbearable. When further tested the next day, the engine block cracked. Dripping gasoline had frozen the bearings, breaking the engine body and frame.

Another two months went by before a second block would be delivered from Pittsburgh. This engine worked fine and as a bonus delivered an unexpected 12 horsepower.

Meantime, the design of the propellers had become a still bigger challenge. "I think the hardest job Will and Orv had was with the propellers," Charlie later said. "I don't believe they ever were given enough credit for that development."

The problem became more complex the more the brothers studied it. Much to their surprise, they could find no existing data on air propellers. They had assumed they could go by whatever rule-of-thumb marine engineers used for the propellers on boats, and accordingly drew on the resources of the Dayton library only to find that after a hundred years in use the exact action of a screw propeller was still obscure. Once more they were left no choice but to solve the problem themselves. "Our minds," said Orville, "became so obsessed with it that we could do little other work."

They began to see the propeller as an airplane wing traveling in a spiral course, and that if they could calculate the effect of a wing traveling a straight course, why could they not calculate the effect of one traveling in a spiral course?

But on further consideration [Orville would explain], it is hard to find even a point from which to make a start; for nothing about a propeller, or the medium in which it acts, stands still for a moment. The thrust depends upon the speed and the angle at which the blade strikes the air; the angle at which the blade strikes the air depends on the speed at which the propeller is turning, the speed the machine is traveling forward, and the speed at which the air is slipping backward; the slip of the air backward depends on the thrust exerted by the propeller, and the amount of air acted upon. When any one of these change, it changes all the rest, as they are all interdependent on one another.

After several months of study and discussion they had come to understand that the thrust generated by a standing propeller was no indication of the thrust when in motion, and that the only realistic way to test the efficiency of a propeller would be to try it out on the flying machine.

During these months their "discussions" became as intense as they had ever been. Heated words flew, filling hours of their days and nights, often at the tops of their voices. "If you don't stop arguing, I'll leave home," a nearly hysterical Katharine cried out at one point.

According to Charlie Taylor, they were never really mad at each other. One morning after one of their "hottest" exchanges, he had only just opened the shop at seven o'clock as usual when Orville came in saying he "guessed he'd been wrong and they ought to do it Will's way." Shortly after, Wilbur arrived to announce he had been thinking it over and "perhaps Orv was right." The point was, said Charlie, "when they were through . . . they knew where they were and could go ahead with the job."

The new Flyer, as they called it, would have two propellers positioned between the two wings just to the rear of the operator. One would turn clockwise, the other, counterclockwise, so the spinning, or gyroscopic action, of the one would balance that of the other. Making the propellers with the proper diameter, pitch, and surface area proved no great problem.

Each had a diameter of 8 and a half feet and were made of three spruce laminations glued together and shaped by hand with a hatchet and spoke shaver, or "drawknife," as used by wheelwrights. That they were different from any propellers ever built before was certain, and the last major problem had been resolved.

Again, the machine would ride on skids, not wheels. The operator would again lie prone at the controls in the middle of the lower wing. The motor and a radiator would be positioned directly beside him on the right.

A little one-gallon gas tank hung overhead on a strut to his left. The drive chains for the propellers were specially made by the Indianapolis Chain Company, and Roebling wire would be used for the trusses between the wings—wire made by the Roeblings who built the Brooklyn Bridge.

On March 23, the brothers applied for a patent on their flying machine, its wing-warping system, and rudder.

In late April came a letter postmarked Paris from Octave Chanute, who, to help recover from the death of his wife, had been on an extended vacation in Europe. Their experiments were attracting much attention in Paris, he reported to the brothers, adding, "It seems very queer that after having ignored all this series of gliding experiments for several years, the French should now be over-enthusiastic about them." While in Paris he had given several talks on the subject, including one at a formal dinner conference at the Aéro-Club de France.

What the genial Chanute did not relate was how, in these talks, he had portrayed his part in the experiments, referring repeatedly to the Wrights as his "devoted collaborators." Perhaps it was his pride in *les frères*, or the glow he undoubtedly felt being a center of attention in his native France where interest in aviation was great. However, the impression he conveyed was that he was their teacher, and they, his daring pupils, were carrying "his" work to fulfillment.

This was not only untrue but grossly unfair. Great as had been Chanute's interest and encouragement, the brothers had never in any way been his pupils or collaborators. All they had achieved was their own doing, gained by their own original study and effort. Exactly when and how they learned of what Chanute had said in Paris is unclear, but it was not something they were happy about or would forget.

Of far greater consequence, however, was Chanute's admirable emphasis on the importance of their glider flights, all of which was a revelation for the French and "even a little disagreeable," as said one of the Aéro-Club's leaders, Comte Henri de La Vaulx. It was time for French aviation experimenters "to get seriously to work if they did not wish to be left behind."

In his speech and in numerous conversations while in France, Chanute had also provided a great deal of information on the details of the Wright glider, and this would indeed have a profound impact on French aviation.

Chanute had agreed to write something for the influential publication *L'Aérophile*, he informed Wilbur, and would need pictures of him and Orville without delay. After allowing a few weeks to slip by, Wilbur replied good-naturedly that they did not know how to refuse when Chanute had put the matter so nicely, but on the other hand they had not the courage to face a camera.

By mid-May, Chanute was back home and wanted to set a date for Wilbur to come again to Chicago and again address the Western Society of Engineers. He also wished to visit the brothers in Dayton quite soon as he had information he wished to deliver in person. He arrived the morning of June 6 and returned to Chicago that same night. In the course of the day's conversation he told the brothers he was giving up his own experiments. From here on, he said, it was all up to them.

―――――

Wilbur spoke before the gathering in Chicago the evening of June 24, and with considerably more confidence and spirit than he had two years earlier. He described in some detail the breakthrough he and Orville had achieved with the glider they tested at Kitty Hawk the previous fall. He said much about the part the study of birds had played in their work, and of the glides they were able to achieve, putting particular emphasis, as he had before, on the necessity of skill at the controls. More than machinery skill was needed.

"A thousand glides is equivalent to about four hours of steady practice," he told the audience, and this was "far too little to give anyone a complete mastery of the art of flying.

> Since soaring is merely gliding in a rising current, it would be easy to soar in front of any hill of suitable slope, whenever the wind blew with sufficient force to furnish support, provided the wind were steady. But by reason of changes in wind velocity there is more support at times than is needed, while at

others there is too little, so that a considerable degree of skill, experience, and sound judgment is required in order to keep the machine exactly in the rising current. . . . Before trying to rise to any dangerous height a man ought to know that in an emergency his mind and muscles will work by instinct rather than conscious effort. There is no time to think.

A continuing study of soaring birds had convinced him that man could build wings that had as little or less resistance than even the best of birds. But that was not the point, or the lesson from birds. "The birds' wings are undoubtedly very well designed indeed, but it is not any extraordinary efficiency that strikes with astonishment but rather the marvelous skill with which they are used."

At the close Wilbur declared still again, "The soaring problem is apparently not so much one of better wings as of better operators."

Asked during a brief discussion period what he thought of experiments being conducted by Alexander Graham Bell to hoist a man into the air with a giant kite, Wilbur replied, "It is very bad policy to ask one flying machine man about the experiments of another, because every flying machine man thinks that his method is the only correct one."

Asked by another in the audience what he thought of the dihedral angle of the wings used by Samuel Langley, Wilbur did not hesitate to point out that Langley's machine was tested only in dead calms when there were no side gusts to contend with and that it must be remembered "the wind usually blows."

Nowhere in the talk had he said a word about the gasoline engine sitting in the back room of the bicycle shop at Dayton; or of his and Orville's intense, often maddening work on propellers; or of what they would be up to at Kitty Hawk in only a matter of months. When the subject of motors came into discussion, he simply kept to the past tense. "As none of our experiments has been with power machines, my judgment . . . may be of little value."

Day after day that June the weather in Dayton remained, as Bishop Wright recorded, "fair and mild." For him all was much as usual. He went to the library, he wrote letters, attended church, accompanied Katharine at a high school commencement. When she headed off to Oberlin for another commencement, the house on Hawthorn Street grew quieter still.

At the shop on West Third Street it was a different story. With the help of Charlie Taylor, the brothers were on the home stretch and working harder than ever to get everything right with every piece and part of the new machine.

From Kitty Hawk Bill Tate sent word that he had installed a gasoline tank at the camp and asked how soon he could expect to see them.

On July 14 came the news that in a matter of days, Samuel Langley was to test his "latest contrivance" on the mosquito-infested banks of the Potomac River near Quantico, Virginia, thirty miles south of Washington. This time it was to be a motor-powered "full-fledged airship" called "The Great Aerodrome," capable of carrying one operator. It had cost $50,000 in public money—in Smithsonian resources and the largest appropriation yet granted by the U.S. War Department. Professor Langley and several of his friends, including Alexander Graham Bell, contributed another $20,000.

Reporters rushed to the scene, and in a flotilla of watercraft comprised of everything from catboats to steam launches converged on the giant houseboat, "the ark" as they called it, on top of which perched Langley's machine, "the buzzard," poised to go.

Langley himself arrived from Washington and went aboard the houseboat only to disappear inside, refusing to show himself, despite earnest pleas for interviews. When a storm struck, he and his party of mechanics and scientists went back to Washington. Then, with the storm over, the young man who was expected to fly the machine, Charles Manly, hurried off to Washington, but on returning the next day refused to say anything.

At last, on the morning of August 8, the air perfectly still, an unmanned, quarter-scale model of the Langley machine was launched and traveled some 1,000 feet before crashing into the river. "AIRSHIP AS A SUBMARINE" ran the mocking headline in the *New York Times*. Manly went before reporters to declare the flight entirely successful, but beyond that would say no more.

How Wilbur and Orville felt about all this, just as they were about to attempt the most important step in their own work, what comments were exchanged in the privacy of the workshop or at home, there is no telling. The only comment on record, in a letter Wilbur wrote to Octave Chanute, was largely an expression of sympathy for Langley:

> Professor Langley seems to be having rather more than his fair share of trouble just now with the pestiferous reporters and windstorms. But as the mosquitoes are reported to be very bad along the banks where the reporters are encamped he has some consolation.

Work on their "whopper flying machine," as they had come to call it, continued through the mounting heat of summer, the brothers and Charlie seeing to the final touches on every component, every small detail, before departure for Kitty Hawk, where, they knew, still more work would be required for the assembly of it all.

"We never did assemble the whole machine at Dayton. There wasn't room enough," Charlie would explain. Just the center section alone when set up in the shop, so blocked passage between the front and back rooms that to wait on customers he or one or the other of the brothers had to slip out a side door and go around to the street entrance in front.

Packing everything for shipment so there would be no damage en route became in itself a major task—motor, frame, and parts adding up to an estimated 675 pounds. By September 18, all was crated and on the train.

There was no ceremony about it or anxiousness, according to Charlie. "If there was any worry about the flying machine not working, they never showed it and I never felt it."

Five days later Wilbur and Orville themselves were packed and on board an eastbound train.

II.

The change from the crowded, stifling hot, noisy confines of the workspace at Dayton to the open reaches of sea and sky on the Outer Banks could hardly have been greater or more welcome. They loved

Kitty Hawk. "Every year adds to our comprehension of the wonders of this place," wrote Orville to Katharine soon after arrival.

The previous winter on the Banks had been especially severe, one continuing succession of storms, the brothers were told, the rain coming down in such torrents as to make a lake that reached for miles near their camp. Ninety-mile-an-hour winds had lifted their building from its foundation and set it down several feet closer to the ocean. Mosquitoes were said to have been so thick they turned day into night, the lightning so terrible it turned night into day.

But the winds had also sculpted the sand hills into the best shape for gliding the brothers had seen, and the September days now were so glorious, conditions so ideal, that instead of turning at once to setting up camp, they put the glider from the year before back in shape and spent what Wilbur called "the finest day we ever had in practice." They made seventy-five glides and with some practice at soaring found it easier than expected. All was looking highly favorable.

With the help of Dan Tate, a new 16 x 44-foot building in which to assemble and store the new Flyer went up in little more than a week's time, its doors hung and hinged just as a terrific storm struck, the wind at one point blowing 75 miles per hour.

Progress on the new machine had to go forward, of course, though indoors. "Worked all day in making connections of sections of upper [wing] surface, putting in wires at rear edge and putting on some hinges," Orville recorded on October 12 the same day Dan Tate reported that five boats had already been driven ashore between Kitty Hawk and Cape Henry.

On October 18, as Wilbur wrote to Katharine, "a storm hove to view" that made "the prayers of Elijah look small in comparison.

> The wind suddenly whirled around to the north and increased to something like 40 miles an hour and was accompanied by a regular cloudburst. In this country the winds usually blow from the north, then from the east, next the south, and then from the west, and on to the north again. But when the wind begins to "back up," that is, veer from south to east and north, etc., then look out, for it means a cyclone is coming. . . .

Maybe it got so in love with backing up that it went forward a little sometimes just to have the fun of "backing up" again. It repeated this process seven times in four days. . . .

The second day opened with the gale still continuing. . . . The climax came about 4 o'clock when the wind reached 75 miles an hour. Suddenly a corner of our tar-paper roof gave way under the pressure and we saw that if the trouble were not stopped the whole roof would probably go.

Orville put on Wilbur's heavy overcoat, grabbed a ladder, and went out to see what could be done. Wilbur, coatless, followed after and, fighting the wind, found Orville at the north end of the building, having succeeded in climbing the ladder only to have the wind blow the coat over his head.

As the hammer and nails were in his pocket and up over his head [Wilbur continued, delighting in telling the story for those at home once the storm had passed], he was unable to get his hands on them or to pull his coattails down, so he was compelled to descend again. The next time he put the nails in his mouth and took the hammer in his hand and I followed him up the ladder hanging on to his coattails. He swatted around a good little while trying to get a few nails in. . . . He explained afterward that the wind kept blowing the hammer around so that three licks out of four [he] hit the roof or his fingers instead of the nail. Finally the job was done and we rushed for cover.

The driving wind and rain continued through the night, Wilbur wrote, "but we took the advice of the Oberlin coach, 'Cheer up, boys, there is no hope.'"

By mail, on October 18, came a newspaper clipping sent by their Hawthorn Street neighbor George Feight reporting the failure of another Langley test flight on October 7, and this time it was the full-sized Great Aerodrome with Charles Manly at what constituted the controls. No sooner had the "buzzard" with a wingspan of 48 feet been launched than it dove straight into the water. Manly, though thoroughly drenched, suffered no injury.

"I see that Langley has had his fling, and failed," Wilbur wrote to Octave Chanute. "It seems to be our turn to throw now, and I wonder what our luck will be."

In the same letter, Wilbur left no doubt that their confidence was at a new high. "We are expecting the most interesting results of any of our seasons of experiment, and are sure that, barring exasperating little accidents or some mishaps, we will have done something before we break camp."

Scratching off a postcard to Charlie Taylor, Orville expressed the same spirit in a lighter vein.

> Flying machine market has been very unsteady the past two days. Opened yesterday morning at about 208 (100% means even chance of success) but by noon had dropped to 110. These fluctuations would have produced a panic, I think, in Wall Street, but in this quiet place it only put us to thinking and figuring a little.

They proceeded on the Flyer much as if they were building a truss bridge, only with the attention to detail of watchmakers, Orville keeping a day-by-day record in his diary.

> *Thursday, October 22* We worked all day on lower surface and tail.

> *Friday, October 23* Worked on skids during morning, and after dinner finished putting on hinges.

> *Saturday, October 24* We put in the uprights between surfaces and trussed the center section. Had much trouble with wires.

On Monday the 26th, they worked again on the truss wires until the afternoon, when the wind veered to the north, and they spent two hours at

Kill Devil Hills flying the glider and succeeded in breaking their previous record for time five times and covering distances of as much as 500 feet.

George Spratt had rejoined them, and on October 27 he and Dan Tate started up the engine on the machine.

> *Monday, November 2* Began work of placing engine on machine. . . .
>
> *Wednesday, November 4* Have machine now within half day of completion.

But when the next day they started up the motor, the magneto—a small generator utilizing magnets—failed to deliver a spark to ignite the gas and the vibrations of the misfiring engine tore loose and badly twisted the propeller shafts.

With little chance of more flight tests anytime soon, George Spratt chose to go home, taking with him the damaged shafts as far as Norfolk to be shipped back to Charlie Taylor in Dayton.

Two days later Octave Chanute appeared. The weather turned miserably cold and rainy, and there was little to do but sit around the stoves and talk. Chanute told the brothers it was as if they were "pursued by a blind fate" from which they were unable to escape.

"He doesn't seem to think our machines are so much superior as the manner in which we handle them," Orville wrote to Katharine and their father after Chanute had left. "We are of just the reverse opinion."

Days passed still too cold to work. Puddles about the camp turned to ice. All the same, the brothers were entirely comfortable and had no trouble keeping warm, as Wilbur wrote reassuringly in another letter home, cheerful as ever and off on another of his wry renditions of coping with the travails of camp life.

> In addition to the classifications of last year, to wit, 1, 2, 3 and 4 blanket nights, we now have 5 blanket nights, and 5 blankets and 2 quilts. Next come 5 blankets, 2 quilts and fire; then 5, 2, fire, & hot-water jug. This is as far as we've got so far. Next comes the addition of sleeping without undressing, then

shoes & hats, and finally overcoats. We intend to be comfortable while we are here.

In the last days of November, snow fell, something they had not seen
before on the Outer Banks. Water in their washbasin froze solid. Cold or
not, they succeeded meantime in getting the engine to run with practically no vibration even at high speed. The Flyer would be launched on
a single wooden track, to serve like a railroad track 60 feet in length on
which it would slide. The total cost for materials for this innovation was
all of $4.

By all evidence the brothers had suffered in spirit not in the least. "After
a loaf of 15 days, we are down to work again," Orville wrote to Charlie on
November 23. "We will not be ready for a trial for several days yet on account of having decided on some changes in the machine. Unless something breaks in the meantime we feel confident in success."

New propeller shafts made of larger, heavier steel tubing arrived from
Charlie, only to crack during an indoor test. With no delay, Orville, the
better mechanic of the two, packed his bag and on November 30 left for
Dayton to see what could be done, with Wilbur remaining behind "to keep
house alone," in his words.

In Washington, by the morning of December 8, the cold wind eased off,
and to Charles Manly and the Smithsonian technicians working with
him, conditions for another test of Samuel Langley's much publicized,
much derided aerodrome looked as favorable as could be hoped for given
the time of year.

Cakes of ice could be seen riding with the current on the Potomac,
but the day was bright, the air calm, and given that money for the project was nearly gone by now, any further postponement seemed out of the
question.

The brave Manly was again to be the "steersman," the only one to risk
his life, and it was he who made the final decision to proceed. As he saw
it, it was "now or never."

The giant airship, with its wings again set at a pronounced dihedral
angle, was to be launched as before by catapult from atop the same mon-

strous houseboat, tied up this time just four miles below the city at Arsenal Point. Some five hours of frantic effort went into the final preparations. Not until four in the afternoon did everything appear ready, and by then it was nearly dark and the wind was rising.

Professor Langley and a few of his associates were watching from small boats. Other boats of every sort were filled with reporters, and crowds of spectators lined the length of the Arsenal seawall.

Having stripped down to a union suit, Manly put on a jacket lined with buoyant cork, climbed aboard the aircraft, and fired up the gasoline engine.

At exactly 4:45 he gave the signal to release the catapult. Instantly the machine roared down the track and leaped 60 feet straight up into the air, only to stop and with a grinding, whirring sound, hang suspended momentarily, nose up, then, its wings crumbling, flipped backward and plunged into the river no more than 20 feet from the houseboat.

Manly, who had disappeared into the river, found himself trapped underwater, his jacket snared by part of the wreckage. Tearing free, he fought his way up through tangled wires only to hit a sheet of ice before at last breaking through to the surface.

He was pulled from the water, uninjured but nearly frozen. After being quickly wrapped in blankets and administered a shot of whiskey, he broke into what one of the Smithsonian staff would describe as "the most voluble series of blasphemies" he had ever heard in his life.

As the newspapers reported, the failure was worse by far than that of October 7, as was the humiliation for Langley and nearly everyone connected with the costly, long-drawn-out project. Halfhearted and unconvincing explanations were offered by Langley and others, fixing the blame on flaws in the launching apparatus. Few were convinced. Langley was compared to Darius Green, the comic fool of the famous poem whose ludicrous machine flew in one direction only, downward.

The government, said the *Washington Post*, should promptly sever its relations with the experiment that had covered eight to ten years and involved a very large outlay of public money without disclosing a single ground for hope.

The whole thing had been a colossal failure, to be sure, but as the *Chicago Tribune* said, it was impossible not to feel some sympathy for Langley.

He has constructed his aerodrome on scientific principles so far as he understands them. He has spent much money, he has shown great patience and perseverance, and he has labored hard. . . . Evidently something is wrong with the scientific principles or the professor's application of them.

The only one whose reputation did not suffer was Charles Manly. Langley, who would die three years later, in 1906, never got over the defeat and humiliation.

Word of what had happened was brought back to Kitty Hawk by Orville. The news had broken on December 9, the morning he was leaving Dayton with a set of new solid steel propeller shafts. It was while waiting at the station that he had picked up the papers with all the details.

Neither brother was ever to make critical or belittling comments about Langley. Rather, they expressed respect and gratitude for the part he had played in their efforts. Just knowing that the head of the Smithsonian, the most prominent scientific institution in America, believed in the possibility of human flight was one of the influences that led them to proceed with their work, Wilbur told Octave Chanute in a letter written some years later.

As for Langley's actual work, his successes and failures, Wilbur thought it "perhaps too soon to make an accurate estimate, but entirely aside from this he advanced the art greatly by his missionary work and by the inspiration of his example.

He possessed mental and moral qualities of the kind that influence history. When scientists in general considered it discreditable to work in the field of aeronautics he possessed both the discernment to discover possibilities there and the moral courage to subject himself to the ridicule of the public and the apologies of his friends. He deserves more credit for this than he has yet received.

The treatment Langley had been subjected to by the press and some of his professional friends had been "shameful," Wilbur said. "His work deserved neither abuse nor apology."

III.

Orville reached Kitty Hawk at midday, December 11, a Friday, and spent that afternoon with Wilbur unpacking "the goods." Saturday the wind was too light to make a start on level ground. Sunday, as always a day off, they passed the time much as they might have at home, reading and visiting with neighbors, in this case, Adam Etheridge from the Life-Saving Station, who with his wife and children came by to say hello and see the new machine so many were talking about.

On the afternoon of Monday the 14th, all final repairs attended to, the brothers were ready. With the help of John T. Daniels, a robust man who looked as though he could lift a house, and two other men from the station, they hauled the 605-pound Flyer the quarter mile over to the Big Hill to the face of the slope where they had positioned the 60-foot launching track.

When the engine was started up with a roar, several small boys who had been tagging along were so startled they took off over the hill as fast as they could go.

Everything was set. There was no debate or extended discussion over which of them should go first. They simply flipped a coin. Wilbur won and worked his way between the propellers and in among the truss wires to stretch flat on his stomach beside the engine, his hips in the padded wing-warping cradle, whereby he could control the wing-warping wires by shifting his body, and head up, looking forward out through the horizontal rudder or elevator that controlled the up or down pitch of the craft.

Orville took hold of an upright bar at the end of the right wings, ready to help balance the whole affair when it started forward on the track.

Then off they went, Orville running as fast as he could, holding on until no longer able to keep up.

But at the end of the track, Wilbur made a mistake. Pulling too hard on the rudder, he sent the Flyer surging upward at too steep an angle. To compensate, he nosed it downward, but again too abruptly and the machine hit the sand a hundred feet from the end of the track.

The brothers were elated. Motor, launching device, everything had proven reliable. Damage was minor. Wilbur's error in judgment, from lack of experience with this kind of apparatus, had been the only cause of trouble, as he told the others and explained in a letter to Katharine and the Bishop.

The repairs took two days. Not until late the afternoon of the 16th was the machine ready. While they were setting it up on the track in front of the building, seeing to final adjustments, a stranger wandered by and after looking the machine over, asked what it was.

> When we told him it was a flying machine, he asked whether we intended to fly it [Orville would write later]. We said we did, as soon as we had a suitable wind. He looked at it several minutes longer and then, wishing to be courteous, remarked that it looked as if it would fly, if it had a "suitable wind."

The brothers were much amused, certain that by "suitable wind," the man had in mind something on the order of the recent 75-mile-an-hour gale.

———

Only five men showed up the morning of Thursday the 17th, after the brothers hung a white bedsheet on the side of the shed, the signal to the men at the Life-Saving Station that their help was needed. Many, as Orville later explained, were apparently unwilling to face the "rigors of a cold December wind in order to see, as they no doubt thought, another flying machine not fly."

Those who did turn out felt differently. "We had seen the glider fly without an engine," remembered John T. Daniels, "and when these boys put an engine in it, we knew that they knew exactly what they were doing."

Adam Etheridge and Will Dough had come with Daniels from the Life-Saving Station. W. C. Brinkley was a dairy farmer from Manteo, and the fifth, Johnny Moore, was a boy of about eighteen who had happened by and was curious to know about the strange-looking machine.

Daniels, known to be "a joker," told him it was a "duck-snarer" and explained how any minute Orville would be going up and out over the bay, where there were ducks by the hundreds, and how he would drop a giant net and catch every one. The boy decided to stay and watch.

Bill Tate, to his subsequent regret, was away at the time in Elizabeth City.

The day was freezing cold. Skims of ice covered several nearby ponds. A gusty wind was blowing hard out of the north. "The wind usually blows," Wilbur had reminded his Chicago audience in June. It was blowing at nearly a gale force of 20 to 27 miles per hour, far from ideal. The difficulty in a high wind was not in making headway in it but maintaining balance.

Reflecting on the moment long afterward, Orville would express utter amazement over "our audacity in attempting flights in a new and untried machine under such circumstances."

Working together they and the men hauled the Flyer to the launching track, four 15-foot-long two-by-fours sheathed with a metal strip, and laid down this time on a flat, level stretch about 100 feet west of the camp, the track running north-northeast straight into the freezing wind.

With everything in place and ready to go, Wilbur and Orville walked off a short way from the others and stood close talking low for some time under an immense overcast sky. Dressed in their dark caps and dark winter jackets beneath which they wore their customary white shirts, starched white collars, and dark ties, they could as well have been back in Dayton on a winter morning chatting on a street corner.

The other five watched and waited together in silence. They had become "a serious lot," John T. Daniels remembered. "Nobody felt like talking."

Because Wilbur had won the toss three days before, it was now Orville's turn. The two shook hands as if saying goodbye. Then Wilbur went over to the others and told them not to look so glum, but to cheer Orville on his way.

"We tried," Daniels said, "but it was mighty weak shouting with no heart in it."

In the time since 1900, when Wilbur had gone off on his first trip to Kitty Hawk bringing a camera as part of his equipment, the brothers had become increasingly interested in photography as essential to their flying experiments. They had even begun selling photographic equipment at the bicycle shop. In 1902 they had made what for them was a major investment of $55.55 in as fine an American-made camera to be had, a large Gundlach Korona V, which used 5 x 7-inch glass plates and had a pneumatic shutter. Early that morning of December 17, Orville had positioned the Korona on its wooden tripod about 30 feet from the end of the starting rail and assigned Daniels to squeeze the rubber bulb to trip the shutter as the Flyer passed that point.

Orville now positioned himself on his stomach at the controls, as Wilbur had, while Wilbur stood to the right at the tip of the lower wing ready to help keep the machine in balance as it started down the track. Minutes passed while the engine warmed up. As they would later emphasize neither had had any "previous acquaintance" with the conduct of the machine and its controlling mechanisms.

At exactly 10:35, Orville slipped the rope restraining the Flyer and it headed forward, but not very fast, because of the fierce headwind, and Wilbur, his left hand on the wing, had no trouble keeping up.

At the end of the track the Flyer lifted into the air and Daniels, who had never operated a camera until now, snapped the shutter to take what would be one of the most historic photographs of the century.

The course of the flight, in Orville's words, was "extremely erratic." The Flyer rose, dipped down, rose again, bounced and dipped again like a bucking bronco when one wing struck the sand. The distance flown had been 120 feet, less than half the length of a football field. The total time airborne was approximately 12 seconds.

"Were you scared?" Orville would be asked. "Scared?" he said with a smile. "There wasn't time."

"It was only a flight of twelve seconds," he would also stress later, "and it was an uncertain, wavy, creeping sort of a flight at best, but it was a real flight at last."

The machine was picked up and carried back to the starting point, after which they all took a short break to warm up inside the camp.

———

At about eleven o'clock, the wind having eased off somewhat, Wilbur took a turn and "went off like a bird" for 175 feet. Orville went again, flying 200 feet. Then, near noon, on the fourth test, Wilbur flew a little over half a mile through the air and a distance of 852 feet over the ground in 59 seconds.

It had taken four years. They had endured violent storms, accidents, one disappointment after another, public indifference or ridicule, and clouds of demon mosquitoes. To get to and from their remote sand dune testing ground they had made five round-trips from Dayton (counting Orville's return home to see about stronger propeller shafts), a total of seven thousand miles by train, all to fly little more than half a mile. No matter. They had done it.

There was talk of going again, of even attempting a flight down the beach to the weather station. But a sudden gust caught the Flyer and tossed it along the sand "just like you've seen an umbrella turned inside out and loose in the wind," remembered John T. Daniels.

Daniels had been standing holding an upright of one of the wings and suddenly found himself caught in the wires and the machine "blowing across the beach, heading for the ocean, landing first on one end and then on the other, rolling over and over, and me getting more tangled up in it all the time"—all 600-plus pounds of the machine, plus Daniels, who weighed over 200 pounds, swept up by the wind as though they weighed nothing at all.

When the machine stopped momentarily, Daniels succeeded in breaking loose. ("His escape was miraculous," Orville later wrote, "as he was in the engine and chains.") "I wasn't hurt much. I got a good many bruises and scratches and was so scared I couldn't walk straight for a few minutes," Daniels would say. The brothers "ran up to me, pulled my legs and arms, felt of my ribs and told me there were no bones broken. They looked scared, too." From that day on Daniels could proudly claim to have survived the first ever airplane accident.

The Flyer was a total wreck, nearly all the ribs of the wings broken, the chain guides badly bent, uprights splintered. Any thought of another flight had vanished.

Daniels and the others said their goodbyes and walked back to the Life-Saving Station. For their part Wilbur and Orville fixed and ate some lunch, then washed the dishes before walking four miles to the Kitty Hawk weather station to send a telegram home.

———

The day in Dayton had been cloudy and freezing cold with snow on the ground. It was past dark when Carrie Kayler, preparing supper in the kitchen at 7 Hawthorn Street, stopped to answer the doorbell. The Western Union man handed her a telegram, which she signed for and carried upstairs to the Bishop.

A few minutes later he came down looking pleased, but with no excitement in his voice, told her, "Well, they've made a flight."

The telegram read:

SUCCESS FOUR FLIGHTS THURSDAY MORNING ALL
AGAINST TWENTY ONE MILE WIND STARTED FROM
LEVEL WITH ENGINE POWER ALONE AVERAGE SPEED
THROUGH AIR THIRTY ONE MILES LONGEST 57
SECONDS INFORM PRESS HOME FOR CHRISTMAS.
                              OREVELLE WRIGHT

(Mistakes in the transmission had caused 59 seconds to become 57 and Orville's name to be misspelled.)

Katharine came in from school, looked at the telegram, and told Carrie to delay supper while she went to tell Lorin.

———

Success it most certainly was. And more. What had transpired that day in 1903, in the stiff winds and cold of the Outer Banks in less than two hours time, was one of the turning points in history, the beginning of change for the world far greater than any of those present could possibly have imagined. With their homemade machine, Wilbur and Orville Wright had shown without a doubt that man could fly and if the world did not yet know it, they did.

Their flights that morning were the first ever in which a piloted machine took off under its own power into the air in full flight, sailed forward with no loss of speed, and landed at a point as high as that from which it started.

Being the kind of men they were, neither ever said the stunning contrast between their success and Samuel Langley's full-scale failure just days before made what they had done on their own all the more remarkable. Not incidentally, the Langley project had cost nearly $70,000, the greater part of it public money, whereas the brothers' total expenses for everything from 1900 to 1903, including materials and travel to and from Kitty Hawk, came to a little less than $1,000, a sum paid entirely from the modest profits of their bicycle business.

Of those who had been eyewitnesses at Kill Devil Hills the morning of the 17th, John T. Daniels was much the most effusive about what he had felt. "I like to think about it now," he would say in an interview years later. "I like to think about that first airplane the way it sailed off in the air . . . as pretty as any bird you ever laid your eyes on. I don't think I ever saw a prettier sight in my life."

But it would never have happened, Daniels also stressed, had it not been for the two "workingest boys" he ever knew.

> It wasn't luck that made them fly; it was hard work and common sense; they put their whole heart and soul and all their energy into an idea and they had the faith.

As they crated up the damaged Flyer to ship home, the brothers were "absolutely sure" in their own minds that they had mastered the problem of mechanical flying. But they also understood as no one else could have how much they had still to do, how many improvements were needed, how much more they themselves needed to learn about flying so different a machine, and that this would come only with a great deal more experience.

The Flyer would go into storage in Dayton. It would never be flown again.

Out at Huffman Prairie

I found them in a pasture lot. . . . The few people who occasionally got a glimpse of the experiments evidently considered it only another Darius Green, but I recognized at once they were really scientific explorers *who were serving the world in much the same way that Columbus had when he discovered America.*

AMOS I. ROOT

I.

I t had been agreed earlier at home that were Wilbur and Orville to succeed at Kitty Hawk, Lorin, acting as press agent, would immediately notify the local papers and the Associated Press. So once Katharine had delivered their "SUCCESS" telegram to him, Lorin took it downtown to the city editor at the *Dayton Daily Journal,* Frank Tunison, who also represented the Associated Press.

Tunison read the telegram and showed no interest. "Fifty-seven seconds, hey?" he said. "If it had been fifty-seven minutes, then it might have been a news item."

No mention was made of the story in the *Journal* the following day, though it did get brief attention in the *Dayton Daily News* on an inside page. Elsewhere in the country, a ludicrously inaccurate account of what the brothers had done got much play as a result of a story that appeared on the front page of the Norfolk *Virginian-Pilot* under a banner headline: "FLYING MACHINE SOARS 3 MILES IN TEETH OF HIGH WIND OVER HILLS AND WAVES AT KITTY HAWK ON CAROLINA COAST."

On the afternoon they had sent their telegram from the Kitty Hawk weather station, the brothers had specifically told the operator on duty, Joseph Dosher, that its content was confidential. When the operator at the Norfolk station asked if he could share the news with a friend at the *Virginian-Pilot,* the brothers had Dosher cable back, "POSITIVELY NO."

It had made no difference. From the scant solid information contained in the telegram, the *Virginian-Pilot* editors concocted an account that was almost entirely contrived. The Wrights' machine, according to the story, had been launched from a platform and soared to an altitude of 60 feet. It was described as having two six-blade propellers, "one arranged just below the frame so as to exert an *upward force* when in motion and the other extends horizontally from the rear to the center of the car to furnish upward impetus." Wilbur's first historic utterance on flying the three miles was reported to have been, "Eureka!"

Variations of the account appeared in the *Washington Post,* the *Chicago Tribune,* the *New York Times,* and the *Cincinnati Enquirer,* among others, but little happened as a consequence.

In Boston, however, two businessmen, brothers Godfrey and Samuel Cabot of the prominent Cabot family, immediately sensed the story's importance. Godfrey wrote at once to congratulate the Wrights and to ask for more details, which he received in a matter of days. More than satisfied with what he read, he sent off a letter dated December 31 to Senator Henry Cabot Lodge of Massachusetts, a distant cousin and known to be a close friend of President Theodore Roosevelt.

> It seems to me [Cabot wrote] that this may fairly be said to mark the beginning of flight through the air by men unaided by balloons. It has occurred to me that it would be eminently desirable for the United States Government to interest itself in this invention.

Senator Lodge passed the Cabot letter on to the War Department where nothing came of it. As for the reaction in Dayton, probably not one person in a hundred believed the brothers had actually flown in their machine, or if they had, it could only have been a fluke.

———

Work at the bicycle shop on West Third Street resumed with, as Charlie Taylor said, no "jig steps" over what had been achieved.

> Of course, they were pleased with the flight. But their first word with me, as I remember, was about the motor being damaged when the wind picked up the machine and turned it topsy-turvy. . . . They wanted a new one built right away. . . . They were always thinking of the next thing to do; they didn't waste much time worrying about the past.

The intention now was to build a heavier version of the Flyer with a more powerful and efficient engine. Nor could they neglect earning an income sufficient to cover expenses both at the shop and at home, not to say the cost of their experiments. As Charlie Taylor would repeatedly remind people, "There wasn't any other money."

As it was during the first several months of 1904, bike repairs were numbering a steady fifteen to twenty a week. Then there were the sales of a great variety of bicycle "sundries," as they were referred to in the shop's large ledger books, including bike tires ($3.25 each), bike bells (10 cents), lamps ($1.00), pedal guards (5 cents), spokes (10 cents), bike pumps (35 cents). Also, as usual in winter, sharpening ice skates (at 15 cents each) provided a steady additional sum.

Sales of the brothers' own line of bicycles, the larger part of their income, would not pick up until April. So to have a sufficient number on hand took up most of their time at the workbenches behind the shop. The only wages to be covered were Charlie Taylor's $18 a week and Carrie Kayler's $2.50.

To help cut expenses for continuing work on their flying machine, it was decided that further expeditions to Kitty Hawk, with all the attendant costs of travel and shipment of tools and material, could be dispensed with by finding a suitable stretch of open land close to home to serve as a practice field. Wilbur and Orville also wanted Charlie Taylor at hand, and there was concern, too, that the wind-driven sands of Kitty Hawk could play havoc with their engine.

The likeliest "flying field," they concluded after some investigation, was a peaceful cow pasture of approximately eighty-four acres eight miles northeast of town called Huffman Prairie. For years a popular science teacher at the high school, William Werthner, had been bringing his students, including Orville and Katharine, on field trips there—outings Orville loved, which probably had something to do with the choice.

The setting was spacious and relatively private, yet nothing like Kitty Hawk, with its broad horizons, wind in abundance, and nearly total privacy. Here, the space to maneuver had clearly defined parameters. Barbed wire and trees lined the borders, and there were besides a number of trees within the pasture, including one fifty-foot honey locust covered with thorns. The field itself, as Wilbur said, was so full of groundhog hummocks it might have been a prairie dog town. In addition the electric interurban trolley line from Dayton to Columbus skirted one side of the property and so could provide passengers on board ample view of whatever might be going on.

The work to be done here, the brothers knew, could well be the final, critical stage in the maturation of their whole idea. Here they would have to learn to do far more than what they had at Kitty Hawk. They must master the art of launching themselves safely into the air, of banking and turning a motor-propelled machine, and landing safely. Therefore, Wilbur stressed, they would have to learn to accommodate themselves to circumstances.

If space was limited, then all the more need to learn to make controlled turns. If the interurban trolley meant daily public exposure, it would also provide ready, inexpensive transportation—a ride of forty minutes for a 5-cent fare—to and from town, and with a handy stop known as Simms Station at the edge of the field. They also knew the trolley's schedule, so if need be they had merely to time their flights to those hours when no one would be passing by.

The pasture belonged to Torrence Huffman, president of Dayton's Fourth National Bank, whom the Wrights knew. When they inquired if they might rent it for their use, he said there would be no charge, so long as they moved the cows and horses outside the fence before flying their machine. While he liked the brothers well enough, Huffman was among the many who had little faith in their project. "They're fools," he told the farmer who worked the adjoining land.

Meanwhile, in what time they had to themselves, the brothers were sawing and planing lumber for the ribs of the new machine and working with Charlie Taylor on the new motor.

Their nephew Milton, who as a boy was often hanging about the brothers, would one day write, "History was being made in their bicycle shop and in their home, but the making was so obscured by the commonplace that I did not recognize it until many years later."

With the advance of the spring of 1904, Wilbur and Orville could be seen out in the grass at Huffman Prairie swinging scythes or working with shovels leveling off ground hog mounds. When it came to building a shed in which to assemble and store their new machine, they put it in a corner as far removed from the trolley stop as the field permitted.

Prior to their first test flight, lest anyone think them overly secretive, the brothers invited friends and neighbors to come and watch. The press would be welcome, too, but on the condition that no photographs be taken. Their concern centered on the chance of photographs being used to study those devices and control mechanisms of their own invention, which set their machine apart from others.

On May 23, a Monday, despite an early morning rain, some fifty spectators gathered at Huffman Prairie. Bishop Wright, Katharine, Lorin and family were all present, as were a dozen or more reporters. But there was too little wind, and the test flight had to be postponed. Motor or not, wind was still essential.

On Wednesday, when the crowd gathered again, rain caused another cancellation. The morning after, May 26, there was more rain. But then, during a brief lull in the afternoon, and with hardly any wind and signs of another storm about to break, the brothers decided to "make a start." With Orville at the controls, Flyer II rose a mere 8 feet and came down at once, within seconds after leaving the starting track. Something had gone wrong with the motor.

It was hardly a premiere to stir excitement or silence the doubters. A few reporters, in an attempt to say something of interest, either praised the sturdiness of the machine or took liberties with the facts, such as to say the plane had gone 75 feet in the air. Bishop Wright, who had been watching with perhaps greater anticipation than anyone present, could only record in his diary, and accurately, that Orville had flown all of 25 feet.

It would be speculated later by some that the failure that day had been a hoax staged as a way to deflate further interest by the public and the press. But this seems absurd given the nature of the brothers and the fact that almost nothing went right for them for the next three months.

On June 10 the machine hit ground because of faulty steering. Another day, a tail was smashed during a landing. "Tail stick broken in starting," Wilbur recorded of his flight on August 2. On another, the tail wires became "disarranged." On August 5, Orville "struck ground at start." Wilbur went again on August 8 and a wing hit the ground before leaving the track. Two days later, a rudder was smashed, a propeller broken. It seemed, as Wilbur would say, they had become "a little rusty" at the art of flying.

"There was nothing spectacular about these many trials," remembered Werthner, the high school science teacher who was lending the brothers a hand with "their great white bird," as he called it, "but the good humor of Wilbur, after a spill out of the machine, or a break somewhere, or a stubborn motor, was always reassuring.

> Their patient perseverance, their calm faith in ultimate success, their mutual consideration of each other, might have been considered phenomenal in any but men who were well born and well reared. These flights, or spurts at flying, they always made in turn; and after every trial the two inventors, quite apart, held long and confidential consultation, with always some new gain; they were getting nearer and nearer the moment when sustained flight would be made, for a machine that could maintain itself aloft two minutes might just as well stay there an hour, if everything were as intended.

At last, on August 13, to their utter amazement, Wilbur flew over a thousand feet, farther than any of the flights at Kitty Hawk and five times what they had been able to do thus far at Huffman Prairie.

"Have you heard what they're up to out there?" people in town would say. "Oh, yes," would be the usual answer, and the conversation would move on. Few took any interest in the matter or in the two brothers who were to become Dayton's greatest heroes ever. Even those riding the interurban line seem to have paid little or no attention to what could occasionally be seen in passing, or to the brothers themselves as they traveled back and forth from town on the same trolley looking little different from other commuters.

An exception was Luther Beard, managing editor of the *Dayton Journal,* who, because of a class he taught occasionally at a school near Huffman Prairie, rode the interurban as far as Simms Station. "I used to chat with them in a friendly way and was always polite to them," Beard would recall, "because I sort of felt sorry for them. They seemed like well-meaning, decent enough young men. Yet there they were, neglecting their business to waste their time day after day on that ridiculous flying machine."

They were also putting their lives at risk, as well they knew. On a flight on August 24, hit by a sudden gust of wind, Orville smashed into the ground at 30 miles an hour and though he suffered no broken bones was so badly shaken and bruised he was unable to fly for another month.

Where Samuel Langley had required the least wind possible for his aerodrome experiments, the Wrights needed more wind. Clearly at Huffman Prairie they would have to make up for what had been so plentiful at Kitty Hawk, to devise, in Wilbur's words, some way to "render us independent of wind." The solution would have to be both simple and inexpensive, and so once again straightforward improvisation solved the problem.

They designed and built their own "starting apparatus," a catapult powered by nothing more than gravity. Its components consisted of a 20-foot tent-shaped tower, or derrick. Made with four wooden poles, it looked like a drilling rig. At the apex, over a pulley, hung by a single rope metal weights totaling as much as 1,600 pounds. The rest of the rope ran from the base of the tower down the launching track on pulleys to the end of the track to another pulley. Then the rope ran back again to the starting point, where it hitched on to the front of the Flyer, which sat on the launching track on a large rimmed bicycle hub.

With a team of horses the brothers would haul the weights up to the top of the derrick. Then, when all was ready, the pilot would release the rope, the weights would drop, the machine would be pulled rapidly down to the end of the track, then shoot into the air at a speed greater by far than possible when attempting takeoff by motor only.

On September 7, with scarcely any wind, Wilbur tested the new catapult for the first time, starting with only 200 pounds of weights. By day's end, having added another 400 pounds, he could take off with no difficulties and flew longer distances than ever. Little more than a week later, on September 15, he not only flew fully half a mile but for the first time succeeded in turning a half circle, a major achievement.

Not one reporter bothered to attend during this time. Nor did public interest increase. With few exceptions there seemed no public interest at all, no local excitement or curiosity or sense of wonder over the miraculous thing happening right in Dayton's own backyard.

Nor did anyone seem to appreciate the kind of minds, not to say the extraordinary skill and courage, needed to succeed at so daring a venture. In five months the brothers were to make no less than fifty test flights at Huffman Prairie, and Charlie Taylor, ever on hand in case of motor trouble, would say that every time he watched either of them head down the starting track, he had the awful feeling he might never again see him alive. To Wilbur and Orville, it seemed fear was a stranger.

Writing his autobiography later, James Cox, publisher of the *Dayton Daily News,* remembered reports coming "to our office that the airship had been in the air over the Huffman Prairie . . . but our news staff would not believe the stories. Nor did they ever take the pains to go out to see." Nor did Cox.

When the city editor of the *Daily News,* Dan Kumler, was asked later why for so long nothing was reported of the momentous accomplishments taking place so nearby, he said after a moment's reflection, "I guess the truth is that we were just plain dumb."

II.

That same September, 200 miles to the northeast in Ohio, a small, elderly gentleman set off in his automobile, as he had before earlier in the summer, for Huffman Prairie on invitation from the Wrights to come see the progress they were making.

He was Amos Ives Root of Medina, a town just south of Cleveland. Always neatly dressed, his short white beard trimmed, he stood no more than five feet three. But his energy and curiosity were great indeed. His bright hazel eyes seemed to miss nothing.

Born in a log cabin, he had started his own business, manufacturing and marketing beekeeping supplies, in 1869, at age thirty, and soon became widely known as "the bee man" of Ohio. At sixty-four, he was extremely well-off, happily married, a father of five, proud grandfather, and quite free to pursue a whole range of active interests. As would be said in the Medina County newspaper, Amos Root bubbled with enthusiasm and a constant desire to "see the wheels go round." He loved clocks, windmills, bicycles, machines of all kinds, and especially his Oldsmobile Runabout. Seldom was he happier than when out on the road in it and in all seasons.

> While I like horses in a certain way [he wrote], I do not enjoy caring for them. I do not like the smell of the stables. I do not like to be obliged to clean a horse every morning, and I do not like to hitch one up in winter. . . . It takes time to hitch up a horse; but the auto is ready to start off in an instant. It is never tired; it gets there quicker than any horse can possibly do.

As for the Oldsmobile, he liked to say, at $350 it cost less than a horse and carriage.

He was also deeply religious, a Sunday School teacher, an active supporter of the temperance movement, and enjoyed conveying his thoughts and ideas on these and a host of other topics in the column he wrote for the Root company's beekeepers trade journal, *Gleanings in Bee Culture.*

It was to be he of all people, the Ohio bee man, who would recognize as no one yet had the genius of the Wrights and the full importance of their flying machine. He would describe in detail what he saw happen at Huffman Prairie, and further, he would describe it accurately. It was not the Dayton papers that finally broke the story—or the *Chicago Tribune* or the *New York Times* or *Scientific American*—but Amos Root's own *Gleanings in Bee Culture*.

He had begun correspondence with the Wrights in February. "I hope you will excuse me, friends, for the liberty I take in addressing you. Let me say briefly that I have all my life had an idea in my head that a flying machine should be made on the principle of flying a kite." He wanted very much, he continued, to be on hand for their experiments and promised never to "undertake to borrow any of your ideas."

In response the brothers had said they would let him know when their new machine was ready for trial. Through spring and into summer, waiting for word to come, Root kept writing. "Please excuse me, friends, but I am so anxious to see that airship I can hardly sleep nights."

When in mid-August word finally came, he was off at once for Dayton in his Runabout, a journey of no little uncertainty then given the state of the roads. He had arrived at the time when the Wrights' machine was not performing well—certainly not as they wished—but for Root the spectacle of actual flight was "one of the bright spots in my life," as he told them in gratitude.

He had promised he would say nothing of what he had seen at Huffman Prairie in anything he wrote in his *Gleanings in Bee Culture*, and good as his word, he described only his venture by automobile.

"In a recent trip of 400 miles through Ohio," he wrote, "I passed through Ashland, Mansfield, Marion, Delaware, Marysville, Springfield, Dayton . . . so many different towns in a brief period of time that I can hardly remember now which was which." He told how he tried and succeeded in not killing any of the numerous chickens on the road, or scaring any of the horses. He wrote of having to give the engine fresh water every ten or fifteen miles, and how wherever he stopped, for water or gasoline, a crowd gathered. He described the torn-up streets and mud roads en route, but then could not resist adding:

And, by the way, we are already, at least to some extent, ignoring not only mud roads, but roads of every kind, and climbing *through the air,* and I do not mean by means of the gas-balloon either. But I am not at liberty just now to tell all I know in regard to this matter.

In the second week of September came word from the Wrights that he should return without delay. He reached Dayton on Tuesday, September 20, 1904, the day Wilbur would attempt something never done before in the history of the world. He would fly a power machine in a complete circle.

Still recovering from his crash in August, Orville would be on the sidelines watching with Root and Charlie Taylor. Apparently no one else was on hand at Huffman Prairie.

"God in his great mercy has permitted me to be, at least somewhat instrumental in ushering in and introducing to the great wide world an invention that may outrank electric cars, the automobiles . . . and . . . may fairly take a place beside the telephone and wireless telegraphy," Root would begin his eyewitness account.

But before describing what he saw happen, he made a point of stressing that the Wrights were not just the sort who love machinery, but were "interested in the modern developments of science and art." He had been "astonished" by the extent of their library and to find in conversation that "they were thoroughly versed not only in regard to our present knowledge, but everything that had been done in the past." In saying this in what he wrote, he would be the first to recognize how much more there was to Wilbur and Orville than most imagined, even among the relative few who took time to give it some thought.

They were not simply "another Darius Green," Root stressed, but "scientific explorers" serving the world much as Columbus had.

He described in his account of September 20 how Wilbur took his place lying flat to offer less wind resistance, how the engine was warmed up to speed, and, how, with everything ready, "a sort of trap" (the catapult) was sprung, and suddenly the machine was aloft.

The plane flew low, never rising more than 20 to 25 feet above the ground. "I was surprised at the speed and I was astonished at the wonderful lifting power." Then it had turned and headed straight back toward him, and with feelings very like those expressed by John T. Daniels after seeing the first flight at Kitty Hawk, he wrote:

> When it first turned that circle, and came near the starting point, I was right in front of it, and I said then, and I believe still, it was one of the grandest sights, if not the grandest sight, of my life.

The plane was still flying low, and Orville, who was standing close by Root, urged him to get to one side, for fear it might suddenly come down. To Root the landing of the plane was hardly less amazing:

> When the engine is shut off, the apparatus glides to the ground very quietly and alights on something much like a pair of light sled-runners [skids], sliding over the grassy surface perhaps a rod or more. Whenever it is necessary to slow up the speed before alighting, you turn the nose uphill. It will then climb right up on the air until the momentum is exhausted, when, by skillful management, it can be dropped as lightly as a feather.

The "skillful management" was breathtaking. It was not just that the machine was like no other on the face of the earth, he wrote, but there was probably no one "beyond these two who learned the trick of controlling it."

When Columbus discovered America, he did not know what the outcome would be, Root would conclude his account. Not even "the wildest enthusiast" could have foreseen. "In a like manner these two brothers have probably not even a faint glimpse of what their discovery is going to bring to the children of men."

As for Huffman Prairie, it was henceforth historic ground. Here man and his machine had " 'learned to fly,' very much like a young bird out of its nest learns by practice to use its wings."

Root pictured a wondrous time near at hand, "when we shall not need to fuss with good roads nor railway tracks, bridges, etc., at such enormous expense. With these machines we bid adieu to all these things. God's free air, that extends all over the earth, and perhaps miles above us, is our training field. . . .

> When you see one of these graceful crafts sailing over your head, and possibly over your home, as I expect you will in the near future, see if you don't agree with me that the flying machine is one of God's most gracious and precious gifts.

In December, Amos Root returned to Dayton—and by the interurban this time—and met with the Wrights at 7 Hawthorn to read aloud what he had written in advance of publication. It was one last step to ensure accuracy and apparently it all went well. What suggested changes, if any, or comments the Wrights may have offered are not known.

Why they had put such trust in Root was never explained. But clearly they had much in common. He, too, in the early days of his beekeeping enterprise had been taken for a "nut." He had succeeded with his ideas only by close study. Importantly, beginning with his first visit in August, he had shown himself true to his word and ready to cooperate in any way he could to achieve accuracy in what he wrote.

Like their father, he was a man of strong religious convictions, and it was of no small importance that Bishop Wright approved. As he wrote in his diary, "Mr. Root seems to be a fine gentleman."

Perhaps above all, Wilbur and Orville knew from their first meeting with Root that his regard for them was altogether genuine, his belief in the possibility of human flight no less than their own.

At the time his article appeared in *Gleanings in Bee Culture* in January 1905, Root sent a copy to the editor of *Scientific American,* saying it could be reprinted at no charge. The editor paid it no mind. Instead, in an article published a full year later, "The Wright Aeroplane and Its Fabled Performances," the magazine chose to cast still more doubt:

> If such sensational and tremendously important experiments are being conducted in a not very remote part of the country, on a subject in which almost everybody feels the most

profound interest, is it possible to believe that the enterprising American reporter, who, it is well known, comes down
the chimney when the door is locked in his face . . . would not
have ascertained all about them and published . . . long ago?

The thought that Amos Root was the "enterprising reporter" apparently never entered the editor's mind.

For their part the brothers refused to get worked up or to speak out.
"If they will not take our word and the word of many witnesses," wrote
Wilbur, ". . . we do not think they will be convinced until they see a flight
with their own eyes."

III.

In October, a month after Amos Root's visit, came the first clear sign
that if the American press and the U.S. government had no interest,
there were those on the other side of the Atlantic who did. An officer
of the British Army's Balloon Section, Lieutenant Colonel John Edward
Capper, appeared in Dayton and did not hesitate to inform the brothers
that he had come at the request of his government.

Reluctant to have him come with them to Huffman Prairie just yet,
they instead showed him photographs of recent flights. But it was they
themselves who impressed the visitor more than anything, and he invited them to submit a proposal for the sale of their Flyer II to the British
government.

They were unwilling to comply, partly because they were "not ready
to begin considering what we will do with our baby now that we have
it," as Wilbur had confided to Octave Chanute. Furthermore, as patriotic
Americans, they would be ashamed to offer it to a foreign government
without their own country having a first chance.

On November 9, in celebration of President Theodore Roosevelt's
resounding election, Wilbur flew almost four circles around the field at
Huffman Prairie. Then, on the third day of the new year 1905, he called on
the newly elected local congressman, Republican Robert Nevin, to explain

the situation. Nevin suggested that Wilbur write a proposal for Secretary of War William Howard Taft.

The letter, dated January 18 and signed by both Wilbur and Orville, stated that their efforts of the past five years had produced a flying machine that "not only flies through the air at high speed, but it also lands without being wrecked." During 1904 they had made 105 flights. They had flown in straight lines, circles, over S-shaped courses, in calms and great winds, and brought flying to the point where it could be of great practical use in various ways, "one of which is that of scouting and carrying messages in time of war."

Congressman Nevin forwarded the letter to the War Department. From there it was passed on to the Board of Ordnance and Fortification, the same agency that had seen the $50,000 it provided to Samuel Langley come to nothing.

Congressman Nevin then received a standard formal rejection from the board, dated January 26, explaining that so great were the number of requests for allotments for experiments in mechanical flight that the device in question must first stage a "practical operation" at no expense to the United States; and from Wilbur and Orville's letter it appeared to the board that their machine had not yet reached that stage. It was a standard reply sent irrespective of the fact that the Wrights had made no appeal for financial support.

Possibly this was an instance of extreme wariness within the board because of the Langley experience of becoming involved again with experimental aviation. Or it could have been a case of plain bureaucratic ineptitude. Or that the claims made by the Wrights for their Flyer, like those in so many crank proposals, seemed too preposterous to be taken seriously.

To Wilbur and Orville it was a "flat turn down," which they seem to have been expecting. "We have taken pains to see that 'Opportunity' gave a good clear knock on the War Department door," Wilbur told Octave Chanute.

> It has for years been our business practice to sell to those who wished to buy, instead of trying to force goods upon people

who did not want them. If the American Government has decided to spend no more money on flying machines till their practical use has been demonstrated in actual service abroad, we are sorry, but we cannot reasonably object. They are the judges.

The brothers had already written to Colonel Capper in England to say they were ready to make their proposal. The British War Office responded at once, and serious correspondence began.

———

As always, they had no time to waste. Work went on. A new 1905 Flyer III was under way, a machine "of practical utility," as the Wrights would say. In fact, the Flyer III would prove to be the first practical airplane in history.

Talk of ideas continued without cease among themselves and with Charlie Taylor while at work in the shop, or standing beside the Flyer between tests at Huffman Prairie, or at work inside the shed, or while riding the trolley.

The fascination with birds continued no less than ever. If Ohio offered nothing comparable to the multitudes of gannets and gulls and buzzards in the skies of the Outer Banks, Ohio provided crows aplenty. In language few others could possibly have understood or appreciated, Wilbur wrote to Octave Chanute:

> The power consumed by any bird or flying machine may be figured from the formula wv/ac, in which w = weight, v = velocity $1/a$ = ratio of drift to lift, and $1/c$ = efficiency of the screws or wings of propellers. In the case of the crow flying at 34 ft. per second, or 2,100 ft. per minute, I would fix the value of $1/a$ at 1/8, and $1/c$ at 1/.75; when we have $(1 \times 2100)/(8 \times .75) = 350$ ft. lbs. per pound of weight. The minimum value of $1/a$ may be rendered independent of velocity by regulating the size of the wings. The value of $1/c$ is about the practical limit of the efficiency of screws under usual conditions, and I

see no reason for believing that wings are more efficient than screws, as propellers. . . .

Birds unquestionably develop power many times greater than is consumed by our Flyer, per pound weight. If you will fix in your mind the distance within which a small bird acquires full speed, say 30 miles an hour, and then figure the power necessary to accelerate its weight to this velocity, I think you will be astonished.

And there was more, always more to learn and think about. The new Flyer III was more sturdily built than its predecessors, its motor more powerful, producing as much as 25 horsepower. The double rudder had been enlarged, the wing area slightly reduced, and the leading edges of the wings made more effective. But the "improvements" this time, as the brothers would stress, resulted mainly from "more scientific design" and changes in methods of balancing and steering. The most important change was to move the forward rudder even farther forward—for better longitudinal, or nose to tail, control. They had discovered that most of their troubles could be remedied by tilting the machine forward a little so its flying speed could be restored.

"The best dividends on the labor invested," they said, "have invariably come from seeking more knowledge rather than more power."

Once the test flights got under way in June, it became clear the improvements were working. Moreover, the two pilots were "rusty" no longer.

In one important close call on September 28, as Orville would recount, he was circling the great honey locust tree when the machine suddenly began to turn up one wing and stall. "The operator, not relishing the idea of landing in a thorn tree, attempted to reach the ground." The left wing struck the tree at a height of 10 or 12 feet and carried away several branches, but by putting the plane into a brief dive Orville was able to nose the plane upward again, and the flight, which had already covered 6 miles, continued on to the starting point. The lesson learned was another step forward—the brief dive had restored the speed needed to increase the lift and thereby straighten the effect of the warp.

Wilbur by then had flown 11 miles on a single run, Orville, 12 miles, then 15. To both of them, this, their Flyer III, with its "improvements," was as big an advance as Flyer I had proven to be at Kitty Hawk.

It was at Huffman Prairie that summer and fall of 1905 that the brothers, by experiment and change, truly learned to fly. Then, also, at last, with a plane they could rely on, they could permit themselves enjoyment in what they had achieved. They could take pleasure in the very experience of traveling through the air in a motor-powered machine as no one had. And each would try as best he could to put the experience in words.

"When you know, after the first few minutes, that the whole mechanism is working perfectly," Wilbur was to say, "the sensation is so keenly delightful as to be almost beyond description. Nobody who has not experienced it for himself can realize it. It is a realization of a dream so many persons have had of floating in the air. More than anything else the sensation is one of perfect peace, mingled with the excitement that strains every nerve to the utmost, if you can conceive of such a combination."

Once into the air Orville would write, the ground was "a perfect blur," but as the plane rose higher the objects below became clearer.

At a height of one hundred feet you feel hardly any motion at all, except for the wind which strikes your face. If you did not take the precaution to fasten your hat before starting, you have probably lost it by this time.

The operator moves a lever: the right wing rises, and the machine swings about to the left. You make a very short turn yet you do not feel the sensation of being thrown from your seat, so often experienced in automobile and railway travel. You find yourself facing toward the point from which you started. The objects on the ground now seem to be moving at much higher speed, though you perceive no change in the pressure of the wind on your face. You know then that you are traveling with the wind.

When you near the starting-point, the operator stops the motor while still high in the air. The machine coasts down at an oblique angle to the ground, and after sliding fifty or a hundred feet comes to rest. Although the machine often lands when traveling at a speed of a mile a minute, you feel no shock whatever, and cannot, in fact, tell the exact moment at which it first touched the ground.

The motor close beside you kept up an almost deafening roar during the whole flight, yet in your excitement, you did not notice it till it stopped!

By now the brothers were openly encouraging family and friends to ride out and see the show. Bishop Wright and Katharine, Lorin and his wife and children, and some seventeen friends and neighbors came by trolley or automobile, and many more than once.

Next-door neighbors John Feight and his son George were among them. Torrence Huffman, a doubter no longer, brought along three of his children. Charles Webbert came to watch, as did Frank Hale, the grocer, and druggist W. C. Fouts, whose respective establishments were close by the bicycle shop on West Third Street; and Frank Hamberger, the hardware dealer whose inventory Wilbur and Orville had helped save at the time of the 1898 flood.

On the afternoon of October 5, 1905, before more than a dozen witnesses, Wilbur circled the pasture 29 times, landing only when his gas ran out.

"I saw Wilbur fly twenty-four miles in thirty-eight minutes and four seconds [in] one flight," wrote the Bishop. In fact, this one flight was by far the longest yet, longer than all the 160 flights of the three previous years combined.

By the time the experiments ended, the brothers had made 105 "starts" at Huffman Prairie and thought it time now to put their creation, Flyer III, on the market.

———

By this point, too, the Dayton press had at last awakened. The Wrights, reported the *Daily News*, were making sensational flights every day as local witnesses were happy to attest. W. C. Fouts, the druggist, was quoted saying:

When I went out to Huffman Prairie I expected to see somebody's neck broken. What I did see was a machine weighing
900 pounds soar away like an eagle. . . . I told a friend about
it that night and he acted as if he thought I had gone daft or
joined the liar's club.

An American correspondent for a German aeronautical journal had
come to Huffman Prairie and begun a series of articles on the brothers.
The French were beginning to make inquiries.

Prodded by Octave Chanute to try one more time to rouse interest in
Washington, on the chance that the new president of the Board of Ordnance and Fortification, Major General J. C. Bates, might be of different
mind, the brothers wrote again. Their earlier proposal appeared to have
been given "scant consideration," they said in their letter of October 9.
"We do not wish to take this invention abroad, unless we find it necessary
to do so, and therefore write again, renewing the offer."

By this time the brothers were routinely making controlled flights in
their aircraft of 25 miles or more. But the response from Washington,
as Katharine wrote to the Bishop, was "the same thing that they had before." The only difference was they were told that before any consideration
of their machine, they must provide "such drawings and descriptions . . .
as are necessary to enable construction," something the Wrights refused
to do.

They tried again, asking what requirements in performance were expected by the board, and were told the board did not care to formulate any
requirements until a machine was produced and able to provide "horizontal flight and to carry an operator."

A sampling of photographs of Flyer III in action could have been re-
quested or a visit to Huffman Prairie by someone from Washington might
well have resolved the issue. Told what the response of the board had been,
Octave Chanute concluded, "Those fellows are a bunch of asses."

Progress with the English having stalled, Wilbur informed an interested group in Paris that he and Orville were ready to discuss sale of the
Flyer III to the French government.

In the last week of 1905, Bishop Wright recorded in his diary:

Thursday, December 28 The morning was beautiful, and a fire hardly needed. A Frenchman by the name of Arnold Fordyce came to investigate and drive a trade for a flying machine. They agreed on terms.

Fordyce represented a syndicate of wealthy French businessmen, but the Wrights assumed the deciding authority would be the French military, which was the case. The syndicate would purchase a Wright Flyer as a gift to the French government. According to the agreement the brothers were to receive one million francs, or $200,000, for one machine, on the condition that they provided demonstration flights, during which the machine fulfilled certain requirements in altitude, distance, and speed.

Details of the final terms were to be negotiated by a French commission assigned to come to Dayton. Meantime, a sum of 25,000 francs, or $5,000, was to be deposited in a New York bank in escrow. $200,000 was an exceedingly large sum and the $5,000 the brothers were to receive, however the further negotiations went, would more than cover all the expenses they had had since first going to Kitty Hawk.

Saturday, December 30 In the afternoon [wrote the Bishop in his diary], Wilbur and Orville sign up the contract with Mr. Arnold Fordyce, of Paris. . . .

A Capital Exhibit A

He inspires great confidence.

HART O. BERG

You people at home must stop worrying! There is no need of it.

WILBUR WRIGHT

I.

The four well-dressed French gentlemen and the American accompanying them were the subject of much talk almost from the moment, on March 20, 1906, when they walked into the lobby of the Beckel Hotel in Dayton to register at the front desk.

Word was out that the "Wright boys" had made arrangements to sell their flying machine to the French. But when a reporter for the *Dayton Herald* inquired of the head of the delegation, Arnold Fordyce, if this were so, his reply was they had come "merely to see the sights." He was writing a book about the customs and industries of America, he said. Dayton was one of four cities on the tour. He did add, however, and most cordially, that they hoped to call on the Wright brothers while in town.

Arnold Fordyce had once been an actor. In truth the men had come with no other purpose than to meet with the Wrights. Three of the group, despite their business suits, were French army officers. Commandant Henri Bonel was chief of engineers of the French General Staff, the only one of the group who spoke no English and an acknowledged skeptic concerning the Wrights and their flying machine. Captains Henri Régnier and Jules Fournier were military attachés from the French embassy in Washington.

The one American, Walter Berry, represented the French ambassador to the United States. An international attorney, Berry spent most of his time in Paris, where he figured prominently in the social life of the noted American novelist Edith Wharton and was well attuned to moving in influential circles on both sides of the Atlantic.

The year 1906 thus far had not been particularly promising for the brothers. Their work proceeded on a new, more powerful engine, but they were doing no flying. Meanwhile, in France there was growing excitement over the progress in aviation being made by French manufacturers and such glamorous aviators as Louis Blériot and the Brazilian-born Alberto Santos-Dumont, while the *Paris Herald*, an English language paper, mocked the brothers in an editorial titled "Fliers or Liars."

> The Wrights have flown or they have not flown. They possess
> a machine or they do not possess one. They are in fact either
> fliers or liars. It is difficult to fly. . . . It is easy to say, "We have
> flown."

Now here were the brothers sitting down with a French delegation that had come to talk seriously. That it could be a most important step forward for all involved went without saying.

As Bishop Wright recorded, they met above the bicycle shop every day for more than two weeks, and with the Bishop, too, sitting in on the discussions. On the evening of March 24, at the invitation of Katharine Wright, Fordyce, Commandant Bonel, and Walter Berry "supped" with the family at 7 Hawthorn Street.

The brothers refused to show the delegation their Flyer III, but willingly provided photographs and eyewitness testimony of the plane in flight. In little time even Commandant Bonel, the skeptic of the group, was convinced, impressed primarily by the Wrights themselves and despite the language barrier.

While no agreement resulted, the possibility of a future working arrangement with the French had been strongly reinforced and respect on both sides greatly strengthened, a point the brothers emphasized in a letter to Bonel written April 6:

> Notwithstanding the failure to reach an agreement at our final conference last evening, we shall always remain very friendly to you personally and to your country. . . . Allow us to express our hearty appreciation of your uniform fairness and courtesy throughout this long conference.

But by now, much of the scientific world and the press had begun to change their perspective on the brothers, with *Scientific American* making the most notable change. In its issue of April 7, 1906, the magazine carried an article titled "The Wright Aeroplane and Its Performances," in which eleven eyewitnesses to flights by the brothers at Huffman Prairie, in answer to twelve specific questions, affirmed that they had seen one or the other of the brothers fly in their machine in varying winds and perform all manner of movements with complete control throughout. Included, too, in the article was a letter from Charles Webbert, from whom the Wrights rented the bicycle shop, telling how in October he had witnessed Orville flying the machine for about half an hour and how the machine had traveled in large circles of about a mile around, and how the Flyer was "absolutely free from the time it left the rail upon which it started until it touched the ground in making its final landing."

On May 22, 1906, the patent applied for in 1903 was at last issued on the Wright Flying Machine, patent number 821,393, and through the rest of that spring and summer, preoccupation with a new engine for Flyer III went on, and flight tests continued at Huffman Prairie into the fall.

In France, Alberto Santos-Dumont, flying what looked like a motor-powered hodgepodge of box kites, had made a public flight covering 726 feet. French aviation enthusiasts went wild with excitement. Santos-Dumont was said to have "gained the greatest glory to which man can aspire." He had achieved "a decisive step in the history of aviation," and "not in secret."

"I fancy that he is now very nearly where you were in 1904," wrote Octave Chanute to Wilbur. "Fear that others will produce a machine capable of practical service in less than several years does not worry us," Wilbur would reply confidently. "We have been over the course and understand how much yet remains for them to do."

Then came overtures from Flint & Company, a New York firm with extensive experience in marketing war materials in Europe. By December the overtures had become serious. Flint & Company was offering the Wrights $500,000 for the sales rights of their plane outside the United States. The Wrights would maintain the American market.

By nature the more entrepreneurial of the two, Orville showed the most interest, and it was he who went to New York, met with the head of the firm, Charles Flint, and made a "deal." Or so it seemed. Further issues required further discussion. So, early in the new year, 1907, both Orville and Wilbur took the train to New York.

The tempo of financial possibilities was picking up considerably. In February, Germany offered $500,000 for fifty Wright Flyers, and the brothers agreed that Flint & Company should be their sales representative—but only their sales representative—on a 20 percent commission everywhere except in the United States.

Then in May came an urgent message from Charles Flint, saying the company's European representative, Hart O. Berg, had become skeptical about the Wrights and their machine and wanted one or the other or both to come to Europe as soon as possible and make their case themselves, all expenses, of course, to be covered by Flint & Company.

Wilbur thought Orville should go. Wilbur wanted to see to the finishing touches on the new engine and prepare the Flyer III for shipment. "I am more careful than he is," Wilbur would explain to their father. Further, the one who went to Europe would have to act almost entirely on his own judgment without much consultation by letter or cable. Wilbur felt he was more willing to accept the consequences of any errors of judgment on Orville's part than to have Orville blaming him if he were to go.

Orville stubbornly disagreed, insisting that Wilbur would make the best impression in France, and Orville was right, as they all knew, including Wilbur, who "grabbed a few things" and left for New York. By Saturday, May 18, he was on board the RMS *Campania,* sailing past the Statue of Liberty on his way out to sea.

An entirely new adventure had begun, unlike anything he, or any of the family, had yet experienced. Wilbur had just turned forty that April and was to be on his own far from home, separated from his family, for longer than he had ever been or ever imagined, and tested in ways he had never been.

II.

"I sailed this morning about 9 o'clock and we are now something over 200 miles out," Wilbur wrote in a letter addressed to Katharine but intended for all at home. "The St. Louis and another ship started at the same time, but we have run off from them." The *Campania,* part of the Cunard Line, was known as one of the finest vessels of its kind, and one of the fastest, a "flying palace of the ocean," which Wilbur particularly liked. The ship was 622 feet in length, with two tall stacks, and burnt some five hundred tons of coal per day. The predominant interior style was Art Nouveau, with staterooms and public rooms paneled in satinwood and mahogany, and thickly carpeted.

The weather was "splendid," the sea smooth, and he had a cabin to himself. With only about half the usual number of passengers on board, he was able to get a $250 cabin for only $100, and he was quite happy about that, too, even if Flint was covering expenses.

"We made 466 miles the first day," he wrote the following evening, "and left the other boats out of sight." The third day out he took a tour of the engine room, marveling at the scale of it all—engines half as high as an office building back home, engines that could deliver 28,000 horsepower, this in contrast to the 25 horsepower of the new engine for Flyer III. There were twelve boilers, and over one hundred furnaces. The ship's propellers measured no less than 23 feet in diameter.

He kept note of the miles made day by day, and walked the promenade deck five to ten miles a day. Though he wrote nothing about the food served or the other passengers, he seemed to be having a fine time.

All went ideally until the sixth day out, when a storm hit and Wilbur had his first experience with pitch and roll on water, not in the air. "The waves are probably 10 feet high and the ship pitches considerably. Fortunately there is but little roll." The spray was such that the promenade decks were useless. The ship had become more like a hospital, though he himself felt only "a little sick" just after breakfast.

The last day at sea, off the Irish coast, he wrote of seeing gulls at intervals, "and how they could skim within a foot or two of the waves and in strong winds did not even have to flap their wings very much."

After landing at Liverpool at first light, Saturday, May 25, Wilbur went by train to London, where, at Euston Station, he was met by the Flint & Company sales representative, Hart O. Berg, an American who recognized Wilbur the moment he stepped off the train.

"I have never seen a picture of him, or had him described to me in any way," Berg would write to Charles Flint, ". . . and either I am a Sherlock Holmes, or Wright has the peculiar glint of genius in his eye which left no doubt in my mind as to who he was."

Berg also noticed Wilbur's luggage consisted of a single leather grip the size of a doctor's bag and his wardrobe left much to be desired. But on the way to the hotel, it was Wilbur who suggested it might be "advisable" for him to buy a new suit. At a tailor shop in the Strand, Berg "fixed him up" with both a dress suit and a tuxedo. When Wilbur's account of these purchases reached home, Katharine wrote at once to tell him how "Orv had marched off to Perry Meredith's [haberdashery] this morning and ordered the same for himself."

Intent on wasting no time, Berg told Wilbur there was little likelihood of doing business in England and the sooner they left for France the better. The main effort would be made in Paris. They also found themselves disagreeing on the best approach—whether to deal with governments primarily or with individuals, Berg much in favor of individuals. Either way, both agreed it would be best not to make much of Wilbur's presence in Europe, not for the time being at least.

Summing things up, at the close of his long memorandum to Charles Flint, Berg stressed how pleased he was with Wilbur's whole bearing and attitude. "He inspires great confidence," Berg wrote, "and I am sure he will be a capital Exhibit A."

How Wilbur felt about Berg at this point is not clear. Though fellow Americans of roughly the same age, their backgrounds and experiences in life could hardly have been more different. Born to a Jewish family in Philadelphia and raised in New York, Berg had attended private schools until sent off to Europe to be trained as an engineer at Liège in Belgium. In the time since he had become a pioneer in the manufacture of pistols, machine guns, automobiles, and submarines. He had worked at the Colt firearms factory in Hartford, Connecticut, maintained his own sales office in Paris, and spent three years in Russia, where he obtained orders from the czar for building ten submarines.

Where Wilbur was lean and rumpled, Berg was stout and immaculate in attire. Berg was fluent in several languages and well connected, with contacts in high places throughout Europe. And though arms dealers— "merchants of death"—were an anathema to many, he seems to have been well liked and respected by nearly everyone. Berg and his wife, Edith, also an American, had lived in Paris for years, and the French held him in high regard. In 1901, he had been made a Chevalier of the Legion of Honor.

From London down to Dover, then across the Channel, Wilbur and Berg were joined by another Flint executive, Frank Cordley. They arrived in Paris on the evening of May 27, when it was still daylight, and checked in to the luxurious Hôtel Meurice on the rue de Rivoli.

———

"The Tuileries Palace and the Louvre are only a couple of squares to our left," Wilbur reported that same night to Katharine and the family.

> The column Vendome is behind us, and the Place de la Concorde and Arc [de] Triomphe are farther up the Champs-Elysées. We are right in the most beautiful and interesting part of the city.

He was also residing in one of the finest hotels in all Paris, indeed, in all Europe. The "New Hotel Meurice," as said, had only just reopened after major "refurbishments." The old "Hotel of Kings" had been made more sumptuous than ever. Its restaurant, in decor and cuisine, was now one of the finest in the city and a "rendezvous of fashion." One could take a magnificent new elevator to a roof garden, and for panoramic views of Paris there were few to compare, or, for that matter, from those guest rooms fronting on the rue de Rivoli, one of which, room 329, Hart Berg had reserved for Wilbur.

"Stay in Paris and taste the pervasive charm, the freshness of beautiful summer nights. The sky dusted with stars is radiant," read an advertisement for the Meurice.

> The electricity shines through little lampshades, the flowers give out a fragrance. We are only a few steps from the Concorde, but one would think himself so far away, transported into a town of dreams.

Wilbur wrote nothing of the roof terrace or the magnificent crystal chandeliers in the main dining room, or the fancy livery worn by the elevator operator. Interestingly, in all he would write about his time in Paris, he never mentioned his plush accommodations. Probably he had no wish to incite envy at home. Or to magnify concern over his being corrupted by high living. Except for the hotel stationery on which his letters were written, one would never have known where he was staying.

Nor did he make mention of the women of Paris, or the fashions on parade, or the shops, the opera, the theater, or the French in general, or the American tourists, of whom there were a great many.

What he did write about in the days that followed, apart from all he reported on his dealings with Berg, Cordley, and the French, were the great buildings and art treasures of Paris, revealing as he never had—or had call to—the extent of his interest in architecture and painting.

Like so many seeing Paris for the first time, he could not get enough of it, and covered more ground on foot than ever before. The five to ten miles a day he walked on board ship would seem to have been only a warm-up. Whatever free time he had away from business, he was out and on his own way. It was spring in Paris, the chestnut trees in bloom.

From the Louvre to the Arc de Triomphe was nearly two miles of gardens and esplanades with thousands of statues, he wrote. He climbed the three hundred steps to the top of the Arc de Triomphe, walked the banks of the Seine to the Île de la Cité, walked to the Opéra, walked down the rue de Rivoli two miles to the Place de la Bastille. On a Sunday morning he hiked to the top of Montmartre, a distance of nearly two miles that included more than three hundred steps.

He loved seeing so much open space used to set off important buildings. "Paris is the most prodigal of land for public purposes," he wrote in a long, descriptive letter to Bishop Wright. There was much to be learned from the French about how to place public buildings.

> There is always an open space as big as a city square in front of each building. . . . And in addition there is nearly always a broad avenue leading directly to it, giving a view from a long distance. It is this, as much as the buildings and monuments themselves, that makes Paris such a magnificent city.

If only a city like New York were arranged the same way. Even New York's skyscrapers, like the Belmont and Knickerbocker hotels, if properly set, would be "wonderful."

He seems to have soaked up everything in view. And whatever he looked at, he looked at closely. Some of the landmarks were "a little shabby." Half the gilding was gone from the dome of Les Invalides, where Napoleon was buried. The same was true of the pedestal of the Egyptian obelisk in the Place Vendôme and he was sorry to see so much of the statuary marred by black streaks.

He spent considerable time at the Panthéon, which, he explained to Katharine, was not used as a church but as commemoration of the great men of France. The dome seen from inside was "not much," he decided— too high in proportion to its diameter, like looking into an inverted well— but the interior was "very grand."

He took architecture seriously, thoughtfully, and made up his own mind, irrespective of whatever was said in his red Baedeker's guidebook. Notre Dame was a disappointment. "My imagination pictures things more vividly than my eyes." He thought the nave too narrow, the clerestory windows too high, the interior far too dark. "The pillars are so heavy and close together that the double aisles on each side form no part of the room when you stand in the nave."

How amazing it was, he wrote in another letter, to see thousands of people dining on the sidewalks up and down the avenues, sitting at little tables outside restaurants, sipping wine and eating in the open air "right on the sidewalks."

Often, as the time passed, he was himself dining handsomely, as the guest of Hart Berg. There was Boivins on the avenue de Clichy in Montmartre, Henri's on the rue Volney, and the famous Café Anglais, where Wilbur enjoyed lunch with both Berg and Mrs. Berg.

He would fill his free time in Paris to advantage and with the same level of intensity he brought to nearly everything, making the most of every waking hour in what, for all he knew, might be his one and only chance for such an opportunity.

Of all that Paris offered, it was the Louvre that he kept going back to again and again, spending hours there and logging still more miles walking the long galleries. His description of the paintings he saw could go on for pages, a sign, it would seem, of how much interest in art there was at home as well, and with Katharine in particular.

He preferred the Rembrandts, Holbeins, and Van Dycks, "as a whole," better than the Rubenses, Titians, Raphaels, and Murillos. His disappointment in the *Mona Lisa* was as great as it had been in Notre Dame. "I must confess that the pictures by celebrated masters that impressed me most were not the ones that are best known." He much preferred Leonardo's *John the Baptist* to the *Mona Lisa*. Above all, he was taken with the work of the seventeenth-century Flemish master Anthony Van Dyck.

In a letter written after a full afternoon at the Louvre, he moved on to a collection of nineteenth-century French masters, including Delacroix, Corot, Millet, and Courbet. "While I do not pretend to be much of a judge, I am inclined to think that in five hundred years it [the collection] will be recognized as some of the greatest work ever done." What appealed especially about Corot was the way he painted the sky. The sky was his source of light.

Such keen interest as he had in art was not only remarkable in someone so committed to technical innovation, but a measure of a truly exceptional capacity of mind. As weeks, then months passed, Wilbur, of his own choice, visited the Louvre fifteen or more times.

What he did not report to those at home was the extent to which he was being scrutinized by the press, and the stir he caused at public occasions. Any hope of anonymity was already gone. To a reporter for the *Washington Post* who stopped him in the lobby of the Hôtel Meurice, Wilbur refused to say anything about his machine or his plans. When the subject turned to the difference between flying and going up in a balloon, Wilbur said he had yet to go up in a balloon, but that it was "entirely another thing from flying which affects one with intoxication. After having once flown it is almost impossible to turn to anything else."

In mid-June he went with Hart Berg to see the balloon races at St. Cloud. Amid a particularly elegant crowd in which were to be seen Gustave Eiffel and the American ambassador, Henry White, Wilbur drew more attention than anyone. A reporter for the *Paris Herald* asked, "You are over here on pleasure, are you not, Mr. Wright?"

"To some extent," Wilbur said. "I am enjoying myself splendidly and seeing all manner of new things."

"You like Paris?"

"It is a marvelous city."

"Mr. Wright talked carefully," the reporter wrote.

> It was obvious that he feared to be caught in a trap concerning his remarkable machine and what he wants to do with it. At the end of each question his clean-shaven face relapsed into a broad sphinx-like smile.

That this same American bicycle mechanic from Ohio was spending hours with the masterpieces of the Louvre was apparently not of interest to the press.

———

The business sessions arranged by Berg had begun their first full day in Paris. Wilbur had been taken to meet an active patron of ballooning with a strong interest in aviation, Henri Deutsch de la Meurthe, whom Wilbur described for Orville as "the Standard Oil King of France." There were sessions with Arnold Fordyce, Commandant Bonel, and officials of the French government. Berg was a "pretty slick hand," Wilbur told Orville, and things were going well. Berg was "very practical," and Wilbur liked the way he was always at hand to explain what was being said in French and said so often at an extremely high speed. Berg could be depended upon to do his utmost. Besides, he was "about as enthusiastic now as a man could be, and he really has a remarkable faculty for reaching people."

The business talks often seemed endless, but thus far the prospects for an agreement looked encouraging. In general outline, the Wrights were to receive $350,000 for their Flyer, once a public demonstration was made in France, before any agreement was struck. The French insisted on seeing the plane and seeing it operate, which was clearly their right.

"The pot is beginning to boil pretty lively," Wilbur reported. But then one French faction tangled with another, political intrigue intervened, progress slowed.

Not so many years before, Wilbur had decided he was unsuited for "commercial pursuits." Now he found himself in the thick of extremely complex commercial dealings, playing for extremely high stakes with highly experienced entrepreneurs, politicians, and bureaucrats, and in a language he neither spoke nor understood. The whole game, the players, the setting, the language were all new to him. Yet he was more than holding his own, and in good spirits, aware as he was of the derision to be found behind the scenes. At the war ministry it was being said the Wrights were "bluffers like all Americans," "worthless people" trying to sell to France "an object of no value" that even the Americans did not believe in.

Alert, patient, closely attentive, Wilbur "never rattled," as his father would say, never lost his confidence. He could be firm without being dictatorial, disagree without causing offense. Nor was there ever a doubt that when he spoke he knew what he was talking about.

Most importantly, he remained entirely himself, never straying from his direct, unpretentious way, and with good effect. If anything, his lack of French, his lack of sophistication, seemed to work to his advantage. He was, indeed, as Hart Berg had anticipated, a capital Exhibit A and more.

That Wilbur neither drank or smoked or showed the least interest in women remained, of course, a puzzlement to the French.

The whole while he was keeping those at home, and Orville in particular, fully abreast of all that was happening, by mail and by cable, often in lengthy detail, describing the various configurations of how they were to profit financially depending on who put in what money. An experienced financial reporter could hardly have provided clearer coverage.

For occasional relief, Hart Berg would treat Wilbur to a pleasant chauffeur-driven drive with him and Mrs. Berg in their grand automobile through the Bois de Boulogne or out to Fontainebleau or Versailles.

One Monday morning, while Wilbur was lying in bed, a hotel clerk knocked at the door to say a dirigible, known as *La Patrie*, was flying over Paris. *La Patrie*, as Wilbur knew, was the first "airship" ordered by the French army. He dressed at once and went up to the roof garden.

La Patrie (The Homeland), was a giant, sausage-shaped gas bag with an open gondola for the crew hanging below. It passed over the Arc de Triomphe and almost directly over the Meurice at what Wilbur estimated to be 15 miles per hour. He judged it a "very successful trial." But as he was shortly to write, the cost of such an airship was ten times that of a Flyer, and a Flyer moved at twice the speed. The flying machine was in its infancy while the airship had "reached its limit and must soon become a thing of the past." Still, the spectacle of the airship over Paris was a grand way to begin a day.

Most mornings only meant more meetings.

The primary question at issue had become whether to sell to the French government or set up a commercial company with Henri Deutsch. The possibility of a contract with the government seemed all but certain, until the French army insisted the Flyer trial be conducted in winds too strong and demanded an exclusive agreement for three years, neither of which Wilbur would agree to.

Then, for the first time, it became clear that Flint & Company was expecting a commission of 20 percent not only on what they sold, as had been agreed on, but also on what the brothers retained. ("Don't worry over Flint's commission," he told Orville. "We can hold them level.")

Next thing, Wilbur was informed confidentially that if he, Orville, and their associates were to raise the price to the French government by $50,000, this sum could be "distributed among persons who had the power to put the deal through." In other words, those in power would need to be bribed substantially. This Wilbur refused even to discuss.

The longer the talk dragged on, the more obvious it became that little would ever be decided until a demonstration was staged, and Wilbur kept urging Orville to speed up progress at home. "I presume you will have everything packed and ready before this letter arrives," he wrote. "Be sure to bring everything needed in the way of spare parts. . . . Bring Charlie Taylor along, of course, when you come. . . . It will pay to have enough trustworthy assistance when we come to experiment."

This was written on June 28. Wilbur had had no word from Orville for nearly a month.

In a letter from Katharine, dated June 30, he was to learn that things were not going at all well at home, that she and Orville felt left out of what was happening in Paris. "Orv can't work any," Orv was quite "uneasy," Orv was "unsettled," "really crazy to know what is going on," "wroth" over how things were being handled in Paris without him. Clearly she was, too.

She and Orville had lost all patience with Flint & Company and questioned whether they could be trusted. She had had little or no experience with Jews, but having seen a photograph of Hart Berg, she wondered if he might be one. "I can't stand Berg's looks," she wrote. "It has just dawned on me that the whole company is composed of Jews. Berg certainly looks it."

A few days later, she let Wilbur know the situation at home had become even worse. She was nearing a crack-up, and it was largely his doing. "What on earth is happening to your letters?"

Her letter became a storm of anger, blame, self-pity, and desperation far beyond her "wrathy" nature. She had had more than enough of the "whole business." "We are all so nervous and worn out with the suspense that we can't any of us keep from being cross. Orv and I regularly fight every time we get together for five minutes. And poor Daddy does nothing but advise us to 'be calm, Bessie, be calm,' while he is so excited that he can't hear anything we say." She had never been so tired in all her life. "I want to cry if anybody looks at me."

Some of their letters to him were being returned because of the wrong address. "Why couldn't you tell us sooner that you weren't getting your mail?

> It makes us desperate to sit here and be perfectly helpless while they [Flint & Company] are working every scheme they can to get advantage of you. What business had they getting you into that French business? You could have done better there by yourselves. . . . I <u>despise</u> the whole lot of them. . . . Orv is so worried and excited and tired out that I feel some concern about him. He can't stand this forever—neither can you, for that matter.

The problem, Wilbur would later explain privately in a letter to his father, knowing the Bishop would understand, was that Orville appeared to be "in one of his peculiar spells" and "not really himself."

The morning of July 17, from his room at the Meurice, Wilbur wrote a long reply to Katharine setting straight for her and Orville the situation in Paris, how he was going about his part in it, his concern for them, how he had tried to spare them aggravation, and why they need not worry. It was noticeably candid and entirely confident in tone, and as revealing of his own estimate of himself as almost anything Wilbur ever wrote, his message being that he was the one on the scene in Paris, he was in command, knew what he was about, knew the people with whom he was dealing, and there was no call for those at home to get worked up.

"In view of the fact that I have written, alone, three or four times as many letters home as I have received from all of you together," he began, "it is a little amusing to read your continual complaints that you get so few from me." In the two and a half months he had been away, he had received, on average, a letter a week from home, whereas he had been writing to them three to four times a week, except for a ten-day stretch when things were in such an unresolved state that there was nothing to report.

He had felt from the start, he continued, that anything he wrote to Orville would unsettle him, but he felt Orville had a right to know what was going on. As for Flint & Company, he did not remind Katharine and

Orville, as he could have, that it was Orville who had most wanted to get involved with them in the first place.

"I have done what I know he would have done if he had been here and understood all the facts. In such cases the man at a distance only does harm by trying to give instructions which do not fit the case."

Within days after reaching Europe, he had felt confident he could handle the situation. His only worry was whether Orville would be ready to follow as quickly as possible with the machine. "It is not my custom to voice my complaints, but this business of never being ready has been a nightmare to me for more than a year."

As for Berg and Cordley, they had at first considered him "merely sort of an exhibit."

> But their eyes have gradually opened, and now they realize that I see into situations deeper than they do, that my judgment is often more sound, and that I intend to run them rather than have them run me. . . . Now I control everything and they give advice and assistance. In this role they can be of great service to us and I see no reason for breaking with them.

He was very sorry those at home were so worn down by excitement. He himself, he assured them, was feeling better than he had in several years.

They must stop worrying. There was no need.

In closing, he reported, arrangements had been made by some Americans for him to go that afternoon on his first balloon flight.

———

They took off from the Aéro-Club grounds at St. Cloud, eventually sailing into the clouds to emerge at about 3,000 feet out into bright sunshine and blue sky. It was higher into the sky by far than Wilbur had ever been, and the view was utterly spectacular. They were fifty miles from Paris by then, crossing open country. "The alterations of rich brown newly plowed soil, with green fields of grass, and grains of different shades and the light brown and yellow fields ready for harvest made a wonderful picture," he

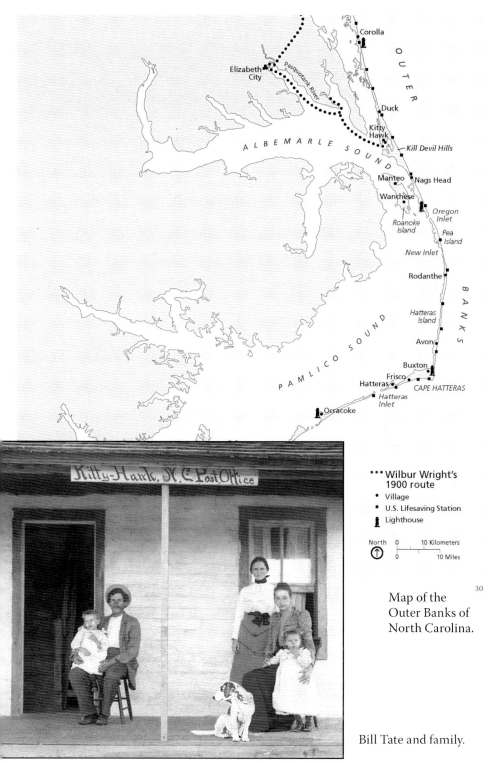

Corolla

OUTER

Elizabeth
City

Pasquotank River

Duck

Kitty
Hawk

Kill Devil Hills

ALBEMARLE SOUND

Manteo
Nags Head

Wanchese

Oregon
Inlet

Roanoke
Island

Pea
Island

New Inlet

Rodanthe

B
A
N
K
S

Hatteras
Island

PAMLICO SOUND

Avon

Buxton
Frisco

Hatteras

CAPE HATTERAS

Hatteras
Inlet

Ocracoke

••• Wilbur Wright's
1900 route
• Village
■ U.S. Lifesaving Station
🗼 Lighthouse

North   0   10 Kilometers
⊕   0   10 Miles

30

Map of the
Outer Banks of
North Carolina.

Kitty-Hawk, N.C. Post Office

Bill Tate and family.

31

Hawks, are better soarers than buzzards but more often want to flapping because they wish greater speed.

A damp day is unfavorable for soaring unless there is a high wind.

No bird soars in a calm.

The object of the tail is to increase the spread of surface in the rear when the wings are moved forward in light winds and thus presses the centre of pressure at about the same spot. It seems to be used as a

rudder very little. In high winds it is folded up very close narrow.

All soarers, but especially the buzzard, seem to keep their fore and aft balance more by shifting the centre of resistance than by shifting the centre of lift. Thus a buzzard soaring in the normal position will be turned upward by a sudden gust. It immediately lowers its wings often much below its body. The momentum of its body now acting above the centre of resistance

Above: Wilbur's notes on the soaring birds of Kitty Hawk.

Wilbur (left) and Orville flying their 1901 glider as a kite.

The first Wright
camp at Kitty Hawk,
1900.

1902 camp kitchen at Kill Devil Hills with all pots,
pans, cups, saucers, and provisions in perfect order.

Camp interior with Wilbur at rear and the 1902 glider at right
foreground. Sleeping quarters were in the rafters overhead.

Octave Chanute.

37

38

Seen during a break in the shade of the Kill Devil shed are (left to right): Orville, Octave Chanute, Wilbur, and Edward Huffaker.

Wilbur takes wing in the 1902 glider soon after the brothers' return to Kitty Hawk in 1903. Their camp and shed stand alone in the distant wind-swept sands.

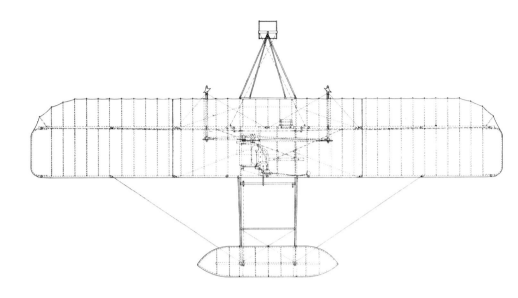

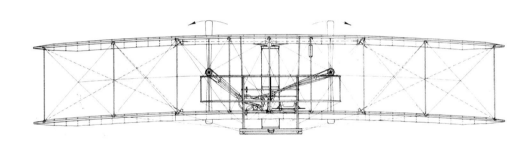

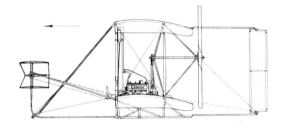

—— KITTY HAWK AEROPLANE ——

CONCEIVED AND BUILT AT DAYTON, OHIO, AND SUCCESSFULLY FLOWN BY ORVILLE AND WILBUR WRIGHT, DECEMBER 17, 1903, AT KITTY HAWK, NORTH CAROLINA.

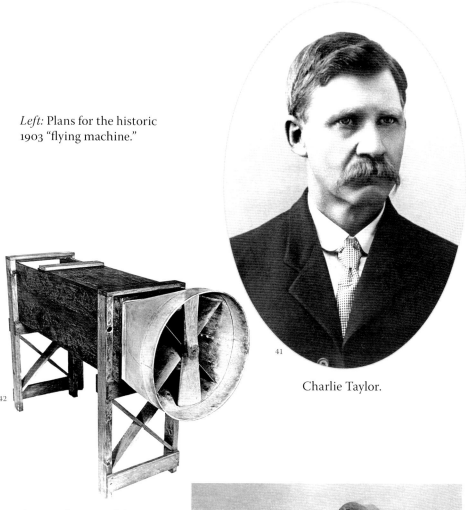

Left: Plans for the historic 1903 "flying machine."

Charlie Taylor.

A reproduction of the Wrights' wind tunnel with which they tested different wing shapes.

A reproduction of the four-cylinder aluminum gasoline engine built by Charlie Taylor.

John T. Daniels (second on the left) and his Kill Devil Hills
life-saving crew, the Wrights' primary support force.

45

AIRSHIP FAILS TO FLY

Prof. Langley's Machine Goes to River Bottom.

PROF. MANLY ABOARD

THE LATTER RESCUED FROM PERILOUS POSITION.

Test of the Airship Off the Arsenal Point Yesterday Afternoon— Large Crowd Present.

The dramatic collapse of Samuel Langley's aerodrome, December 8, 1903. The story at left is from the Washington *Evening Star*.

by noon and got the machine out on the tracks in front of the building ready for a trial from the level. The wind was gradually dying and by the time we were ready was blowing only about 4 to 5 meters per sec. After waiting several hours to see whether it would breeze up again we took the machine in.

Thursday, Dec. 17th

When we got up a wind of between 20 and 25 miles was blowing from the north. We got the machine out early and put out the signal for the men at the station. Before we were quite ready, John T. Daniels, W.S. Dough, A.D. Etheridge, W.C. Brinkley of Manteo, and Johnny Moore, of Nags Head arrived. After

running the engine and propellers a few minutes to get them in working order, I got on the machine at 10:35 for the first trial. The wind according to our anemometers at this time was blowing a little over 20 miles (corrected) 27 miles according to the Government anemometer at Kitty Hawk. On slipping the rope the machine started off increasing in speed to probably 7 or 8 miles. The machine lifted from the truck just as it was entering on the fourth rail. Mr. Daniels took a picture just as it left the tracks. I found the control of the front rudder quite difficult on account of its being balanced too near the center and thus had a tendency to turn itself when started so that the rudder was turned too far on one side and then too

Left: Orville Wright's own diary account of what happened at Kill Devil Hills the morning of December 17, 1903. *Above:* One of history's turning points recorded in one of the most famous photographs ever, as the Wright Flyer takes off for the first time. Orville is at the controls; Wilbur runs beside him. The picture was taken by John T. Daniels. The time was precisely 10:35 A.M.

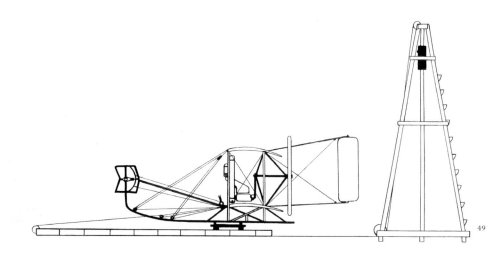

49

Diagram of the "starting apparatus" or catapult
devised by the Wrights to compensate for a lack
of sufficient winds at Huffman Prairie.

50

The Wrights' 1905 Flyer, the world's first practical airplane, takes
to the air over Huffman Prairie with Orville at the controls,
September 29, 1905, a day when he flew 12 miles in 20 minutes.
On October 5, Wilbur flew 24 miles in 39 minutes.

51

Volume XXXIII.   JANUARY 1, 1905   Number 1

GLEANINGS
IN BEE CULTURE

CONTENTS

MARKET QUOTATIONS............4
STRAWS, by Dr. Miller...................11
BEE-KEEPING AMONG THE ROCKIES......13
CONVERSATIONS WITH DOOLITTLE 15
EDITORIALS.................. 16
  Government Apicultural Work......................16
  Sidelights from the St. Louis Convention......16
GENERAL CORRESPONDENCE....................19
  De Luxe Comb Honey.......... 19
  Queens Mating More than Once...................22
  The Wings of the Bee..............................24
  Judging Honey at Fairs........................25
  The Danzenbaker Hive 26
  How I Manage Swarming..........................27
  Lizards and Bees.................................28
  Hoffman Frame and Follower Defended.........29
  The Hoffman Frame Come to Stay 30
  Food Commissioners and Adulterated Honey...31
HEADS OF GRAIN................. 32
  Shaken Swarms a Success, and When...........32
  Feeding Bees in the Cellar, etc...............32
  How to Wash Out Kerosene-cans 32
  Paint for Hives—What Color to Use..........33
  Perforated Zinc Reduce Amount of Honey?....33
  Information Wanted by St. Nicholas Editor...33
  Failure to Cure; What's the Trouble?.........33
  Noises above a Bee-cellar.....................33
  V vs. Square Edges on Hoffman Frames....34
OUR HOMES............................36
SPECIAL NOTICES.................49

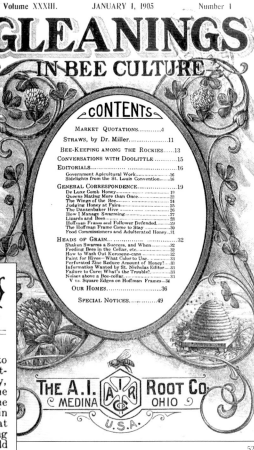

THE A.I. ROOT Co.
MEDINA   OHIO
U.S.A.

52

Amos I. Root, the Ohio beekeeper who, in the January 1, 1905 edition of his publication, *Gleanings in Bee Culture,* provided the first full, eyewitness, accurate account of the magnitude of what the Wright brothers had achieved.

OUR HOMES, BY A. I. ROOT.

What hath God wrought ?—NUM. 23:23.

Dear friends, I have a wonderful story to tell you—a story that, in some respects, out-rivals the Arabian Nights fables—a story, too, with a moral that I think many of the younger ones need, and perhaps some of the older ones too if they will heed it. God in his great mercy has permitted me to be, at least somewhat, instrumental in ushering in and introducing to the great wide world an invention that may outrank the electric cars, the automobiles, and all other methods of travel, and one which may fairly take a place beside the telephone and wireless telegraphy. Am I claiming a good deal? Well, I will tell my story, and you shall be the judge. In order to make the story a helpful one I may stop and turn aside a good many times to point a moral.

In our issue for Sept. 1 I told you of two young men, two farmer's boys, who love machinery, down in the central part of Ohio. I am now going to tell you something of two other boys, a *minister's* boys, who love machinery, and who are interested in the modern developments of science and art. Their names are Orville and Wilbur Wright, of Dayton, Ohio. I made mention of them and their work on page 241 of our issue for March 1 last. You may remember it. These two, perhaps by accident, or may be as a matter of taste, began studying the flights of birds and insects. From this they turned their attention to what has been done in the way of enabling men to fly. They not only studied nature, but they procured the best books, and I think I may say all the papers, the world contains on this subject.

53

wrote. He loved seeing the little towns with their red tile roofs and the white roads reaching off in every direction.

They flew nearly eighty miles in just over three hours and landed in a wheat field about ten miles west of Orléans. But beautiful as it had been, ballooning was not for him any more than it had been for Otto Lilienthal. Once on the ground you had to hike to a nearby village, find somewhere to spend the night, then, because of the prevailing winds, go back to where you started by a slow local train. ("What we are seeking is the means of free motion in the air, in any direction," Lilienthal had written.)

On the evening of the same day that Wilbur was heading back to Paris by train, Orville left Dayton on an overnight express for New York, also on his way to Paris. The Flyer III had at last been finished, packed, and shipped off to France, to be stored in the customs house at Le Havre until needed. Orville, as Katharine said, had gone off looking "pretty well fizzled out." He had also, as he discovered en route, forgotten to bring Wilbur's hotel address in Paris.

III.

Early on a Sunday morning in late July, the brothers were reunited. Having enjoyed an uneventful crossing on the steamer *Philadelphia*, Orville succeeded in finding his way to the Meurice, where he discovered Wilbur looking better than he had in years.

Following breakfast at the hotel, they went for a long walk together, talking the whole time. They lunched at the Café Alcazar on the Champs-Elysées, after which they spent most of a sultry afternoon sitting and talking in the park along that boulevard. And by all signs they succeeded in clearing the air between them.

The following day they met with Hart Berg and Frank Cordley for what Wilbur described as "a rather warm heart-to-heart talk," meaning it was extremely heated. They took up the matter of patents, Wilbur making it clear from the start that Flint & Company was in no way entering into a partnership with them. "We are, and intend to be, the sole owners of the patents," he said, according to his own notes on the conversation.

They talked of expenses, and of stock in the enterprise. "The point is this," Wilbur told Berg. "We do not intend you to own twenty percent of any stock. We intend to own the stock. You are the selling agents." And so it went back and forth, Berg making his case, Wilbur and Orville holding firm.

From all Wilbur had reported and explained to him, and from his own judgment of Berg, and from the meeting, Orville had his suspicions absolved, his mind put to rest. He was ready to proceed with Wilbur and as Wilbur directed. "Our friends F [Flint & Company] and B [Berg] are not in the bandit crew," Orville was glad to assure Katharine.

Wilbur led Orville on a first stroll through the Louvre and to celebrate Orville's arrival in Paris, Frank Cordley hosted an evening at the legendary and highly expensive Tour d'Argent by the Seine on the Left Bank, where a table-side preparation of duck, *canard au sang*, the main course, performed by the restaurant's celebrated owner-chef, Frédéric Delair, seems to have made a far greater impression on Orville than anything he had seen at the Louvre. Delair worked in a formal tailcoat and with his flowing side whiskers and pince-nez eyeglasses, looked, as Orville would report to Katharine, more like a college professor than a chef and had a way of swinging his head as he carved up the duck into small pieces that in itself was worth the full price.

> The legs, wings, etc., [Orville continued] are sent to another room where we cannot see them receiving the finishing touches; but the carcass, after most of the meat has been removed is put in a fancy press, and all the juice and marrow extracted. The meat and juices are then placed over the alcohol flame and cooked together. Mr. Frederic basting the meat the entire time. Finally the duck is served with the enclosed card and folder which gives the serial number of the duck we ate.

When, in a letter, Bishop Wright expressed dire warnings over the temptations of Paris, Wilbur wrote to assure him they would do nothing to disgrace the training they had received at home, and that all the wine he had tasted thus far would not fill a single glass. "We have been real good over here," Orville added. "We have been in a lot of the big churches and haven't got drunk yet."

Their prospects in France were at a low ebb, thanks in large part to the number of government officials departing for their customary August vacations. But with interest in Germany still active, Wilbur and Berg decided to leave for Berlin, departing August 4.

On the way to Berlin, seeing a sign from the train window of the small town of Jemappes in Belgium, Wilbur began talking about the historic battle fought there in 1792, and, to Berg's amazement, went on at length about the importance of the victory won by the army of the infant French Republic over the regular Austrian army. It was for Berg yet another example of the extraordinary reach of Wilbur's mind. He had read about it in his youth, Wilbur explained.

A week later, when Charlie Taylor arrived, Orville had him check into a less conspicuous hotel on the rue d'Alger, around the corner from the Meurice, and register simply as C. E. Taylor of Lincoln, Nebraska. "We do not want the papers or anyone here to know that he has come over," Orville wrote Katharine. In the time since Orville's arrival the press had been following the brothers everywhere, and it was becoming ever more bothersome.

To the reporters the brothers were like no one they had ever tried to cover. A correspondent for the London *Daily Mail* told Orville he was "the toughest proposition" newspapermen had yet run up against. He himself, said the correspondent, had already spent more money on cab fares trying to learn what the brothers were up to than he could ever hope to recover, but that he could not give up for fear some other reporter would get the "scoop."

In mid-August, when it looked as though French interest in an agreement had revived, Wilbur and Berg returned from Berlin. Still there was no real progress with the French. Nor had there been with the Germans.

By early September the brothers had little to do but bide their time, and to judge from what Orville recorded, they had become occupied primarily with sitting in the park watching the passing parade. If Wilbur had his Louvre, Orville had the garden of the Tuileries.

"You need not worry about me missing the use of the front porch," Orville wrote to Katharine, "I spend at least half of my time while awake in the park across from the hotel." There were hundreds of little iron chairs in the park, the rent for which was 2 cents a day, he explained. "A number of women are employed in going about to pounce down on every unsuspecting chap that happens to be occupying a chair and to collect the two cents."

He especially enjoyed watching the French children, amazed by how well behaved they were. He described the small merry-go-rounds, each operated by a man turning a crank, and thought it was pathetic that the children could so enjoy something so tame, hanging on as if riding a bucking bronco. Then, every so often, along would come some American children to liven things up.

> They jump on and off the horses while the affair is going at full speed—which is never fast—seize the rings by the handful, which they are supposed to spear one at a time with an ice pick, and when the ride is over begin tossing the ice picks (I don't know what they are called here) about among themselves when the man comes to collect them, till the poor fellow that runs the affair is driven nearly crazy.

"Of course, we feel ashamed of the youngsters," he added, "and know that they need a good thrashing, but it does seem pleasant to have something once in a while that is a little more exciting."

Greatest by far was the spectacle of seeing so many—children, men, and women of all ages—playing with "diabolo," a simple, age-old toy that had lately become all the rage. It consisted of a wooden spool the shape of an hourglass and two bamboo sticks about two feet in length, joined by a string four to five feet in length, and it cost about 50 cents. The player would slip the string around the spool, then, a stick in each hand, lift the spool from the ground and start it spinning and by spinning it faster, keep it balanced in the air. It was because the spool would so often fall to the ground, until the beginner got the knack, that it was called "the devil's game." It had originated in China a hundred years or more earlier, and to the brothers it was irresistible.

The whole course of their lives, they liked to say, had begun in childhood with a toy, and a French toy at that, and now here they were in middle age in France, enjoying themselves no less than if they were children still.

With the diabolo the magic was not that the toy itself flew, as did Alphonse Pénaud's helicopter. Here you yourself had to overcome the force of gravity with skill. You had to learn the trick by practice, and more practice, with the sticks and string, to keep the spool flying—just as an airplane was not enough in itself, one had to master the art of flying.

The time the brothers devoted to playing diabolo so publicly did not go unnoticed and added still more to the growing puzzlement over *les frères mystérieux*. The "mystery" of the Wrights, wrote the *Paris Herald*, remained as dense as ever, and quoted an American visitor who frequently observed them in the garden of the Tuileries and became convinced they had laid aside their flying machine and quit thinking about it. "Everybody knows," the man had said, "that when a person has contracted the diabolo habit he cannot possibly attend to anything else."

Apparently the brothers caught on quickly to the diabolo art and became quite good at it. But for Charlie Taylor, the spool kept falling to the ground nine tries out of ten. As for what else Charlie Taylor may have been doing to pass the time, besides diabolo, there is no record.

When Katharine read about the hours spent in the park, she bristled as a schoolteacher must. "You never told me whether you learned to talk any French," she wrote to Orville. "Instead of sitting around in the park everlastingly, it seems to me that I would have been getting around to see everything about Paris. Couldn't you get someone to talk French with you?" Just the same, she asked them to "be sure" to bring home a diabolo for her.

His sense of humor plainly in play again, Orville told her he had indeed met a Frenchman in the park who spoke English, but that he thought it hopeless to try to learn both diabolo and French at the same time.

Schools had reopened in Dayton, Katharine was back in the classroom, and all was well at home, the atmosphere entirely different from what it had been. She and father were "getting along famously." He had bought a new typewriter. She had ordered a new stove. "You can stay as long as you please," she told the brothers.

"What plans do you suggest?" Wilbur asked Orville at the end of September in a letter from Berlin, where he had returned again. "We cannot afford to spend much more time on negotiations, nor can we afford to return to America without some arrangements for our European business."

So stay they did and for a while Orville joined Wilbur in Berlin. Not until the start of November, back in Paris, did they decide it was time to go.

But not before going with Hart Berg to see a demonstration put on by the French aviator Henri Farman, "Monsieur Henri," a former artist, champion bicycle rider, and automobile racer, who was considered Europe's outstanding pilot. Large crowds gathered at Issy-les-Moulineaux southwest of Paris. Farman had been getting a great deal of publicity, and even in the United States. ("Aren't you getting worried over 'Farman's flights'?" Katharine had asked.) Farman flew a biplane made by a French aircraft manufacturer, Voisin Frères. Many of his trials were unsuccessful. On the longer flights, he had trouble getting off the ground, and the same was true when trying to make a circle. But in one flight he covered more than half a mile and flew an almost complete circle.

Yet from what he saw, Orville felt he and Wilbur had no cause to worry. When asked by a reporter what he thought, Orville said only that he and his brother never liked to pass criticisms on the work of others, and that time would show whether the methods used in the Farman machine were sufficient for strong winds.

French aviation enthusiasts had no doubt, however, that France was now clearly in the lead. France could boast of the Voisin brothers, Gabriel and Charles, who had formed their aircraft company only that year, and other French aviators beside Henri Farman, including Léon Delagrange, who also flew a Voisin biplane, and Louis Blériot, who had taught himself to fly in a monoplane of his own design. Like Henri Farman, these French pilots flew in public and greatly to the public's delight.

Also, quite unlike the Wright brothers, most of the pilots in France— Farman, Santos-Dumont, Delagrange, Blériot, Comte Charles de Lambert—were men of ample private means for whom the costs of their aviation pursuits were of little concern.

"It seems that to the genius of France is reserved the glorious mission of initiating the world into the conquest of the air," said the president of the Aéro-Club. To his eminent fellow member of the club, Ernest Archdeacon, the Wright Flyer was no more than a "phantom machine."

For the time being, the Flyer III and all its parts would remain in storage at the customs house at Le Havre. Wilbur and Charlie Taylor left for home first. Orville followed soon after.

Writing from on board the RMS *Baltic,* his spirits high, Wilbur told his father:

> We will spend the winter getting some more machines ready for the spring trade. Then we will probably put out a sign, "Opening day, all goods below cost." We will probably return to Europe in March, unless we make arrangements with the U.S. Government before that.

While Charlie went directly to Dayton after arriving in New York, Wilbur stopped off in Washington to check on developments there before reaching home in time for Thanksgiving. He was extremely pleased to report that at long last the U.S. Army was seriously interested in doing business.

With the onset of a new year, all that the brothers had worked to achieve in the way of sales agreements began to happen. On February 8, 1908, their bid of $25,000 for a Flyer was at last accepted by the War Department. Less than a month later, on March 3, they signed an agreement with a French company, to be known as La Compagnie Générale de Navigation Aérienne, with the understanding that public demonstrations of the Flyer in France would follow by midsummer.

Triumph at Le Mans

Gentlemen, I'm going to fly.

WILBUR WRIGHT

I.

"**I** am on my way to Kitty Hawk to get a camp in shape for a little practice before undertaking the official trials at Washington and in France," Wilbur wrote to Octave Chanute from Elizabeth City on April 8, 1908. The decision to proceed for the first time with large public demonstrations of their Flyer—as important and difficult a step as the brothers had yet faced—had finally been made, and "a little practice" was indeed called for. Neither had flown a plane for two and a half years, not since the fall of 1905.

Though he had been forewarned that the camp at Kill Devil Hills was in shambles, what Wilbur found was worse than he had imagined. Of the original building, only the sides still stood. The new building was gone, carried off by violent storms or vandals who figured the brothers were never coming back. The water pump was gone. The floors of both buildings had disappeared under more than a foot of sand and debris. Walking among the ruins he kept turning up pieces and parts of the 1901, 1902, and 1903 machines.

It was an altogether discouraging prospect to face, and particularly, one might imagine, for somebody who had so recently resided at the Hôtel Meurice.

He arranged to room temporarily at the Kill Devil Hills Life-Saving Station and, with the help of two local carpenters, began building anew. High winds, driving rain, and a severe attack of diarrhea made things no easier. "Conditions are almost intolerable," he wrote in his diary. Nor did the fact that so many of those he and Orville worked with in earlier years had either died or moved away. Bill Tate was tied up with work of his own; John T. Daniels had transferred to the Nags Head Life-Saving Station; Dan Tate had died.

A Dayton mechanic the brothers had hired to help, Charlie Furnas, appeared on the scene and by Saturday, April 25, the day Orville arrived, bringing the crated parts of the Flyer, the camp was close to ready.

> Spent afternoon cleaning out trash and making the building habitable [Wilbur recorded in his diary]. I slept in a good bed of regular camp pattern. Orville slept on some boards thrown across the ceiling joist. Furnas slept on the floor. Each pronounced his own method a success.

The morning of Monday, April 27, was spent uncrating boxes, brushing off wings, and setting up a workbench. That afternoon they repaired a few ribs broken in transit and began sewing the lower sections together. Mounting the engine and chain guides, and work on the launching track occupied another several days.

The big change this time was that the Flyer had been modified to carry two operators. They were to ride sitting up side by side, primarily to provide better control over the wing warping. It also meant no more stretching flat on their stomachs straining their necks to see ahead. The wind resistance would be greater but the advantages counted more.

In the three weeks since Wilbur arrived on the Outer Banks not a single reporter had appeared. Then the Norfolk *Virginian-Pilot* ran a wholly fabricated story picked up by newspapers everywhere that the Wright brothers, back again at Kitty Hawk, had already made a 10-mile flight out to sea against a wind of 15 miles an hour. In no time the rush of the press was on to the Outer Banks. In the lead was a young freelance reporter for the *New York Herald,* D. Bruce Salley, who could now be seen crouching among the scrub pine on a distant hill, spying on the camp with field glasses.

Test flights got started on May 6. Orville went first and flew just over 1,000 feet. Two days later, taking turns, he and Wilbur both were making flight after flight until interrupted by Salley, who came rushing into camp unable to contain his excitement over what he had seen. Once he left, Wilbur took off again and flew more than 2,000 feet.

A stream of reporters kept arriving. The advance of the press on their lives, a factor the brothers would have to contend with for years to come, had begun in force. The reporters to be seen hanging about on the hills with field glasses and telescopes represented the *New York Times,* the *New York American Weekly,* the *New York World, Collier's, Technical World,* the *Paris Herald,* and the London *Daily Mail.*

A writer named Byron Newton, sent by the *Paris Herald,* did full justice to the wild and unimaginably remote setting he and the others found themselves confronted by after landing at Manteo on Roanoke Island:

> The Wrights we found were some twelve or fourteen miles distant from that point, among the great sand dunes on the coast near Kitty Hawk life saving station. Their place was on the narrow stretch of marsh and jungle that lies between the Atlantic and the mainland. . . . I have never viewed or traversed a more forbidding section of country. To reach this stretch of land we had to cross Roanoke Sound in an open boat and then walk about six miles, at times climbing over great mountains of gleaming white sand . . . and other times we were forced to pick our way through swamps and jungle infested with poison snakes, mosquitoes, wild hogs, and turkeys, with the air heavy with fever breeding vapors.

Kill Devil Hills and Kitty Hawk seemed "the end of the world," wrote the correspondent for *Collier's Weekly,* Arthur Ruhl, who then stressed that this end of the world had in fact become "the center of the world because it was the touchable embodiment of an Idea, which, presently, is to make the world something different than it has ever been before."

It was not newspaper reporters, he said, but the world's curiosity that had ridden, climbed, waded, and tramped all those miles and now lay hiding there, hungry and peering across the intervening sands. "There was something weird, almost uncanny about the whole thing," wrote another correspondent. "Here on this lonely beach was being performed the greatest act of the ages, but there were no spectators and no applause save the booming of the surf and the startled cries of the sea birds."

Wilbur and Orville wondered why the reporters remained at such a distance. Only later were they told that it had been said the brothers kept rifles and shotguns at the ready to guard their machine. Asked what he and Wilbur would have done had the correspondents come into camp and sat there to watch, Orville replied, "We couldn't have delayed our work. There was too much to do and our time was short."

Describing what the scene looked like from where they were posted, another of the correspondents wrote of "dazzling white sand dunes, almost monumental, to the right, and to the left in the distance more sand dunes, and a glimpse of the sea, and the Carolina sun, pouring down out of a clear blue sky, immersed everything in a shimmer and glare." The two brothers, moving their machine about near the shed, looked like "two black dots." The engine, when it started up, sounded like that of "a reaper working a distant field." The propellers "flashed and whirled," and the next thing the plane swept by "fast as an express train."

"[We were] all seasoned campaigners in the field of unexpected events," wrote the *Paris Herald* correspondent, Byron Newton, "but for all that, this spectacle of men flying was so startling, so bewildering to the senses in that year 1908, that we all stood like so many marble men."

A photographer for *Collier's Weekly,* James Hare, snapped what would be the first photograph ever published of a Wright Flyer in the air.

Early the morning of May 14 the onlookers were treated to a sight never before seen anywhere—two men in a motor-powered flying machine—when Wilbur took Charlie Furnas up for a short ride.

To the newsmen from their distant vantage point, it appeared Wilbur and Orville had taken flight together and so some of their dispatches reported. But the brothers, ever conscious of the risks involved, had already decided they must never fly together. That way, if one were to be killed, the other could still carry on with the work.

Days as hot as summer had returned to the Outer Banks, and that afternoon, when Wilbur went up alone, the heat was nearly unbearable. Flying at something over 50 miles per hour, he made one big circle and was starting into another when, still unfamiliar with the new control levers, he made a mistake with the rudder and suddenly plunged to the ground about a mile from camp.

"I was watching with the field glass," Orville would recount. "The machine turned on end—the front end—with the tail in the air. There was a big splash of sand—such a cloud that I couldn't see from where I was exactly what had happened. . . . It was probably thirty seconds before Will appeared."

He had been violently thrown against the underside of the top wing and had to be pulled from the wreckage. There was a cut across his nose, and though hit hard and bruised on both shoulders, an arm, and one hand, he was not seriously injured. No bones were broken.

The plane, however, was a total wreck, and thus as Wilbur announced, the tests had come to an end. Two days later he was on his way again. It was agreed he would go to France to proceed with the required demonstrations there, and that Orville would do the same in Washington.

During little more than a week of test flights at Kill Devil Hills, he and Orville had been the subjects of far more attention and praise in the press than they had ever known. They had become a popular sensation. Still no major public performance had yet been made. The rabbit had still to be pulled from the hat for all to see.

Passage was arranged for him on the *Touraine,* Wilbur reported to Katharine from New York. "I hate like anything to go away without first coming home."

"Write often," she told him in response. "Don't come home without getting me several pairs of gloves—number six—black and white, short and long. . . . Don't get them unless they are cheap."

II.

The voyage to Le Havre proved uneventful—"smooth but foggy much of the time" was about all Wilbur had to say of the crossing. He reached Paris on May 29, and for the next week he and Hart Berg were on the move, touring possible sites for the public demonstrations, including Fontainebleau and Vitry, but found nothing suitable.

The French press, aware of Wilbur's return, had a "tendency" to be hostile, he reported to Orville. But to almost anyone else it would have seemed considerably more than a "tendency." The popular *L'Illustration*, as an example, ran a heavily retouched photograph of the Flyer taken at Kitty Hawk, saying, "Its appearance seems quite dubious and one finds in it every element of a 'fabrication,' not especially well done moreover."

Further, there was a resurgence of popular enthusiasm over French aviators and their daring feats. Earlier in the year Henri Farman had flown for nearly two minutes, and that spring at the end of May, Farman made news when he took a passenger up for a ride. As Wilbur reported to Orville, Farman and Delagrange were also putting on demonstrations elsewhere in Europe and with much success.

As for themselves, Wilbur wrote, "The first thing is to get some practice and make some demonstrations, then let the future be what it may."

Hart Berg assured a correspondent for *L'Auto* that within two months the Wright plane would fly before the people. The period of secret trials was over, Berg said. The French public would be the first to see with their own eyes.

But where? On June 8, he and Wilbur went by train to Le Mans, a quiet, ancient town of some 65,000 people on the Sarthe River in the department of the Sarthe, 125 miles southwest of Paris. A prominent automobile manufacturer, ballooning enthusiast, and leading local citizen named Léon Bollée, hearing of Wilbur's need for a suitable field, had sent a message to Berg suggesting Le Mans, where there was plenty of flat, open space.

Bollée met Wilbur and Berg at the station in one of the largest and handsomest of his automobile line and took them off on a tour. As it turned out, no one could have been more genial or helpful or generous with his time than Léon Bollée.

Short and dark bearded, he was extremely fat, weighing 240 pounds. The physical contrast with Wilbur was more pronounced even than between Wilbur and Hart Berg. Like Wilbur, Bollée had not attended a university, but instead joined his father's bell foundry business and eventually began building automobiles with much success. ("Léon Bollée automobiles are constructed using only top quality materials in the vast and beautiful factories of Le Mans," read a recent advertisement.) His English was reasonably good and Wilbur liked him at once. As things turned out Bollée would do more to help Wilbur than anyone, and never asked for anything in return.

Of possible sites, the Hunaudières horse racetrack, about five miles out from town, seemed to Wilbur most suitable. The course was entirely enclosed by trees and the ground was rough. Still, as he would report to Orville, he thought it would serve their purpose. Bollée said he would see what could be arranged. He also offered Wilbur full use of a large room at his factory in which to assemble the Flyer, in addition to the help of some of his workers.

Three days later, back in Paris, Wilbur received word from Bollée that the Hunaudières racetrack was available, and the day after Wilbur was busy getting ready, buying overalls, work shoes, and a straw hat.

One evening in the elegant Louis XVI salon of Berg's apartment, Wilbur sat for an interview with a young French aviation journalist, François Peyrey, who knew it was the first interview Wilbur had agreed to do in France. Berg had made the arrangements. They talked of the experiments at Kitty Hawk, of motors and patents, and why Le Mans had been the choice for the demonstrations. But it was Wilbur himself, about whom Peyrey had had his doubts, who became the subject of greatest fascination.

"Mr. Hart O. Berg warmed up for the interview by offering me a cup of coffee and laid out a box of cigars," Peyrey would write. "I felt my doubts fly away one by one in the blue smoke. Through curls of smoke I examined Wilbur Wright, his thin, serious face, lit by the strangely gentle, intelligent and radiant eyes. . . . I had to admit: no, this man is not a bluffer."

The interview marked an important beginning. In the months to come,

François Peyrey was to provide some of the most insightful, firsthand observations about Wilbur ever published.

———

Wilbur arrived back in Le Mans close to midnight, June 16, and settled in at the Hôtel du Dauphin in a room overlooking the main square, the Place de la République. Eager to get started on the reassembly of the Flyer, he began opening the crates at the Bollée factory first thing the following day and could hardly believe what he saw. At Kitty Hawk two months before, he had found the old camp a shambles. Now he was looking at the Flyer in shambles and could barely control his fury.

A dozen or more ribs were broken, one wing ruined, the cloth torn in countless places. Everything was a tangled mess. Radiators were smashed, propeller axles broken, coils badly turned up, essential wires, seats, nuts, and bolts, all missing.

In a letter written that same day he exploded at Orville as he rarely had, charging him with the worst example of packing he had ever seen. "I am sure that with a scoop shovel I could have put things in within two or three minutes and made fully as good a job of it. I never saw such evidences of idiocy." It was going to take much longer than he had figured to get everything ready to go, and there was no Orville or Charlie Taylor to help.

He set immediately to work, putting things in order and making repairs. "Worked all today and a few hours yesterday replacing broken ribs in the surfaces," he recorded in his diary June 18.

> Had to take one wing entirely down to fix it. Found many things not as well as in the old machine. Rear wire not inside of cloth right; little washers on this wire not on the proper side of ribs; no blocks to hold end ribs of sections from slipping back; no steel ferrules on front lower spar under heavy uprights; not play enough in rear hinges joining sections; no cloth wrapping around spar where screw frames fasten on.

The mechanics at the Bollée factory did as best they could to help, but were of little use at first. "I have had an awful job sewing the section together," he informed Orville in another letter. "I was the only one strong enough in the fingers to pull the wires together tight, so I had all the sewing to do myself. . . . My hands were about raw when I was not half done."

"In putting things together," he added, "I notice many evidences that your mind was on something else while you worked last summer."

But then Wilbur learned that the chaos and damage had not been caused at Dayton, but at Le Havre by careless French customs inspectors, and he apologized to Orville at once. Orville, knowing the stress his brother was under, made no issue of the matter.

Wilbur labored on steadily, installing uprights and wires, and fixing the old engine after finding work he had had done on it by French mechanics "so bad," he had to give a full day to it. "I have to do practically all the work myself, as it is almost impossible to explain what I want in words to men who only one fourth understand English."

True to the Wright rules of life, he did not work on Sundays, but instead wrote letters or went sightseeing. He was living most comfortably at the Hôtel du Dauphin, where, according to the *Motor Car Journal,* one found "*nothing of luxe*—simply plain, bountiful fare cooked and served by the *patron-chef,*" which proved exactly to Wilbur's liking. And Le Mans, he was pleased to say, was an "old fashioned town, almost as much out of the world as Kitty Hawk." He loved the sound of the chimes—Bollée bells—from the church across the square and was happy to provide those at home with a lengthy description of the town's crowning edifice, the colossal Cathédrale Saint-Julien.

Set on a hill first settled by the Romans above the Sarthe River, it rose high over a thick cluster of medieval buildings and houses that constituted the oldest part of town. There was no steeple. Instead, the cathedral's singular exterior distinction was its prominent double buttresses. But beyond that was the rare combination of both the Romanesque and Gothic styles all in one building and best seen within. That part built in the Romanesque manner dated back nearly nine hundred years, to the eleventh century, while the larger, more spectacular segment had risen out of the fourteenth and fifteenth centuries, and it was this, so plainly in evidence, that so moved Wilbur.

As he wrote to Katharine, "The arches forming the openings between the aisles and the choir keep increasing in height so that a person standing against the outside wall of the outer aisle can see way up to the top of the choir and take in the magnificent stained glass windows of the clerestory." One saw not only the light and brilliant color of the ancient windows, but all the light and color that the windows threw onto the upper reaches of the arches some 108 feet above the cathedral floor.

If at the time he felt or reflected on any connection between the upward aspiration of this stunning human creation and his own unrelenting efforts in that direction, he made no mention. But it seems most unlikely that he would not have.

Attending a Sunday service at the cathedral some days later, Wilbur found the only part he could understand or participate in was the collection. Still, the great structure, he told Katharine, "impresses me more and more as one of the finest specimens of architecture I have seen."

Meanwhile, just outside the cathedral, as he added, a farmer's market filled the public square and, to cap it all, a traveling circus had set up camp.

He wrote of the comforts of the hotel, praising the food especially. The meals were better than any he had had since coming to Europe—better in that they were both plentiful and not overly fancy. He described a lunch that included sliced tomatoes, cucumbers, roast tongue with mushrooms, lamb chops with new potatoes, "some sort of cake," and almonds. He had never been so comfortable away from home, he said, implying perhaps that a place like the Meurice had been far too luxurious for comfort. No one at the hotel understood a word of his English, but all did their best to serve him well.

A first encounter with alphabet soup provided opportunity for a touch of the wit he knew Katharine especially would appreciate:

> I was a little astonished and disturbed the other evening, when I sat down to dinner to find my soup which was a sort of noodle soup, turning into all sorts of curious forms and even letters of the alphabet. I began to think I had the "jim jams." On close investigation I found that the dough had been run through forms so as to make the different letters of the alphabet and figures, too! It was like looking into the "hell box" of a printing office, and was all the more amusing because every mouthful of soup you take out, brought up a new combination.

Progress at the Bollée factory was hardly improving, however. "I have to do all the work myself as there are no drawings to show anyone how things go together, and explanations take more time than doing things myself.

> I have a man but he is not a first class mechanic; he has no invention or initiative, and his vocabulary is limited. When I say to him, "Hand me the screwdriver," he is liable to stand and gawk or more often rush off as though he really understood me, and it is only after I have waited a long time and finally got it myself that I realize that he does not understand the special meaning of the word "hand" as I used it.
>
> Most of my time has been spent on things I should not have to do at all. . . .
>
> So far I have the main surfaces [of the wing] together and wired with new wires in a number of places. The skids are on and the engine is mounted and adjusted ready to run with the jump spark magneto in place. I have yet to put on the transmission and screws [propellers] which should be a small job. But I have the front rudder and framing and wiring yet to do and also the rear rudder.

Those who worked with him at the factory marveled at his meticulous craftsmanship, how he would make his own parts when needed, even a needle if necessary, and how at the sound of the factory whistle he would start or stop working just as they did, as though he were one of them.

On the evening of July 4, at about six o'clock, Wilbur, contrary to his usual work pattern, was still on the job. Only Léon Bollée remained on hand to keep him company. Having by then mounted the engine, Wilbur was standing close by, his sleeves rolled up, giving it a speed test, when suddenly a radiator hose broke loose and he was hit by a jet of boiling water. His bare left forearm took the worst of it, but he was scalded as well across his chest.

Bollée eased him to the floor and ran for help. "Fortunately we had picric acid in the factory's pharmacy," he would report to Hart Berg, "so that in less than a minute after the accident he was swathed in bandages soaked in picric acid."

Bad as it was, the press, as usual, made the accident sound still worse, and for the family at home Wilbur, as usual, made light of it, spending much of a letter, written three days later, describing how the local physician went about tending the wounds as would a horse doctor. Nonetheless, Wilbur insisted, all was practically healed, the pain gone, when in fact it would be a month before he could use his left arm and the stress he was under had been greatly compounded.

Yet despite everything, by the first days of August he was seeing to the finishing touches on a machine reconstructed from the smashed and broken remains of the original, an airplane that was thus different from those he and Orville had built at home and one he had never yet flown. Testing it, even under ideal conditions, could be highly dangerous. Besides it had been three months since his last flight and that had ended in a crash.

———

It was nearly dark, the evening of August 6, when Wilbur, Léon Bollée, and Hart Berg folded back the front framing of the Flyer, set a couple of wheels under the skids, hitched the whole affair to Bollée's stately automobile, and hauled it down the road to the Hunaudières racetrack five miles to the south. There it was put away in a shed, and to Wilbur's delight the press was never the wiser. For all the hovering, all the surveillance by reporters, none had taken notice.

To keep guard over the plane Wilbur would sleep beside it that night and the nights to follow. The shed was much like those at Kitty Hawk, except here there was a privy and an outdoor hose for bathing. In addition, a small nearby restaurant served "very good meals," and at a farmhouse not more than a hundred feet from the shed, he could get milk and enjoy visits with a small boy of five or six who spoke some English and had all the appearance of "a truthful little chap."

Neither his left arm nor the Flyer was in a condition he would have liked, and a first public demonstration that failed in almost any way would be a serious setback.

Reporters on the scene were becoming increasingly impatient and, to Wilbur, increasingly annoying. A correspondent for the London *Daily*

Mail, Joseph Brandreth, would write, "We voted him 'mule-headed,' 'eccentric,' 'unnecessarily surly,' in his manner toward us, for it was impossible to discover from such a Sphinx what he intended to do or when he intended to do it."

"I did not ask you to come here," Wilbur told them. "I shall go out when I'm ready. No, I shall not try and mislead you newspaper men, but if you are not here I shall not wait for you."

When the exasperation with the press became acute, the genial Berg would appear out of the shed and tell them some amusing story that would almost always put everyone in good humor again.

Bollée talked happily to reporters about Wilbur and his ways, describing how he would not let anyone touch his machine or handle so much as a piece of wire. He even refused to allow mechanics to pour oil into the engine, Bollée said, so sure was he that "they don't do it the correct way." Their nickname for him was *Vieille Burette,* "Old Oilcan."

Somehow the *Daily Mail* reporter, Brandreth, managed to get a peek at how the American eccentric was living:

> In a corner of the shed was his "room." This consisted of a low packing case from which the top had been removed. Resting on the edges of the case was a narrow truckle bed. Nailed to the side of the shed was a piece of looking glass and close by a camp washstand. This together with a cabin trunk, a small petrol cooking stove—he cooks his own breakfast—and a camp stool, comprised the whole furniture. He takes his baths from a hosepipe attached to a well sixty feet away. He sleeps practically under the wings of his aeroplane. And early in the day he starts to work, whistling the while.

III.

Saturday, August 8—the eighth day of the eighth month of the eighth year of the new century—was as fine as could be hoped for. The sky overhead was a great blue vault with not a cloud. A northwest breeze was a little gentler than Wilbur would have wished, but he was up to go.

Word of the preparations at the racetrack had spread rapidly, and by the looks of the day it seemed certain the show could now begin. Those who gathered were nearly all from Le Mans and though not impressive in numbers, they looked appropriately festive as they began filling the little wooden grandstand, quite as if turning out for the horse races—gentlemen sporting straw boaters and Panama hats, ladies in full summer skirts, their oversized summer hats covered by veils as further protection against the sun.

Here and there in the trees encircling the track could be seen perched a number of youngsters from the town. The spirit was of a summer outing, the whole scene as different, as far removed from Kitty Hawk, North Carolina, as could be imagined. Some couples carried baskets with picnic lunches. As the hours passed, waiting for something to happen, nearly all kept on happily chattering.

Here and there among the crowd could be seen several notables not from Le Mans. There were two Russian officers in uniform and Ernest Archdeacon of the Aéro-Club de France, noted for his skeptical opinion of the Wrights, and, of greatest interest to the others gathered, the celebrated French aviator-hero Louis Blériot. What Blériot may have been thinking as he sat waiting is unknown, but Archdeacon was busy proclaiming his confidence that Wilbur Wright would fail and was happy to explain to those close by in the grandstand all that was "wrong" with the Wright plane.

Archdeacon's open scorn of the Wright brothers had been made especially clear at an Aéro-Club dinner in Paris in October 1907 when he declared:

> The famous Wright brothers may today claim all they wish. If it is true—and I doubt it more and more—that they were the first to fly through the air, they will not have the glory before History. They would only have had to eschew these incomprehensible affectations of mystery and to carry out their experiments in broad daylight, like Santos-Dumont and Farman, and before official judges, surrounded by thousands of spectators.

On hand, too, and in substantial numbers as expected, were the repre-
sentatives of the press, reporters and correspondents from Paris, London,
and New York, all waiting for what could well be one of the biggest stories
of the time.

———

Wilbur, who had been up early as usual, showed no sign of nervous ten-
sion or excitement. Such "quiet self-confidence" was reassuring, said Hart
Berg afterward:

> One thing that, to me at least, made his appearance all the
> more dramatic, was that he was not dressed as if about to do
> something daring or unusual. He, of course, had no special
> pilot's helmet or jacket, since no such garb yet existed, but
> appeared in the ordinary gray suit he usually wore, and a cap.
> And he had on, as he nearly always did when not in overalls, a
> high, starched collar.

Inside the shed he proceeded to work on preparations, checking everything with total concentration. As would be said by one observer from the
press, "Neither the impatience of waiting crowds, nor the sneers of rivals,
nor the pressure of financial conditions not always easy, could induce him
to hurry over any difficulty before he had done everything in his power to
understand and overcome it."

For the spectators the only signs of what might be about to take place
were the launching track and the tall, four-legged catapult set in place at
the center of the field, the track placed at right angles to the grandstand,
pointing directly at the trees at the opposite end of the field.

About noon Hart Berg walked out onto the field to announce over a
loudspeaker that no photographs would be permitted. After much show
of despair, the press photographers, who had been waiting day and night,
held a brief meeting, after which they gave their word that if Mr. Wright
agreed to allow photographs on Monday, they would take none until then.
To be sure that no photographs were taken by amateurs, one press photographer would patrol the field on a bicycle.

It was nearly three in the afternoon by the time Wilbur opened the shed doors and the gleaming white Flyer was rolled into the sunshine, where he continued to fuss with it. He then walked the full length and width of the field, made sure the starting rail was headed exactly into the wind, checked the catapult to see if all was in order, and supervised the raising of the iron weight, never hurrying in the least.

With Berg, Bollée, and several others helping, the aircraft, mounted temporarily on two sets of wheels, was gently rolled to the middle of the field, and positioned on the starting rail.

Finally, at six-thirty, with dusk settling, Wilbur turned his cap backward, and to Berg, Bollée, and the others said quietly, "Gentlemen, I'm going to fly."

He took the seat on the left. Two men started the engine, each pulling down a blade on the two propellers. Not satisfied with something he heard as the motor was warmed up, Wilbur called to a mechanic who was standing at the back of the machine to ask if some small, last-minute adjustment had been made on the motor. The man said it had. According to an eyewitness, "Wilbur sat silent for a moment. Then, slowly leaving his pilot's seat, he walked around the machine just to make sure, with his own eyes, that this particular adjustment had, without the slightest shadow of a doubt, been well and truly made."

Back again in his seat, Wilbur released the trigger, the weight dropped, and down the rail and into the air he swept.

Cheers went up as he sailed away toward a row of tall poplars, where, at what seemed the last minute, the left wing dropped sharply, he banked off to the left, turned in a graceful curve, and came flying back toward the grandstand.

Those in the crowd who had brought field glasses had seen how he twisted the wings as he turned and rounded corners as naturally as though he were on a bicycle. Very near the point where he had started, he made another perfect turn to fly full circle once again, all at about 30 to 35 feet, before coming down to a gentle landing within 50 feet from where he had taken off. In all he was in the air not quite 2 minutes and covered a distance of 2 miles.

The crowd was ecstatic, cheering, shouting, hardly able to believe what they had seen. As said in the *Paris Herald,* it was "not the extent but the nature of the flight which was so startling." There were shouts of *"C'est l'homme qui a conquis l'air!"* "This man has conquered the air," and *"Il n'est pas bluffeur!"* "He is not a bluffer." One of the French pilots present, Paul Zens, who had been waiting since morning, told a reporter, "I would have waited ten times as long to have seen what I have seen today."

"We are children compared to the Wrights," said another pilot, René Gasnier, and Louis Blériot declared outright, "I consider that for us in France, and everywhere, a new era in mechanical flight has commenced." Then, catching his breath, Blériot said he was not yet sufficiently calm to express all that he felt, except to say, *"C'est merveilleux!"*

Spectators waving hats and arms raced onto the field, everyone wanting to shake the hero's hand. Hart Berg, knowing how Wilbur felt about such things, did all he could to keep the men from kissing Wilbur on both cheeks. "The enthusiasm," reported *Le Figaro,* "was indescribable." Even Wilbur lost his customary composure, "overwhelmed by the success and unbounded joy which his friends Hart O. Berg and Léon Bollée shared."

Then, "very calmly," his face beaming with a smile, he put his hands in his pockets and walked off whistling. That night, while the normally sleepy town of Le Mans celebrated, the hero retired early to his shed.

That summer Saturday in Le Mans, France, not quite eight years into the new twentieth century, one American pioneer had at last presented to the world the miracle he and his brother had created on their own and in less than two minutes demonstrated for all who were present and to an extent no one yet had anywhere on earth, that a new age had begun.

In less than twenty-four hours it was headline news everywhere— "WRIGHT FLEW" (*Le Matin*); "MR. WILBUR WRIGHT MAKES HIS FIRST FLIGHT: FRENCH EXPERTS AMAZED BY ITS SMOOTHNESS" (*Paris Herald*); "MARVELOUS PERFORMANCE, EUROPEAN SKEP-TICISM DISSIPATED" (London *Daily Mail*); "A TRIUMPH OF AVIA-TION" (*Echo de Paris*); "WRIGHT BY FLIGHT PROVES HIS MIGHT" (*Chicago Tribune*); "WRIGHT'S AEROPLANE ASCENDS LIKE A BIRD" (*Dayton Journal*).

"It was not merely a success," said *Le Figaro*, "but a triumph . . . a decisive victory for aviation, the news of which will revolutionize scientific circles throughout the world."

"The mystery which seemed inextricable and inexplicable is now cleared away," declared *Le Matin.*

> Wright flew with an ease and facility such that one cannot doubt those enigmatic experiments that took place in America; no more than one can doubt that this man is capable of remaining an hour in the air. It is the most extraordinary vision of a flying machine that we have seen. . . .

Wilbur Wright, wrote Joseph Brandreth of the London *Daily Mail,* had made "the most marvelous aeroplane flight ever witnessed on this side of the Atlantic." The length of the flight was not what mattered, but that he had complete control and, by all signs, could have stayed in the air almost indefinitely.

Leaders of French aviation joined in the chorus of acclaim. "Not one of the former detractors of the Wrights dare question today the previous experiments of the men who were truly the first to fly," announced the greatly respected publication *L'Aérophile.* Even the stridently skeptical Ernest Archdeacon, who had run on with so many negative comments while waiting in the grandstand, stepped forth at once to say he had been wrong. "For a long time, for too long a time, the Wright brothers have been accused in Europe of bluff. . . . They are today hallowed in France, and I feel an intense pleasure in counting myself among the first to make amends for the flagrant injustice."

An exuberant Hart Berg wanted Wilbur to keep flying the next day, but Wilbur would have no part of it. As was explained in the French press, "Today, because it is Sunday, M. Wright, a good American, would not think of breaking the Sabbath." The crowd that came to Hunaudières would have to be content with looking at the closed hangar.

On Monday, August 10, when the demonstrations resumed, more than two thousand people came to watch, including a number of Americans this time. Nearby inns and cafés were reaping "a harvest of money." Those who had made the effort to attend were to be even more dazzled by what they saw than those who had been there two days before. It was another perfect summer day, but as the hours passed, with nothing happening, the heat became intense. Still no one left.

Sitting among the crowd was a French army captain in uniform carrying a camera. Previously told he was to take no photographs, he had given his word he would not. But shortly afterward he began using the camera and was spotted by Wilbur, who, "ablaze with anger," climbed directly into the grandstand and demanded both the camera and the plates. At first the captain hesitated, offering excuses, but as reported in the papers, "Mr. Wright set his mouth firm, folded his arms and waited." The captain handed over the camera and plates and left the field.

Perhaps it was the heat, or the stress he was under, or a combination of both that caused Wilbur to do what he did. Quite upset afterward, he said he was not in the habit of making trouble, but it had been too much for him when he saw the man deliberately break his word.

Wilbur's performance that afternoon was surpassing. On one flight, heading too close to some trees, he had to turn sharply. As the correspondent for the *Daily Mail* reported, "In a flight lasting 32 seconds, he took a complete turn within a radius of thirty yards and alighted with the ease of a bird in the midst of the field." It was "the most magnificent turning movement that has ever been performed by an aviator."

That evening, the light fading, Wilbur flew again, this time making two giant figure eights in front of the crowd in the grandstand and landing exactly at his point of departure. An aircraft flying a figure eight had never been seen in Europe before.

Blériot had been so impressed by what he had seen on Saturday that he had returned to watch again. Present also this time was the pioneer French aviator Léon Delagrange, who, after hearing of Wilbur's performance on Saturday, had halted his own demonstrations in Italy to hurry back. Both men were as amazed as anyone by Wilbur's figure eight. "Well, we are beaten! We just don't exist!" Delagrange exclaimed.

As a thrilled Léon Bollée declared, "Now all have seen for themselves."

———

With the mounting popular excitement over the news from Le Mans came increasing curiosity about the man making the news. The Wright machine had been shown to be a reality. But what of the American flying it? Of what sort was he?

Correspondents and others on the scene did their best to provide some clues, if not answers. In a memorable portrait written for the *Daily Mail*, Joseph Brandreth seemed a touch uncertain whether he liked Wilbur. (Nor, it is known from a letter he wrote to Katharine, did Wilbur much like him.) Brandreth was struck most by how greatly Wilbur resembled a bird, an odd bird. The head especially suggested that of a bird, "and the features, dominated by a long prominent nose that heightened the bird-like effect, were long and bony." From their first meeting, Brandreth wrote, he had judged Wilbur Wright to be a fanatic.

A writer for *Le Figaro*, Franz Reichel, fascinated with the flecks of gold in Wilbur's eyes, came to much the same conclusion. "The flecks of gold," wrote Reichel, "ignite a passionate flame because Wilbur Wright is a zealot.

> He and his brother made the conquest of the sky their existence. They needed this ambition and profound, almost religious, faith in order to deliberately accept their exile to the country of the dunes, far away from all. . . . Wilbur is phlegmatic but only in appearance. He is driven by a will of iron which animates him and drives him in his work.

Without wanting to diminish the value of French aviators, Reichel wrote that while Wilbur Wright was flying, they were only beginning to "flutter about."

Léon Delagrange, who before becoming an aviator had been a sculptor and painter, could not help puzzling over what went on behind Wilbur's masklike countenance, and, being French, found it hard to comprehend or warm to someone who seemed so devoid of the elemental human emotions and desires. "Even if this man sometimes deigns to smile, one can say with certainty that he has never known the *douceur* [sweetness] of tears. Has he a heart? Has he loved? Has he suffered? An enigma, a mystery."

That said, Delagrange openly declared in the article he wrote for *L'Illustration*, "Wilbur Wright is the best example of strength of character that I have ever seen.

In spite of the sarcastic remarks and the mockery, in spite of the traps set up from everywhere all these years, he has not faltered. He is sure of himself, of his genius, and he kept his secret. He had the desire to participate today to prove to the world he had not lied.

To François Peyrey, who had seen more of Wilbur than had others and knew more, he was *"un timide"*—shy, a simple man, but also a "man of genius" who could work alongside the men of the Bollée factory, just as he could work entirely alone, who could cook his own meals and do whatever else was necessary under most any conditions and quiet by nature. He went his way always in his own way, never showing off, never ever playing to the crowd. "The impatience of a hundred thousand persons would not accelerate the rhythm of his stride."

Further, Peyrey, unlike others, had discovered how exceptionally cultured Wilbur was, how, "in rare moments of relaxation," he talked with authority of literature, art, history, music, science, architecture, or painting. To Peyrey, the devotion of this preacher's son to his calling was very like that of a gifted man dedicating his life to a religious mission.

At the close of one long day at Le Mans, Peyrey had caught Wilbur gazing off into the distance as if in a daydream. It reminded him, Peyrey wrote, "of those monks in Asia Minor lost in monasteries perched on inaccessible mountain peaks. . . . What was he thinking of this evening while the sun was dying in the apricot sky?"

On Thursday, August 13, Wilbur flew again, this time circling the field several times. It was his longest flight yet at Le Mans and before the biggest crowd, which cheered every round he made. So loud was the cheering that he flew to nearly 100 feet in the air, in part to lessen the distracting effect of the noise.

He was trying to master the use of the control levers and after one turn he found himself flying too low. To compensate he made a "blunder," as he would later explain to Orville. He pushed the left lever

forward instead of back and the left wing hit the ground. It was, he acknowledged, "a pretty bad smash-up." He himself, however, had been uninjured.

The admiration of the crowd diminished not at all. Those who
knew the most about the art of flying were more impressed than ever.
One French aircraft designer told a reporter for the *New York Herald*,
"Mr. Wright is as superb in his accidents as he is in his flights."

Wilbur could scarcely believe the change that had come over nearly
everyone—the press, the public, the French aviators and aircraft builders.
"All question as to who originated the flying machine has disappeared,"
he wrote Katharine. The popular "furor" could be irksome at times, to be
sure. "I cannot even take a bath without having a hundred or two people
peeking at me. Fortunately everyone seems to be filled with a spirit of
friendliness."

A new song, "Il Vole" ("He Flies"), had become a popular hit. Also,
much to Wilbur's liking, a stray dog had been added to his camp life by
Hart Berg and christened "Flyer."

Much of the feeling back in Dayton was expressed in a wholehearted
home-town tribute published in the *Dayton Herald*. All were extremely
proud of the brothers, declared the paper, and not because that was the
fashion of the moment, but because of "their grit, because of their persis-
tence, because of their loyalty to conviction, because of their indefatigable
industry, because of their hopefulness and above all, because of their sterling American quality of compelling success."

A letter from Katharine assured Wilbur that the whole family was
thrilled by the news from Le Mans, but that thrilled and proud as they
were, their minds were greatly on edge over young Milton, Lorin's fifteen-
year-old son, who had been stricken by typhoid fever and was in a struggle
for his life. "How many, many times have we wished for Jullum, since Milton has been sick," she wrote. "Of course we were 'de-lighted' over your
flight . . . but we can't half enjoy anything now. . . . If we weren't so poor—
we'd cable congratulations!"

A week later she could happily report that Milton was out of danger
and the Dayton papers were still going wild over the news from Le Mans.
They were even proposing a big "welcome home."

With the demonstrations at a standstill momentarily until repairs were made, Wilbur had more time to appreciate those around him and enjoy the attention they were giving him. A local manufacturer of canned goods was providing "all kinds of the finest sardines, anchovies, asparagus, etc., etc., you ever saw," he reported to his father.

> The people of Le Mans are exceedingly friendly and proud of the fame it [the experiments] is giving their town. I am in receipt of bouquets, baskets of fruit, etc., almost without number. The men down at Bollée's shop have taken up a collection to buy me a testimonial of their appreciation. They say that I, too, am a workman.

When the French army offered Wilbur a larger field for his demonstrations, he accepted and so the Flyer, its damages fully repaired, was moved seven miles east to Camp d'Auvours. "The new grounds are much larger and much safer than the old," he reported home. "I can go four miles in a straight line without crossing anything worse than bushes." He resumed flying at d'Auvours on August 21 and the crowds arriving by special trains grew larger by the day, the "excitement almost beyond comprehension."

Though Camp d'Auvours was "lost in the middle of the woods," as said and less convenient to town than the racecourse of Hunaudières, the crowds came in numbers greater than ever. "They flock from miles," their "curiosity too strong," reported *Le Figaro*, only to find that Wilbur, for some reason or other, was not flying that day. "Never mind," was the response. "We'll come back." It was almost as though the less he flew the greater the curiosity of the crowd.

> The public is of an untiring and admirable patience. It waits for hours on end to see nothing . . . but the famous launching pylon. . . . When it is late and they know that Wright won't fly . . . these good people gather at the foot of the pylon, measure it with their eyes, touch it, because they know what they will have to do tomorrow: come back.

———

Brother Orville was much on Wilbur's mind, for by then Orville had gone to Washington to begin preparing for the flights he was to make at Fort Myer, Virginia. Earlier, in midsummer, as Wilbur had been about to proceed with his demonstrations for the French, he had received a letter from his father urging him to "avoid all unnecessary personal risk." Now Wilbur sent off much the same kind of warning to Orville, as older brother but also as one who had now experienced a number of turns onstage before enormous crowds and an ever-eager, ever-demanding press.

> I tell them plainly that I intend for the present to experiment only under the most favorable conditions. . . . I advise you most earnestly to stick to calms, till after you are sure of yourself. Don't go out even for all the officers of the government unless you would go equally if they were absent. <u>Do not let yourself be forced into doing anything before you are ready.</u> Be very cautious and proceed slowly in attempting flights in the middle of the day when wind gusts are frequent. . . . Do not let people talk to you all day and all night. It will wear you out, before you are ready for real business. Courtesy has limits. If necessary appoint some hour in the daytime and refuse absolutely to receive visitors even for a minute at other times. Do not receive <u>anyone</u> after 8 o'clock at night.

Then, after some technical discussion about the rudder, he wrote again. "I can only say be extraordinarily cautious."

On the evening of August 25 in Le Mans, a celebration banquet in Wilbur's honor took place at the Hôtel du Dauphin. This time he was happy to join in the festivities.

Part III

CHAPTER NINE

The Crash

[He] rode the air as deliberately as if he were passing over a solid macadam road. Nothing I have ever seen is comparable.

GUTZON BORGLUM

I.

With her young nephew Milton much improved in health and her classes at the high school soon to resume, Katharine was feeling more herself. Orville was in Washington preparing for the demonstrations at Fort Myer, staying at the elegant Cosmos Club and meeting "stacks of prominent people." And hardly a day passed without something in the papers about the continuing clamor over Wilbur in France.

Both brothers wrote when they had time, but Katharine longed for more than just aviation talk. "Suppose you tell me about a few things when you write!" she admonished Wilbur in one letter. "What do I care about the position of the trees on the practice ground? Hey! Hey! Sterchens wants to hear all about the beautiful young ladies and the flowers and champagne!"

Wilbur would go only so far as to tell her Mrs. Berg was a "very smart" and "charming woman, like yourself."

Orville said he could hardly get any work done, so much time was taken up "answering the ten thousand fool questions people ask me about the machine." A *Washington Post* reporter noted with amazement how "Mr. Wright stood and talked and talked and talked to his questioners." Still, with it all, Orville was frank to tell Katharine, "I am meeting some very handsome young ladies!" The trouble was if he were to meet them again, he would have a hard time remembering their names.

"I don't know when Pop has been in such good health," she was happy to report to Wilbur. "Now, if you and Orville don't do some wild things to get me crazy, I think I'll weather the thing through."

———

Fort Myer occupied a stretch of high ground on the Virginia side of the Potomac River, just west of Arlington National Cemetery. With its neatly arranged, handsome red-brick buildings, it looked not unlike an attractive college campus, and offered a panoramic view of Washington five miles in the distance. At the center was the parade ground, measuring approximately 1,000 feet by 700 feet, and there Orville was to perform his test flights.

It was a space smaller even than what Wilbur had to work with at Les Hunaudières, but with it came an ample shed for a hangar and a dozen army men ready to assist. To get there from the city he traveled back and forth by streetcar.

After several days of trouble with the motor, and with help from Charlie Taylor and Charlie Furnas, both of whom had come from Dayton, he had all in order as scheduled. It would be the first full-scale public performance of a Wright plane in the United States, and the machine Orville was to take into the air had never been flown until now.

Not until late in the afternoon of September 3 was it wheeled into place. That Orville was extremely on edge was plainly evident. "For the first time since his arrival in this city," wrote a reporter for the *New York Times*, "Mr. Wright betrayed obvious signs of nervousness. The lines on his face seemed deeper than ever, and there was a furtiveness and an uneasiness of manner which was noticeable to everyone. He seemed to be making a tremendous effort to control himself."

He could hardly hold still. One minute he would be up on a sawhorse examining the upper wing, the next, down on his hands and knees helping adjust the starting mechanism. "That man's nerves are pretty near the jumping off place," another correspondent was heard to say.

The crowd on hand was small. Washington had yet to catch on to what was happening at Fort Myer. At last, at about six o'clock, Orville climbed into his seat, the motor was started, and the big propellers were "cutting the air at a frightful rate," when he called out, "Let her go!"

The weights of the catapult dropped, the plane shot down the rail, but then for 50 feet or more it skimmed barely above the grass before lifting into the air. Everyone was shouting.

At the lower end of the drill field, Orville banked, turned, and started back, the white canvas of the double wings standing out sharply against the dark border of trees at the edge of Arlington Cemetery.

The crowd broke into a "frenzy of enthusiasm" as the plane circled overhead at about 35 feet and headed away down the field again. Suddenly it veered off toward the wooden hangar, descended at an abrupt angle and hit the ground.

The crowd rushed forward to find Orville calmly brushing the dust from his clothes. "It shows I need a great deal of practice," he said.

By his estimate he had flown somewhat less than a mile at a speed of about 40 miles per hour. According to their contract with the army, the brothers were to receive $25,000 if the Flyer achieved 40 miles per hour in its speed test.

The day after, Friday, September 4, Orville and the Flyer remained in the air more than four minutes, circling the parade ground five and a half times under perfect control, covering three miles with no mishap. Major George Squier, president of the board in charge of the tests, thought the flight "splendid." The Flyer "seemed to respond perfectly to your every touch, and that landing was a marvel," he told Orville. Other officers were calling it the most wonderful exhibition they had ever seen.

In the days that followed, Orville provided one sensational performance after another, breaking one world record after another. As never before the two "bicycle mechanics" and their flying machines were causing simultaneous sensations on both sides of the Atlantic. They had become a transcontinental two-ring circus. Only now it was the younger, lesser known of the two whose turn had come to steal the show.

Early the morning of Wednesday, September 9, with relatively few spectators present, Orville circled the Fort Myer parade ground 57 times, remaining in the air not quite an hour. When word reached Washington that he might fly again that afternoon, offices were closed and a thousand or more government officials—members of the cabinet, department heads, embassy personnel, members of Congress—came pouring across the Potomac by automobile and trolley to see for themselves.

"At 5:15, as the sun was disappearing below the Virginia horizon," wrote the *Dayton Journal* correspondent on the scene, "the latest invention of man to change the laws of nature, rose grandly into space and sailed over the drill grounds.

> Higher and higher it rose, turned at a slight angle as the aviator brought it round the far side of the field, and raced along at increasing speed. . . . Round after round the machine traveled on cutting short turns, shooting along the stretch and presented somewhat the appearance of an automobile racing about an imaginary course in the air.

He had flown around the circle 55 times and was in the air altogether an hour and three minutes, another new world record. At home in Dayton the *Herald* called it "the most marvelous feat in aviation yet recorded."

The next day, September 10, against a stiff wind, Orville stayed in the air longer still by several minutes.

Worried that Orville might be losing count of the number of times he had circled the field, Charlie Taylor climbed on top of the Flyer's shed with a pot of white paint and a brush and began marking off the times on the tar paper roof in figures big enough for Orville to see. As the numbers 50 and 55 appeared, the excitement of the crowd became "acute." Charlie began signaling with his arms. Not until after dusk, upon completing 57½ circles, did Orville start back down to earth.

Swooping in for a landing, the plane headed straight in the direction of the crowd, but then, sending up a cloud of dust as its skids hit the ground, came to a stop not more than 20 feet short of the crowd.

One of those watching that day was the noted sculptor Gutzon Borglum, who was later to carve the faces on Mount Rushmore. When he first saw Orville's plane sitting on the ground, he had not been particularly impressed. It looked to him like something any boy might build, not at all how he had imagined a flying machine. But then Orville had taken off. "He could fly as he wished, move as he willed.

> [He] rode the air as deliberately as if he were passing over a solid macadam road. Nothing I have ever seen is comparable. . . . There is no action of the wings, so you do not think of birds. It has life, power.

And yet it was so simple, Borglum wrote, that one wondered why in the world human beings had not built one long before.

Automobile horns were honking, people cheering, as Orville stepped from his seat. At the same time he was handed a letter from Wilbur. Orville smiled. It was the first letter he had received from his brother in two weeks, he said, and it seemed to please him quite as much as the triumphant flight he had just made.

He had been in the air nearly an hour and six minutes, a new world record.

To the crowd that quickly surrounded him he seemed "the coolest man around and entirely free from nervousness." Nor did he show any sign of fatigue. Indeed, seeing Lieutenant Frank Lahm, one of the committee that would pass on the trials, standing nearby, Orville asked if he would like to go up while there was still some light left. So the two took off for a brief ride just as a full September moon was rising.

The day after Orville set yet another record with a flight of an hour and 10 minutes, during which he thrilled the crowd with two figure eights. He tried one maneuver after another, as if he were an acrobat performing, at times turning corners so sharply that the plane seemed nearly on edge.

> He dipped down low to earth [wrote a reporter for the *New York Herald*]. He skimmed it at twice a man's height. He rose steadily and gracefully until 150 feet of space lay be-

tween him and the ground. . . . He all but brushed the trees in Arlington Cemetery. He tried every combination of the levers and planes in his run of 58 turns around the field. There was never a misfire of the engine and never a symptom of distress.

On Saturday the 12th, five thousand people encircled the parade grounds. As they had never been able to do until now the American people were seeing with their own eyes one of their country's greatest inventions in action. Among those who rushed to congratulate Orville was Octave Chanute, who, a bit out of breath, exclaimed, "Good for you, my boy!," then asked him how it felt to be making history. "Pretty good," Orville said, "but I'm more interested in making speed." The remark made more headlines back in Dayton.

It had not gone unnoticed that the secretary of war was another of those who had come to see the demonstrations, and future weapons of war were very much on the minds of the officers at Fort Myer and figured prominently in their conversations. Buoyant with his successes, Orville would write to Wilbur, "Everyone here is very enthusiastic and they all think the machine is going to be of great importance in warfare."

A new book by the popular British novelist H. G. Wells featured a terrifying illustration of New York City in flames after an aerial bombing. "No place is safe—no place is at peace," wrote Wells. "The war comes through the air, bombs drop in the night. Quiet people go out in the morning, and see the air fleets passing overhead—dripping death, dripping death!"

Until now the brothers had spent little time dwelling on such possibilities, not at least to judge by how very little they wrote or had to say on the subject.

———

The excitement at home in Dayton was like nothing in memory, and at 7 Hawthorn Street especially, as Katharine recorded in a long Sunday letter to Wilbur.

Orv telegraphed after he made his long flight Wednesday morning. . . . Our telephone rang steadily all evening. Everybody wanted to say something nice. I finally got to bed and had just dozed off when I was startled by the ringing of our doorbell. . . . I bounced out and was half way down the stairs when I realized what I was doing. I saw a man standing at our front door so I went up to the keyhole and said, "What is it?" "I am from the Journal and I would like to speak to Mr. Wright. I have a telegram which I think would interest him." It scared me just a little because he acted as if he didn't want to tell me. I demanded, "What is your telegram?" He said that the Journal had a telegram saying that Orville Wright had made a record breaking flight. When he got that far I discovered that he was the young idiot who had been out here once before to write up Pop and hadn't returned a picture that Netta loaned him. So I said, "You can't see father. He's too old to be called up at such an hour as this. We knew about that before noon today." Now the joke is that he had some news—the second long flight— and I wouldn't wait until he could tell it. I departed for bed and heard him talking through the crack in the door—until I was on the stairs. The next morning I found the picture which he had borrowed, sticking in the front door screen. . . . Maybe I wasn't wrathy at being waked up at that hour of the night! I didn't sleep again until after one.

The mayor had come to see them. He wanted to appoint a committee to plan a grand welcome home for the brothers. People were wild over the idea.

Hasn't Orv had good luck with his motor? [she continued] I am afraid that your health as well as your motor is interfering with your doing your best. You are doing well enough, but we know that you would have made an hour long's flight long ago if you had had as good a chance as Orv. Since you didn't, I am glad Orv did just what he did—to shut up the ever-lasting knockers. We hope every day that we will see that you have made a record. We know that there is some reason for it when you don't and that makes us uneasy about your health. Those burns were so much more serious than we thought for a long time. That has pulled you down, I have no doubt. You look mighty thin in all the pictures.

She had made up her mind that the Bishop should go to Washington to see Orville fly. She would go, too, but there was not money enough for both to make the trip.

"Do you suppose we could scratch up the cash? Daddy has about a hundred dollars."

The Bishop liked to preach the futility of craving fame. "Enjoy fame ere its decadence, for I have realized the emptiness of its trumpet blasts," he had written to Wilbur, and quoted favorite lines from the Irish poet Thomas Moore:

> *And false the light on glory's plume*
> *As fading lines of even.*

But for all that he was as eager as the thousands in Washington to see Orville in action. "He wants to go alright," Katharine wrote.

That same Sunday, September 13, on the other side of the Atlantic, Wilbur wrote to tell Orville the sensation he, Orville, was in Europe. "The newspapers for several days have been full of stories of your dandy flights, and whereas a week ago, I was a marvel of skill, now they do not hesitate to tell me I am nothing but a 'dub,' and that you are the only genuine sky scraper. Such is fame."

Wilbur's longest time in the air at Camp d'Auvours thus far was just over 21 minutes, and only the week before, Léon Delagrange had made the longest flight ever in Europe, staying in the air slightly less than half an hour.

He was having motor troubles, Wilbur explained, and the weather had been "something fierce." To Katharine he reported he had had almost as many congratulations on Orville's success as he himself had had a month earlier.

But in a letter to his father, also written that same Sunday, Wilbur confided the real trouble was the constant fuss being made over him. It had become more than he could take. Everyone seemed a genuine friend and looked upon him as an adopted citizen of France. Nearly every evening two or three thousand people came out to see if he would fly and went home disappointed if he did not. One old man of seventy who lived thirty miles away made the round-trip on a bicycle almost every day for a week.

> The excitement and the worry, and above all the fatigue of an endless crowd of visitors from daylight till dark had brought me to such a point of nervous exhaustion that I did not feel myself really fit to get on the machine. . . . I can't stand it to have people continually watching me. It gets on my nerves.

As he explained to Katharine, he carried on his correspondence sitting in his shed, the door locked to keep people out.

Close to midnight in Washington, from the privacy of his room at the Cosmos Club, Orville wrote to Wilbur that he had never felt so rushed in his life, and that he had a stack of unanswered letters a foot high. To Katharine he wrote that the weather, being what it was, would probably take another few days to "quiet down." In any event, he added, "I do not think I will make any more practice flights."

In his brief time thus far at Fort Myer, Orville had set seven world records.

Rumors in Washington and in an article in the *New York Times* on September 15 saying that President Roosevelt would soon announce his intention of going up in the plane with Orville provided still more excitement. To many it seemed perfectly in keeping with a president so "given to the espousal of the unusual." Two years before he had startled the country by diving beneath the waters of Long Island Sound in a submarine.

"Of course, if the President asks me to take him on a flight, I cannot refuse," Orville said when reporters questioned him. However, he was not enthusiastic about the idea. "I'm sorry," he said. "I don't believe the President of the United States should take such chances."

II.

O n Thursday, September 17, the day was clear and cool, wind conditions were ideal. The crowd by the time Orville was ready to take off
numbered more than 2,600. Expectations were higher than ever.

A young army officer had been assigned, at his own request, to go with
Orville as a passenger, as two other officers had already done and to which
Orville had had no objections. This time, however, the young man was
someone Orville did not like or trust.

Lieutenant Thomas Selfridge was a twenty-six-year-old West Point
graduate from San Francisco with two eminent military figures in his
family background with the same name, a grandfather and great-uncle,
both rear admirals. The great-uncle Thomas Selfridge had been the naval
officer assigned in 1870 to survey the isthmus of Central America to determine the place to cut a canal from the Atlantic to the Pacific.

In little time Lieutenant Selfridge had become one of the army's most
knowledgeable and enthusiastic aviation specialists. He was tall, handsome, and personable and had been made a member of the Signal Corps
Aeronautical Board. In addition, he was a member of what was known
as the Aerial Experiment Association, or AEA, founded and headed by
Alexander Graham Bell, in the interest of progress in the design of flying
machines, and that in particular troubled Orville. The young man had a
good education and a clear mind, Orville had told Wilbur in a letter, but
he was almost certainly a spy for Bell and others of the AEA. "I don't trust
him an inch."

"Selfridge is endeavoring to do us all the damage he can behind my
back, but he makes a pretense of great friendliness," Orville told his father.
The thought of someone like that seated beside him in the air was not easy
to accept.

Selfridge also weighed 175 pounds, more than anyone Orville had yet
taken up. Still, as a member of the appraisal board, Selfridge was clearly
entitled to a flight, and so Orville had agreed.

Looking extremely happy, Selfridge removed his coat and campaign
hat, handed them to a friend, and took his place next to Orville, who was

attired in his customary dark suit, starched collar, black tie, and Scottish plaid cap.

Charlie Taylor and Charlie Furnas turned the propellers to get them going and at 5:14, the plane headed down the track and lifted more slowly than usual, it seemed to those watching. For 30 to 50 feet it was barely above the grass before it began to "creep" into the air.

The plane was at about 75 feet by the time it reached the lower end of the field, went neatly into its first turn, and came sweeping back at about 100 feet.

"It was noticed that Lieutenant Selfridge was apparently making an effort to talk with Mr. Wright," reported the *Washington Post*. "His lips were seen to move, and his face was turned to the aviator, whose eyes were looking straight ahead, and whose body was taut and unbending."

The plane circled the field three times at about 40 miles per hour. On the fourth turn, heading for Arlington Cemetery, Orville slowed down somewhat and all seemed to be working well.

Then, suddenly, just as the plane was passing over the "aerial garage," a sizable fragment of something was seen to fly off into the air.

"That's a piece of the propeller," shouted one of the army officers.

Orville would later describe hearing an unexpected sound, "a light tapping" behind him, in the rear of the machine. A quick backward glance revealed nothing, but he slowed the engine and started toward a landing.

Then, at an altitude of about 125 feet came two loud thumps and "a terrible shaking." Orville shut off the engine, hoping to glide to a landing. He pulled as hard as he could on the steering and lateral balance levers, but to no effect. "Quick as a flash, the machine turned down in front and started straight for the ground."

Lieutenant Selfridge, who had remained quiet until now, was heard only to say in a hushed voice, "Oh! Oh!"

Those below watched in horror as the plane twisted this way and that, then plunged straight down, "like a bird shot dead in full flight," in Orville's words.

It hit the ground with terrific force, throwing up a swirling cloud of dust. A half dozen army men and reporters, along with Charlie Taylor, rushed out to help, led by three cavalrymen on horseback.

Orville and the lieutenant lay pinned beneath bloodstained wreckage, faces down. Orville was conscious but moaning in pain. Selfridge lay unconscious, a great gash across his forehead, his face covered with blood.

The scene around the wreckage became one of wild confusion. Officers were shouting orders, automobiles honking. Hundreds of people from the crowd who dashed forward had to be held back by the cavalrymen, one of whom was heard to shout, "If they won't stand back, ride them down."

Several army surgeons and a New York doctor in the crowd did what they could for the two men until the stretchers arrived and they were carried off to the base hospital at the far end of the field.

A reporter wrote of having seen Charlie Taylor bend down and loosen Orville's tie and shirt collar, then, stepping back to lean against a corner of the smashed plane, sob like a child.

Among the crowd that gathered outside the hospital as night came on were Charles Flint and Octave Chanute.

Not until well after dark did word come from within the hospital. Orville was in critical condition, with a fractured leg and hip, and four broken ribs, but was expected to live. Lieutenant Selfridge, however, had died at 8:10 of a fractured skull without ever having regained consciousness. His was the first fatality in the history of powered flight. Speaking for the Army's Signal Corps, Major George Squier praised Lieutenant Selfridge as a splendid officer who had had a brilliant career ahead of him.

But no one who had witnessed the flights of the previous days could possibly doubt that the problem of aerial navigation was solved. "If Mr. Wright should never again enter an aeroplane," Squier said, "his work last week at Fort Myer will have secured him a lasting place in history as the man who showed the world that mechanical flight was an assured success."

That Orville's passenger that day could well have been Theodore Roosevelt was not mentioned.

The telegram from Fort Myer arrived at 7 Hawthorn Street just after Katharine returned from school. Bishop Wright was in Indiana attending a church conference.

There was never a question of what she must do. Moving into action without pause, she called the school principal, told her what had happened, and said she would be taking an indefinite leave of absence. Then, quickly as possible, she packed what clothes she thought she would need and was on board the last train to Washington at ten that same evening.

Bishop Wright, too, had received the news, but from the little he wrote in his diary there is no telling how stunned or alarmed he was. Nonetheless, he excused himself from the conference and returned to Dayton without delay. Once there he wrote to Orville and clearly from the heart.

> I am afflicted with the pain you feel, and sympathize with the disappointment which has postponed your final success in aeronautics. But we are all thankful that your life has been spared, and are confident of your speedy though tedious recovery, and of your triumph in the future, as in the past.

Then, in the way of a fatherly sermon, he added, "We learn much by tribulation, and by adversity our hearts are made better."

It was eight o'clock at Camp d'Auvours the morning of September 18 when Hart Berg arrived at Wilbur's shed to tell him the news. At first Wilbur seemed not to accept what he heard. A thousand people had already gathered at the field. The weather was ideal for flying, Le Mans more crowded than ever with people eager to see him fly. But out of respect for Lieutenant Selfridge, Wilbur postponed all flights until the following week, then, shutting himself in his shed, refused to see anyone except Berg and one or two others who came to console him.

"Now you understand why I always felt that I should be in America with Orville," he said. "Two heads are better than one to examine a machine."

Left alone, he sat with head in hands. When another friend came in— Léon Bollée most likely—Wilbur looked up, his eyes full of tears, and said if anything could make him abandon further work in solving the problem of flight, it would be an accident like this. Then, springing to his feet, he declared, "No, we have solved this problem. With us flying is not an experiment; it is a demonstration."

Others present saw him struggle with his emotions. He asked for fuller details, but there were none.

Since coming to Camp d'Auvours, he had acquired a bicycle on which he now went riding eight miles to Le Mans in the hope of hearing further word from Fort Myer. For some time he could be seen pacing nervously about the porch at the Hôtel du Dauphin. He felt very bad about "this business," he told a reporter for the *Paris Herald* who approached him. "It seems to me that I am more or less to blame for the death of poor Selfridge, and yet I cannot account for the accident.

> Of course, when dealing with aeroplanes, or indeed anything mechanical, there is always the possibility of something breaking, and yet we imagined that we had eliminated all danger. . . .
>
> The thing which is worrying more than anything is that my father, who is almost eighty years of age, will take this matter very much to heart. He has always been nervous about our trials, but up to the present he has never had occasion to be so.

Toward dusk, Wilbur took his bicycle and rode back to Camp d'Auvours.

In a letter to Katharine written the following day, he told her he could not help thinking over and over that if he had been with Orville the accident would never have happened. "I do not mean that Orville was incompetent to do the work itself, but I realized that he would be surrounded by thousands of people who with the most friendly intentions in the world would consume his time, exhaust his strength, and keep him from having proper rest.

> If I had been there I could have held off the visitors while he worked or let him hold them off while I worked. . . . People think I am foolish because I do not like the men to do the least

important work on the machine. They say I crawl under the machine when the men could do the thing well enough. I do it partly because it gives me opportunity to see if anything in the neighborhood is out of order.

He presumed their father was terribly worried about Orville's condition, he wrote in conclusion, but things would turn out right at last. Of this he was sure.

At his upstairs desk in Dayton that same day, September 19, Bishop Wright wrote to Wilbur in much the same spirit.

It is sad that Orville is hurt and unpleasant that his success is delayed. It is lamentable that Lieut. Selfridge lost his life. I am saddest over his death. But success to your invention is assured. The brighter day will come to you.

On Monday, September 21, at Camp d'Auvours, Wilbur was back in action taking "the bull by the horns," as he liked to say, before ten thousand spectators. He flew one hour, 31 minutes, and 25 seconds, over a distance of 40 miles establishing another sensational world record.

Among the enormous crowd was the American ambassador to France, Henry White, who was reported to have been the most excited man present and who, "quite forgetting his usual diplomatic dignity" went racing across the field to be the first to shake Wilbur's hand.

III.

Katharine reached Washington early the morning of September 18 and found Charles Flint and two army officers waiting at the station, ready to drive her immediately in a Signal Corps automobile across the river to Fort Myer. At the hospital she was met by the young army surgeon and shown into Orville's room.

"I found Orville looking pretty badly," she reported in a letter home to Lorin. His face was cut in several places, the deepest of the gashes being over his left eye. He was so sore everywhere he could not bear to be touched. His leg was not in a cast, as she had expected, but "in a sort of cradle" held up by a rope to the ceiling, she wrote to Wilbur.

"When I went in his chin quivered and the tears came to his eyes, but he soon braced up again. The shock has weakened him very much, of course." As the day went on Orville turned extremely nervous and on edge. "I suppose the working with his leg has made him so. I bathed that side of his face that was exposed, and his chest and shoulders. That quieted him, some."

She liked the doctor and the male nurse on duty. The room, she was also pleased to report, was full of flowers and there was a great basket of fruit and a pile of telegrams on a side table, including one saying, "The thousand proud pupils and teachers of Steele High School unanimously extend sympathy and encouragement."

"I will acknowledge the notes and telegrams," she said. "There is a desk in the room, and I can sit there and write. After a bit I can read to him." How long she would be staying was impossible to say. He was not dangerously injured, she stressed, but she was sure it would be weeks before he would be able to leave.

At first she lived with a couple named Shearer, relatives of a Dayton friend. To get to the hospital from their home in Washington by trolley required three transfers and took fully an hour. Still, she was at Orville's bedside every day without fail. Some nights, too tired for the return trip to town, she slept at the hospital.

Orville's progress was not steady. "Last night was a rather bad time for little brother and this morning, too," she wrote to her father. His leg was broken in two places, she explained, but the breaks were "clean and in as favorable places as they could be," in the thigh bone of the left leg. The doctors were making a great effort not to let the leg be shortened and apparently they were succeeding. The broken ribs made it necessary to bandage him tightly and that made his breathing hard.

"Tonight I am staying all night with him. After I came today he quieted down and was so much easier that I made up my mind to see him through the night. It is after eleven now and he has been asleep nearly an hour. Last night codeine had no effect. Tonight it has."

Her letter was written September 21, the same day Wilbur made his record-breaking flight at Camp d'Auvours.

> Will had his nerve with him sure enough [she wrote, knowing how her father must feel]. One hour, thirty-one minutes, twenty-five seconds! All the newspapermen began calling up the hospital to tell me. Orville did a great deal of smiling over it. That did him an immense amount of good.

"It's midnight now and I am very tired," she wrote at last. "Orville is still sleeping. The night nurse has gone down to get a sandwich and some tea for me."

Meanwhile, the army's Aeronautical Board had begun a formal investigation to determine the cause of the crash. "Orville thinks that the propeller caught in one of the wires connecting the tail to the main part," Katharine wrote. "That also gave a pull on the wings and upset the machine."

As would eventually be determined, Orville was correct. One of the blades of the right propeller had cracked; the propeller began to vibrate; the vibration tore loose a stay wire, which wrapped around the blade, and the broken blade had flown off into the air. Because the stay wire had served to brace the rear rudders, they began swerving this way and that and the machine went out of control.

Until now both of the Wright brothers had had close scrapes with death. Wilbur had crashed two times with slight injuries, Orville four times, twice at Kitty Hawk and twice at Huffman Prairie. But as Wilbur wrote to their father, this was "the only time anything has broken on any of our machines while in flight, in nine years experience." Nor had either of them ever plunged "head foremost" straight to the ground from an elevation of about 75 feet.

For Katharine especially, the one member of the family there at Orville's side seeing the condition he was in, it was truly a miracle he had escaped with his life.

Charlie Taylor and Charlie Furnas—"the two Charlies" as they had become known at Fort Myer—came to the hospital to show Orville the piece of the propeller blade that had broken away. The wreckage of the machine, they assured him, was secure in the shed, where the windows and doors had been nailed shut, and a guard stationed. They were packing the plane's engine and transmission parts that were undamaged to be shipped home. That accomplished, they, too, would be on their way.

On September 23, Alexander Graham Bell and two members of his Aerial Experiment Association came to the hospital to see Orville, but learned he was not yet ready for visitors. The group then crossed the parade field toward Arlington Cemetery to view Lieutenant Selfridge's casket still awaiting burial. On the way they stopped at the shed. Charlie Taylor, who had not as yet shipped the wreckage of the Flyer back to Dayton, had taken a break for lunch. The only one on duty was the guard, who agreed to let the visitors into the building where the crate containing the Flyer stood open, the wreckage on display. Bell took a tape measure from his pocket and made at least one measurement of the width of a wing.

Word of this was not to reach Katharine or Orville for another week, but when it did they were extremely annoyed. Katharine asked Octave Chanute for his view on the matter and after talking to the soldier who had witnessed the incident, Chanute felt it was not something to be overly concerned about.

When Charlie Taylor, on his return to Dayton, told Bishop Wright what had happened, the Bishop, in a letter to Katharine, allowed it was "very cheeky" of Bell, but "a very little piece of business anyway." No more was said of the matter and exactly what Bell's intentions were was never made clear.

———

Everyone at the hospital continued to be extremely kind and helpful to Katharine, and while she did not find the military hospital quite up to standards, no other hospital would have permitted her to stay there and without a single restriction. The doctors and the day nurse were "splendid." But having learned that the night duty nurse looked in on Orville only once every half hour and that he was stationed on the floor below, she felt she had to be on hand for Orville. She stayed day and night, which Orville greatly preferred. Often he was delirious at night and could not be left alone.

The strain on Katharine was taking a toll. "Brother has been suffering so much . . . and I am so dead tired when morning comes that I can't hold a pen," she wrote to Wilbur in explanation of why he had heard so little from her.

She fended off reporters and received visitors who were denied access to Orville. She continued to answer mail and telegrams, and it was she who represented Orville at the funeral ceremony on September 25 when Lieutenant Selfridge was laid to rest in Arlington Cemetery with full military honors.

The role she had taken upon herself did not go unnoticed or unappreciated. Some of the press concluded she had to be a nurse and so described her. "Your sister has been devotion itself," wrote Octave Chanute to Wilbur. Most important by far, Orville told her he never could have gotten through the ordeal were it not for her.

Others tried to show their empathy and respect in other ways. Alexander Graham Bell invited her to take a drive one evening along with Octave Chanute, after which they dined at the Bell home on 33rd Street in Washington. It was the only time she had been anywhere, she told her father.

She was growing dreadfully homesick and worried over earning no income. "Have lost eighty-two and a half dollars already," she reported to Wilbur on October 2, knowing she still had a long time to go before a return to Dayton would be possible. Orville seemed to be improving but was still in no shape to leave for home. The night of October 3, his temperature jumped to 101 degrees and for no apparent reason.

Orville was thirty-seven, but in his present condition, lying there, he looked older by far. The chances that he might ever fly again—or ever want to fly again—seemed remote, if not out of the question.

Letters from home and letters from Le Mans helped greatly. The postscript of one letter from Wilbur gave her and Orville both a particularly welcome lift. "I took Bollée (240 pounds) for a couple of rounds of the field," he wrote. "It created more astonishment than anything I have done."

"We are both fairly wild to get home," Katharine wrote to him. She had been thinking of going back for a week or so, if only to get some sleep. But then Orville would turn miserably uncomfortable, unable to get his breath. "I think I will have to stay until I bring him home," she wrote to her father on October 17, a month to the day since the crash.

Orville continued having his "ups and downs," which the doctors attributed to indigestion. So she began cooking for him—broiled steak, beef broth, soft-boiled eggs. When Walter Berry, the American attorney who three years before had come to Dayton with the French delegation, invited her to dinner, she had to turn him down. She was refusing nearly all invitations, she explained to her father, being "too tired to talk!"

By the last week of October, it was decided Orville should be moved to Dayton, not because he was sufficiently recovered, but in the hope that being back in familiar surroundings might help alleviate his nervousness. Three days before he was to leave, two nurses helped him out of bed to try standing with crutches and the blood rushed down within his left leg as if the leg were about to burst and he nearly fainted.

But on October 31, after five weeks and five days in the hospital and with Katharine still at his side, Orville was taken aboard a train at Washington's Union Station.

———

A good-sized crowd stood waiting at the Dayton station as the train pulled in the next morning. Katharine stepped out first onto the platform. Then Orville appeared on crutches, supported by two train officials. "Many had come there to cheer the return of the man who had been instrumental in placing the fair name of Dayton before the eyes of the civilized world," wrote the *Dayton Journal*. But instead of cheers there was silence and murmurs of pity and sympathy, so drawn and wasted did the hero look. No one was allowed to speak to him except members of his family. Her brother was still a very sick man, Katharine explained.

Brother Lorin had come to the station to meet them and a carriage stood waiting. But the vibrations on the train ride had been an agony for

Orville and any more of that in the carriage, it was decided, should be avoided. So he was moved slowly along the twelve and a half blocks to Hawthorn Street in a wheelchair.

Bishop Wright was at the house to greet them, and Carrie Kayler (who had been married and was now Carrie Grumbach) was on hand to prepare dinner. Orville's mind was "good as ever," the Bishop would record that night, "and his body promises to be in due time." A bed had been set up for him in the front parlor. As for herself, Katharine allowed she was "tired to death."

In the days that followed Orville still required "a good deal of attention," as Katharine recorded, but was "tolerably active," able to stay up longer through the day, sometimes for several hours. A local surgeon who looked him over found his left leg had been shortened about an inch—not the one eighth of an inch he had been told at the Fort Myer hospital—but with proper padding in the heel of his shoe he should have no serious trouble.

Neighbors, old school friends, came to call on Orville. By the second week in November, Charlie Taylor was pushing him in the wheelchair to the shop on Third Street, where the engine from the Fort Myer Flyer had been uncrated for inspection.

"I have an awful accumulation of work on hand," Orville told Wilbur on November 14, in the first letter he had written since the accident. Home and a little work seemed to do exactly what had been hoped. So improved was he in health and outlook, and such was his progress walking on crutches, that by late December he and Katharine were letting it be known they would soon be sailing together for France to join Wilbur, Wilbur having told them they were needed.

A Time Like No Other

*Every time we make a move, the people on the street stop
and stare at us.*

KATHARINE WRIGHT

I.

Wilbur's days at Le Mans had never been so full. In the months since Orville's accident, he had become an even bigger sensation. Not since Benjamin Franklin had any American been so overwhelmingly popular in France. As said by the Paris correspondent for the *Washington Post,* it was not just his feats in the air that aroused such interest but his strong "individuality." He was seen as a personification of "the Plymouth Rock spirit," to which French students of the United States, from the time of Alexis de Tocqueville, had attributed "the grit and indomitable perseverance that characterize American efforts in every department of activity."

The crowds kept coming to Le Mans by train and automobile and from increasingly farther distances. "Every day there is a crowd of people not only from the neighborhood," Wilbur reported to Orville, "but also from almost every country in Europe."

During the six months Wilbur was flying at Le Mans 200,000 people came to see him. The thrill of beholding the American wonder in action, the possibility, perhaps, even to shake his hand or be photographed with him, the constant fuss made over him by young and old, men and women, were all part of the excitement, as was the sight of prominent figures daring to ride with him in the sky.

First there had been the rotund Léon Bollée, then Hart Berg, and after that Berg's wife, Edith, who was the first American woman to go up in a plane. To avoid the embarrassment of having her long skirts lifted aloft by the winds, she tied them around her ankles with a rope. On her return she said she had felt no nervous strain or "the least bit of fear." Her admiration for "Mr. Wright," strong as it already was, had increased tenfold by his master-working of the machine. She would be ready anytime, she said, to fly the English Channel with him.

A photograph of Madame Berg seated on the Flyer at Wilbur Wright's side, beaming with pleasure in advance of takeoff, made an unprecedented magazine cover, and the famous Paris dress designer Paul Poiret, quick to see the possibilities in the rope about the ankles, produced a hobble skirt that became a fashion sensation.

Arnold Fordyce, who had led the French delegation to Dayton in 1906, took a turn to ride with Wilbur for a full hour, and for the chief of the French army's aeronautical department, a Colonel Boutioux, Wilbur made several rounds at only 18 inches or so above the ground, which astounded everyone.

Another passenger, like Edith Berg, marveled at how "steady" was the entire time in the air. It seemed as if Wilbur and he were "progressing along an elevated track," wrote an English officer and aeronautical enthusiast, Major Baden Fletcher Smyth Baden-Powell, brother of the founder of the Boy Scouts. But he was astonished, too, by the noise.

> Mr. Wright, with both hands grasping the levers, watches every move, but his movements are so slight as to be almost imperceptible. . . . All the time the engine is buzzing so loudly and the propellers humming so that after the trip one is almost deaf.

A reporter from the *Paris Herald* took a turn, then another reporter from *Le Figaro*, then several Russian officers. The "accommodating attitude of this man that we took great pleasure in depicting as a recluse, is inexhaustible," wrote the reporter from *Le Figaro*. Clearly Wilbur was having a grand time.

"Queen Margherita of Italy was in the crowd yesterday," he wrote on October 9. "You have let me witness the most astonishing spectacle I have ever seen," she told him. "Princes and millionaires are as thick as fleas on the 'Flyer,' " he added, knowing Katharine would love hearing that.

That women found him increasingly appealing became quite evident. One highly attractive Parisian lady, the wife of a prominent politician, spoke freely and at some length to a reporter on the matter, with the understanding that her name would not be mentioned.

Her first impression was not altogether favorable, she admitted. "M. Wright appeared a bit too rough and rugged. His expression was fixed and terribly stern.

> But the moment he opened his lips to speak, the veil of severity vanished. His voice is warm, sympathetic and vibrating. There is a kindly look that imparts exceptional charm and refinement to his bright intelligent eyes. . . . The frank honest way in which he looks straight in the eyes of the person to whom he speaks, and the firm grip of his wiry, muscular hand seem to give true insight into his character and temperament. . . .
>
> He impressed me as one of the most remarkable men I have ever met.

Having finished the number of test flights required by the French syndicate, Wilbur began training the first of three French aviators, as was also required. He was Comte Charles de Lambert, a slim, blond-haired Russian-born aristocrat, age forty-three, who spoke English and to whom Wilbur took an immediate liking. With the plane fitted out with a second set of levers, he would ride to Wilbur's right. For his part Wilbur would sit with his hands between his knees, ready if necessary to take control.

Never had it been more important that Wilbur perform to perfection, for any mishap now, coming after Orville's crash, would be seen in a very different light, and so, as much as he was enjoying himself, the pressure on him was greater than ever. Only by escaping out into the countryside on his bicycle could he have time to himself. "How I long for Kitty Hawk!" he wrote to Octave Chanute.

In his honor the Aéro-Club de France was planning its biggest banquet ever at which Wilbur was to receive the club's Gold Medal and a prize of 5,000 francs ($1,000) and in addition a gold medal from the Académie des Sports. "I will have quite a collection of bric-a-brac by the time I return home," he wrote to brother Reuchlin. What he valued still more, he said, was the friendship of so many of the good people of Le Mans.

When he had arrived a few months earlier he had known no one. Now he counted some of his warmest friends among those he had come to know. It seemed all the children within a dozen-mile radius would greet him as he rode by on his bicycle. They would politely take off their caps and smile and say, "Bonjour! Monsieur Wright."

"They are really almost the only ones except close friends who know how to pronounce my name," he told Reuchlin. "People in general pronounce my name, 'Vreecht' with a terrible rattle of the 'r.' In many places I am called by my first name, 'Veelbare' almost entirely."

———

The Aéro-Club de France's banquet took place in Paris the evening of November 5, 1908, in the *salle de théâtre* of the Automobile Club on the Place de la Concorde. As reported, the "brilliantly illuminated" room had been "transformed" by plants and flowers "in profusion." The 250 guests, nearly all men in full dress, included almost every major figure in French aviation—Léon Delagrange, Louis Blériot, Alberto Santos-Dumont, Ernest Archdeacon—in addition to Léon Bollée, Hart Berg, and Comte Charles de Lambert. Conspicuous, too, was the great structural engineer Gustave Eiffel. Among the few women present was Edith Berg.

A military band provided appropriately rousing music and, as the guests read in the menus at each of their places, the evening's sumptuous feast included *jambon d'York aux épinards* (ham with spinach), *faisan rôti aux croutons* (roasted pheasant with croutons), *salade Russe* (Russian potato salad), and *Glace a lananas* (pineapple ice cream).

All was quite befitting the occasion—as a statement of national pride and the elegant taste of the time, and as recognition of an infinitely promising turning point in history.

In presenting the Gold Medal, the president of the Aéro-Club, M. L. P. Cailletet, spoke of the great change in public opinion that had swept over France and the world in general since Wilbur Wright began his performance at Le Mans. He spoke of how Wilbur and his brother had endured a period of ridicule and abuse such as had seldom been known in the history of scientific investigation. France, he said, was now at last showing its appreciation of their merit.

Wilbur received a sustained ovation, and Louis Barthou, minister of public works, delivered a "hearty speech of congratulation," lauding Wilbur and Orville for achieving "through straightforwardness, intelligence, and tenacity . . . one of the most beautiful inventions of the human genius.

> Mr. Wright is a man who has never been discouraged even in the face of hesitation and suspicion. The brothers Wright have written their names in human history as inventors of pronounced genius.

Photographs were taken. Then Wilbur rose from his place at the center of the head table. Baron d'Estournelles de Constant translated as Wilbur spoke.

> For myself and my brother I thank you for the honor you are doing us and for the cordial reception you have tendered us this evening.
>
> If I had been born in your beautiful country and had grown up among you, I could not have expected a warmer welcome than has just been given me. When we did not know each other, we had no confidence in each other; today, when we are acquainted, it is otherwise: we believe each other, and we are friends. I thank you for this. In the enthusiasm being shown around me, I see not merely an outburst intended to glorify a person, but a tribute to an idea that has always impassioned mankind. I sometimes think that the desire to fly

after the fashion of birds is an ideal handed down to us by our ancestors who, in their grueling travels across trackless lands in prehistoric times, looked enviously on the birds soaring freely through space, at full speed, above all obstacles, on the infinite highway of the air. Scarcely ten years ago, all hope of flying had almost been abandoned; even the most convinced had become doubtful, and I confess that, in 1901, I said to my brother Orville that men would not fly for fifty years. Two years later, we ourselves were making flights. This demonstration of my inability as a prophet gave me such a shock that I have ever since distrusted myself and have refrained from all prediction—as my friends of the press, especially, well know. But it is not really necessary to look too far into the future; we see enough already to be certain that it will be magnificent. Only let us hurry and open the roads.

Once again, I thank you with all my heart, and in thanking you I should like it understood that I am thanking all of France.

At the point when Wilbur expressed his gratitude for the warm friendship he had experienced in a country not his own, his "habitually rigid mask softened," according to one account, "his voice, usually so clear, quavered slightly."

The members and guests responded with a standing ovation. The band played "The Star-Spangled Banner," and for some time afterward Wilbur stood patiently signing two hundred or more menus. "He knows the little chores that are incumbent upon our heroes to perform," observed the account in *L'Aérophile* approvingly.

In the weeks that followed, Wilbur returned several times to Paris to receive additional tributes and awards and to be hosted at more dinners in his honor. When not being celebrated at such gatherings, he could be seen striding alone up and down the Bois de Boulogne or exploring the avenues, looking in the windows of curio shops or standing quietly studying the architecture of one of the city's monuments.

"He has a half dozen invitations for every day," wrote a correspondent for the *New York World,* "and some few of them he accepts, putting on his hat and coat to go out and meet ladies and gentlemen who have spent an hour or two with their maids and valets in order to make themselves sufficiently beautiful for the honor of meeting him.

> They drive up in carriages and pairs with gold-braided coachmen and footmen, and Wright shoulders an umbrella for a walk through the rain to the house where the dinner happens to be. . . . He is just himself in the most refreshing way.

During an extended conversation with Wilbur one evening at the Bergs' apartment on the Champs-Elysées, it became clear to the correspondent how greatly Wilbur enjoyed Paris. "He has too keen an appreciation of the beautiful not to do so."

———

In early December, with winter setting in, Wilbur sent the Comte de Lambert to the southern reaches of France to look over the fashionable resort town of Pau, close to the Pyrénées Mountains and the border of Spain, as a possible location at which to continue the demonstrations. It was where de Lambert had grown up, a town of some 34,000 people known for its fourteenth-century castles, its foxhunting and eighteen-hole golf course (the first on the continent), and what was considered one of the most appealing winter climates in Europe.

The prospect of visiting a destination so popular with the high society of England and Europe might also, Wilbur hoped, further entice Orville and Katharine—Katharine especially—to join him there for an extended stay. A few months in such a place would do them both great good, he wrote to her. "I know that you love 'Old Steele' [her high school], but I think you would love it still better if the briny deep separated it from you for a while. We will be needing a social manager and can pay enough salary to make the proposition attractive. So do not worry about the six [dollars] per day the school board gives you."

But she had already made up her mind. "Brother and I are coming over as soon as we can," she wrote only a few days later, in advance of his letter reaching Dayton. She had only to make satisfactory arrangements for the Bishop, who had just turned eighty and was not up to such a trip.

In Paris, where new toys being sold were part of the "streets sights" of the Christmas season, the most popular was a little reproduction of the Wilbur Wright airplane, of which much was made in the newspapers, including the *Chicago Tribune.*

> It is quite a wonderful toy, for even the smallest details have been perfectly carried out, and the tiny machine will start from the ground, make its miniature flight, and then descend in a manner that is most remarkable. "Mr. Wright" himself is seated in the toy and operates it in the most life-like way. The features of the inventor have a distinctly more Parisian than an American cast, but for all that no one but knows for whom it is intended and the sale of them has been quick and large.

In Le Mans, despite increasingly cold days, Wilbur, having switched to wearing a black leather motorcycle jacket, was busy practicing takeoffs without the use of a catapult. He had decided to compete for the Michelin Cup, a prize newly established by the French tire company, and in the competition such launching devices were not allowed.

On the day of the event, December 31, the last day of the year and Wilbur's last big event at Camp d'Auvours, in spite of rain and cold he was barely able to endure, he put on his most astonishing performance yet, flying longer and farther than anyone ever had—2 hours, 20 minutes, and 23 and one fifth seconds during which he covered a distance of 77 miles. He won the Cup.

He was sorry to have missed Christmas at home, he wrote his father the next day. "But I could not afford to lose the Michelin Prize, as the loss of prestige would have been much more serious than the direct loss. If I had gone away, the other fellows would have fairly busted themselves any record I left. The fact that they knew I was ready to beat anything they should do kept them discouraged."

After landing he prepared to go up again, no matter the cold and rain, and this time took the minister of public works, Louis Barthou, with him.

"He informed me that the government had decided to confer the Legion of Honor upon both Orville and myself."

II.

For many, even veteran travelers, the prospect of crossing the Atlantic in the middle of winter would have kept them happily safe and comfortable at home. But Katharine Wright, who had never been to sea, never even set foot on board an ocean liner, seems to have had no misgivings or hesitation whatever. On January 5, 1909, in New York, she and Orville went aboard the German liner *Kaiser Wilhelm der Grosse*, Orville hobbling up the gangplank as best he could beside her, bound for France. She who had so long been confined by work and family responsibilities was now at last, at age thirty-four, embarking on a venture such as she had only been able to dream of, scarcely imagining it might one day happen.

She had made her first visit to the dress shop in Dayton in early December to choose a traveling ensemble and hat, and ultimately packed her trunk with two new evening dresses as well, one pink, the other black. When asked by friends and reporters about the purpose of the trip, she and Orville would say it was for "a sort of family reunion." In their absence, Bishop Wright would be looked after by Carrie Grumbach, who, with her husband and child, had moved in with him at 7 Hawthorn Street.

Katharine's primary responsibility would be Orville, who was walking now with a cane instead of crutches, but was still quite unsteady on his feet, with a decided limp, and needed somebody with him to make sure he did not fall. Except for one rough day at sea, the crossing turned out to be extremely smooth. Even so, Orville had trouble walking the deck.

They were traveling first-class, enjoying good service and in "pleasant company," as Katharine wrote their father. Clearly all was as she would wish.

They landed at Cherbourg the afternoon of January 11 and by boat-train reached Paris at one in the morning to find Wilbur waiting at the station to greet them—"in silk hat and evening clothes," no less, Katharine was delighted to record. He had come all the way from Pau, and with him were the Bergs and Arnold Fordyce, who stepped forward to present Katharine with a large bouquet of American Beauty roses from which protruded an American flag.

They all went to the Myerbeer Hotel on the Champs-Elysées, near the Bergs' apartment. Once the others said good night, the three Wrights sat up talking until three in the morning.

The following day the brothers met for lunch with André Michelin, the automobile tire manufacturer, who presented Wilbur with the $4,000 that went with the Michelin Cup. Katharine, meanwhile, went shopping with Edith Berg, "a pretty woman and very stylish," Katharine reported to the Bishop later that night. "She will be down at Pau with me and that will make it more pleasant. She will take her automobile and take me about in the country." Wilbur and Hart Berg had already left for Pau. She and Orville would follow shortly.

Orville asked her also to tell the Bishop that as of now, from French syndicate payments, prize money, and cash awards, Wilbur and he had $35,000 in the bank in Paris.

Orville and Katharine left Paris for Pau, 194 miles to the south, by overnight train the evening of Friday the 15th. En route, at about seven A.M., the train crashed head-on into a freight train, killing two passengers and seriously injuring a half dozen others. She and Orville were "not even scratched," Katharine assured their father. "We happened to take a compartment 'de-luxe' which was all that saved at least one of us from a bad fall." In fact, Orville, while not injured, had been badly shaken up and subjected to severe pain.

After a delay of five hours, they reached Pau the following afternoon and checked into the Grand Hôtel Gassion, next door to the birthplace of France's most popular king, Henry IV.

The hotel was grand indeed and set on the brink of a steep bluff with a commanding view of the green valley below and the spectacular, snow-capped peaks of the Pyrénées, some ten thousand feet in elevation, that stretched the length of the horizon approximately thirty miles to the south. To provide further enjoyment of the spectacle there was also a beautiful promenade running a mile along the top of the bluff. Never in their lives until now had Katharine and the brothers seen such mountains. "I never saw anything so lovely," wrote Katharine, struggling to find words to express what she felt.

Wilbur would not be staying at the hotel but at a flying field called Pont-Long about six miles from town, or twenty minutes by automobile, where the city fathers had provided him with luxurious living quarters—or at least luxurious by his standards—and with most all the comforts, including his own personal French chef. The chef did not last long, however, Wilbur finding the cuisine too fancy. Neither did a successor satisfy. Finally, a third chef caught on to what the American liked to eat and all seems to have gone well thereafter.

At a reception for the three Wrights put on by the mayor of Pau, some five hundred guests gathered in the Pau Garden, at the Grand Hall du Palais d'Hiver at the eastern end of the promenade. Outside the encircling palm trees and flowers another thousand people or more looked on.

Wilbur had yet to conduct any of his "experiments," but as reported in the *Paris Herald,* Pau had "simply gone mad about aviation.

> Nothing is talked about but mechanical flight, everyone is buying a new camera to snap aeroplanes, painters are busy at their canvases, the long-neglected roads are being repaired, and society is inviting the Wrights to many more gatherings than they can possibly attend.

A few days later a photograph of Wilbur, Orville, and Katharine out for a stroll in Pau appeared on the front page of the *Herald.* She and her brothers were "the whole show" everywhere they went, wrote Katharine. Until a year ago Wilbur and Orville had worked practically in secret. Now they were the toast of Europe and she was with them.

"Every time we make a move, the people on the street stop and stare at us. . . . We have our pictures taken every two minutes." She minded this not in the least. "The <u>Daily Mirror</u> of London had a man here who got a dandy picture of Orv and me."

———

With the onset of February and warmer days came a marked increase in the arrival of notables of the kind Pau was known for—counts and countesses, dukes and duchesses, lords and ladies, many of them English. There were members of the French cabinet, generals, lords of the press, and a number of American millionaires, as well as a former prime minister of England and two kings.

Never in their lives had the three Wrights been among so many who, by all signs, had little to do but amuse themselves. Nor did they feel out of place or the least intimidated by such company. They felt that they, in their way, were quite as well-born and properly reared as anyone. Never did they stray from remaining exactly who they were, and more often than not, they found themselves most pleasantly surprised by those they were meeting.

At a luncheon at their hotel, their host, Alfred Harmsworth, Lord Northcliffe, publisher of the London *Daily Mail,* was much to their liking, though a man worlds apart from Wilbur and Orville. He had immense wealth and all the glamour of power and success, but appealed greatly all the same. Further, he was keenly interested in the development of aviation and he liked Americans.

On another occasion, they were with Joseph Pulitzer, publisher of the *New York World,* and his wife. "We all liked them very much," wrote Katharine. She wrote also of a "rousing good time" at lunch with Lord and Lady Balfour.

Arthur Balfour, former prime minister of England, was so eager to take part in preparations for Wilbur's flights at Pont-Long that along with Lord Northcliffe he helped haul on the rope that lifted the catapult weight into place. Seeing a young British lord also assisting, Northcliffe remarked to Orville, who was standing close by watching, "I'm so glad that young man is helping with the rope, for I'm sure it is the only useful thing he has ever done in his life."

Katharine had the thrill of a day's expedition to the Pyrénées by automobile with a wealthy Irish couple and, as she reported to her father, knowing how it would please him, she had begun taking French lessons for two hours every morning, and with her background in Greek and Latin her progress was rapid. One of those helping her with her French was the son of Prime Minister Georges Clemenceau. Another she greatly liked was the Comtesse de Lambert, the attractive wife of Wilbur's student the Comte de Lambert.

Her complaints were few. On those days when there was no sun, the cold and dampness were such as she did not care for. Besides, Edith Berg, whom she had liked at first in Paris, was getting on her nerves. She was "a regular tyrant and as selfish as anyone can be. We will be glad when she goes." But to judge by her letters, that was as "wrathy" as Katharine turned during the time in Europe, and though Edith Berg stayed on, Katharine appears to have had no further complaints about her.

More press arrived, more photographs were taken, more articles written for *Le Figaro*, the *Paris Herald*, the London *Daily Mail*, the *New York Times*, and papers back in Ohio. One story sent by the United Press from Paris claimed a French army lieutenant had charged Wilbur in a divorce case. The story was a complete fabrication that none of the French papers carried, but in Dayton, where it did appear, it caused a temporary embarrassing sensation. Wilbur wrote an angry denial. Family and friends at home rose quickly to his defense, saying he was not that sort of man.

Since arriving in Paris in January, Orville had told reporters that, given his physical state, it would be foolish for him to attempt any exertion. At Pau, he mainly stood and watched, saying little. With his derby hat, well-pressed suit, his polished shoes and cane, he could have been another of the European aristocrats.

A writer for *Flyer* magazine. H. Massac Buist, was surprised to see how small Orville was, indeed, how different both brothers were from what he had expected, judging from press accounts. "I have never seen them taciturn, or curt, or secretive, or any of the other things which I had been led to believe were their outstanding characteristics." Recalling a line attributed to Wilbur—"Well, if I talked a lot I should be like a parrot, which is the bird that speaks most and flies least."—Buist wrote that in the course of a day Wilbur talked quite as much as most men; the difference was his words were to the point.

The less Orville had to say, the more Katharine talked and with great effect. She had become a celebrity in her own right. The press loved her. "The masters of the aeroplane, those two clever and intrepid Daytonians, who have moved about Europe under the spotlight of extraordinary publicity, have had a silent partner," went one account. But silent she was no longer and reporters delighted in her extroverted, totally unaffected Midwestern American manner.

Some of what was written went too far. She was said to have mathematical genius superior even to that of her brothers, and that she was the one financing their time in Europe. In the main, however, it was fullhearted, long-overdue, public recognition of the "mainstay" of her brothers in their efforts.

> Who was it who gave them new hope, when they began to think the problem [of flight] impossible? . . . Who was it that nursed Orville back to strength and health when the physicians had practically given him up after that fatal accident last September?

Besides, wrote one correspondent, "Like most American girls, the aviators' sister has very decided views of her own."

Wilbur made his first flight at Pau on February 3 and from that day on remained a sensation. As said one headline, all Pau was "AGOG."

Virtually every day but Sunday a steady stream of elegant carriages and automobiles headed out to the flying field to see the doors of the huge red "aerodock" swing wide and the four-year-old Flyer come rolling out, showing signs of much wear and tear, the canvas soiled and torn, patched and tattooed with tin tacks. Wilbur would examine it up and down with his usual care, oil can in hand, pockets bulging with twine, a screwdriver, a wrench, touching a wire here, a bolt there, and never hurrying. Then, with all to his liking, off he would go, "right up into the air, turning, wheeling up and down, graceful as an albatross, showing the perfect command of the aviator." For a second or two, the plane would seem to hang motionless against the high white line of the snowcapped Pyrénées, "absolutely a scene of beauty quite impossible to describe."

One of the few problems to contend with was the ground filled with bumps, some the size of a bowler hat, that made takeoffs difficult. Someone suggested that with a bit of spade work the ground could be leveled. It was just what Wilbur and Orville had done preparing for their first test flights at Huffman Prairie, but Wilbur by now felt he could dispense with that. "If we have to alter the face of the earth before we can fly," he replied, "we may as well throw up the proposition." Such was the way of the man, observed a writer who was present. "He never sought to escape by the easy way round."

Most of Wilbur's time was devoted to training the Comte de Lambert and another of the French aviators he was expected to teach, Paul Tissandier. Like de Lambert, Tissandier was a wealthy aristocrat who had been an automobile racer before taking up aviation. The third student was a French army officer, Captain Paul N. Lucas-Girardville. Of the three, de Lambert was the best pilot and Wilbur's favorite.

In none of his flights at Pont-Long was Wilbur attempting to set a record, and so other passengers, too, went aloft seated beside him, as many as a dozen altogether, including Katharine, who went up before a large crowd on February 15, just as night was coming on. It was her first time in the air.

A spell of cold weather had set in. ("Southern sunny France is a delusion and a snare!" she had told her father.) But all that was forgotten when Wilbur at long last invited her to go with him.

She was most happily surprised by how smoothly they sailed along and how easily she could recognize faces below. She thought they were flying at about 30 feet, but found out later it was 60 feet, and they were moving at 42 miles per hour. Yet she had a feeling of complete tranquillity and forgot completely about the cold. The flight lasted seven minutes. To show her the ease with which he could maneuver the machine, Wilbur made several sharp turns, but again she experienced no ill effects and never showed the least sign of fear.

Asked later if she had felt like a bird when flying with her brother, Katharine responded, "I don't know exactly how a bird feels. Birds sing,

I suppose, because they are happy. I sang, I know, and I was very happy indeed. But like the birds, I sang best after the flight was over."

By now Wilbur was making flights with passengers five or six times a day. Who got to go was entirely up to him, and while it was assumed by many that he was charging a fee for so rare a privilege, and many were prepared to pay, and pay handsomely, he charged nothing, which made a great impression.

When a wealthy American from Philadelphia was told by Lord Northcliffe that only Wilbur decided who went with him, the man replied, "Oh, I dare say that can be arranged."

"I would like to be around when you do the arranging, just to see how it's done," Northcliffe replied. The man did not get his ride.

Northcliffe would later say he never knew more unaffected people than Wilbur, Orville, and Katharine Wright, and that he did not think the excitement over them and the intense interest produced by their extraordinary feats had any effect on them whatsoever.

Katharine filled her assignment as social manager for the brothers to perfection, taking active part in all manner of events night and day, and availing herself of every opportunity to make use of her rapidly improving French. "I understand a great deal now and talk fairly well," she told her father. That neither of her brothers had made such an effort annoyed him greatly. "A year in France and not understand nor speak French!" he had written in reference to Wilbur in particular. It was about as critical as the Bishop ever was when it came to Wilbur.

In addition, the brothers depended on Katharine to maintain correspondence with their father, and so she did, sending off letters and postcards several times a week. In more than a month's time at Pau, Orville never wrote a word to the Bishop, while Wilbur wrote only once, on March 1, to say he would be going to Rome next, that Orville was much better than when he arrived, though still "not entirely himself," and that he, Wilbur, would be very glad to get back home again.

For his part Bishop Wright kept them regularly posted on events at home, his health (which was good), Carrie Grumbach's cooking (also good), his travels on church work, the weather, and the fact that he was "not a bit lonely." He had too much to do. He had begun work on an autobiography and had already produced fourteen typewritten pages. A few weeks later, he was up to fifty pages.

As noted in the press, the airfield at Pont-Long continued to shine as a "place of pilgrimage for men of eminence." In the last week of February, the king of Spain, Alfonso XIII, arrived to witness "the miracle." He watched Wilbur take off and fly high above in great circles, never taking his eye off the spectacle. Afterward, as his entourage, Orville, Katharine, and others crowded around, he stood close to hear Wilbur explain each of the control mechanisms on the machine. The king, who spoke English and clearly knew a good deal about aviation, had many questions for Wilbur. At one point, turning to Katharine, he asked, "And did you really ride it yourself?" When she said she had, he said he wanted very much to go up with Wilbur but had promised his wife he would not. Katharine judged him "a good husband."

Turning to Wilbur, the king inquired whether it would be asking too much to request another demonstration. "I have seen what you can do," he said. "I want to see what one of your pilots can do."

Wilbur at once consented, taking off this time with the Comte de Lambert for a flight of twelve minutes, during which Wilbur never once touched the levers. That a student pilot could have learned to handle the plane with such skill in such a short time seemed to impress the king more than anything.

Orville had told the press he would do no flying while in France. Nor did he plan to go up with Wilbur. But only days later Wilbur took Katharine for another ride, this time for a thirteen-mile flight cross-country. "It was great," she told her father. Not long after that she would take off in a balloon with a French count, and this time Orville went, too, sailing some thirty miles to land at Ossun in the Pyrénées.

That accomplished, Katharine gave out. Close to collapse from "too much excitement," she stayed in her hotel room for two days.

———

On March 17, the most beautiful day yet—"royal weather," as people were saying—the king of England arrived, having driven more than seventy miles over to Pau from his customary holiday headquarters at Biarritz and with a considerable royal party accompanying him in a stream of gleaming black automobiles.

Edward VII was in his sixty-eighth year, a stout, white-bearded, affable figure whose enjoyment of life, whose manner of dress—the homburg hats, tweed suits, the habit of never buttoning the bottom button on his vests—along with his love of fast automobiles and unmasked enthusiasm for beautiful women, had led to his being taken as a kind of emblem for the years since 1900, the Edwardian Era. The oldest son of Queen Victoria, he was an altogether refreshing personification of escape from the Victorian Age. That he was also keenly interested in aviation and had come in person to witness for himself the wonder of Wilbur Wright seemed entirely in keeping.

The crowd at the airfield was large, the excitement great. Katharine was presented to the king, who, as noticed, was wearing a small bunch of shamrock in his buttonhole in honor of St. Patrick's Day.

He was taken first to see the Flyer inside the shed. Wilbur apologized for the plane's worn appearance, but was proud to point to the very spic-and-span new Flyer being built right beside it, which, Wilbur explained, was to be used in Rome.

As Wilbur saw to the positioning of his plane on the field and did his final inspection, Orville explained its workings to the king. Then Wilbur took off, performed to perfection, and after about seven minutes made a perfect landing at the point where he took off. The king watched it all with "bated breath," as he said.

As he had for King Alfonso, Wilbur offered to go again to show how he carried a passenger, and once again, Katharine went with him. She had by now flown longer and farther than had any American woman.

Later that same day, much to the pride of all three Wrights, and to every French man and woman in the crowd, the Comte de Lambert performed a solo flight.

The clamor and amazement over what the Wrights had achieved—all they had shown to be true time after time at Le Mans and Pau—was by no means limited to Europe. At home in the United States, newspapers and magazines from one end of the country to the other gave the story continual attention. Nor was the potential of so miraculous a creation lost sight of.

In a long article in the Waco, Texas, *Times-Herald* on "The Monarchs of the Air," James A. Edgerton wrote as follows:

> Most of us can remember when the automobile was a novelty. The writer is under forty, yet recalls the time when the first "horseless wagon" was used, and it was only about a score of years ago. . . . The machine was a big clumsy affair, with large wheels, uncertain steering apparatus, and was run by a very noisy steam engine. This was so great a failure that it was some years before another crossed my field of vision. Now they are as common as millionaires.
>
> If the automobile could be so vastly improved in so short a time, who can predict what may occur in the field of aerial navigation now that the principle has actually been discovered and is before the world? Is it not possible that it will revolutionize human affairs in as radical a way as did the discovery of the use of steam?
>
> In all this stupendous change going on before our very eyes the Wright brothers are the chief magicians. They are the leaders and pioneers.

It had been announced that the Aero Club of America would present the brothers with a gold medal on their return. Congress, too, had voted a medal to be presented by President William Howard Taft, and Dayton was making preparations for the biggest celebration in its history.

But for all the attention being paid to the Wrights, there was at the same time increasing realization of how much else was happening in aviation in France. Six months earlier the number of builders of airplanes in Paris and vicinity amounted to less than a half dozen. On April 25, the *New York Times* reported that no fewer than fifteen factories were now in full operation. If the Wrights were front and center in the show of inventive change, the cast onstage in France was filling rapidly.

Scores of inventors are constructing their own machines [the *Times* article continued]. There is an aerodrome where pupils are taught to fly. Three new papers devoted to aviation have been founded within the past six months. There are three societies in France for the encouragement of aviation, and over $300,000 in prizes will be open to competition in the course of the year.

The largest of the competitive events, an international flying meet, was scheduled for the coming summer, at the town of Reims, northeast of Paris in the champagne country.

III.

With his demonstrations concluded at Pau, Wilbur spent his final few days there packing the new Flyer for shipment in sections to Rome—the Flyer used at Le Mans and Pau would ultimately wind up in a museum in Paris—and supervising the final stages of training for his French students to the point where all three had soloed. Orville and Katharine had already returned to Paris, and on March 23, Wilbur, too, left Pau for Paris.

A few days later the three Wrights went to Le Mans to be received at a heartwarming farewell banquet. Three days after that Wilbur and Hart Berg were on board a train from Paris to Rome, where, a week later, Orville and Katharine were to join them.

In Paris, to Katharine's delight, the social pace continued full speed. As she informed her father, she was the only woman ever invited to a dinner at the Aéro-Club de France. "You ought to seen it," she wrote in the Ohio vernacular. "Me—sitting up there big as you . . . talking French as lively as anyone! It was a performance I can tell you." Best of all, she also told the Bishop, he had been toasted. "They drank a champagne in your honor!"

Katharine and Orville left for Rome on April 9 and arrived the next afternoon to find the city overrun with tourists, including an estimated thirty thousand Americans. Apparently no one had prepared them for such crowds. Hotels, restaurants, monuments, and museums were swarming with people. Hart Berg had found rooms for Orville and Katharine opposite the Barberini Palace. Wilbur was staying several miles south of the city at a flying field called Centocelle, but instead of a shed this time he was living in a nearby cottage on an estate belonging to a countess.

In terms of the purpose for which the Wrights had come there, Rome was an unqualified success. From April 15 to the 26, Wilbur completed more than fifty flights, all to great acclaim and without mishap. He trained Italian military officers how to fly his plane, lectured to schoolteachers and students, and took a variety of passengers for a ride, one of whom, a news cameraman, produced the first motion picture films ever shot from an airplane in flight.

The weather was ideal and as in France, large crowds watched in amazement. And again there was no shortage of prominent figures among the onlookers. King Victor Emmanuel III of Italy strolled about with a camera slung over his shoulder as though one of the tourists. There were princes, dukes, cabinet members, the American financier J. P. Morgan and his sister and daughter, and James J. Hill, the famous American railroad builder. The American ambassador to Italy, Lloyd Griscom, was one of those who went flying with Wilbur.

But for Orville and Katharine, Rome, after the time they had had in France, left much to be desired. That April was "the choice season" in Rome, that the palaces of the Caesars, the Arch of Constantine, and the Colosseum were even more impressive than expected, was not sufficient. As Katharine told her father, "I was homesick for the first time when we reached Rome." She and Orville both were "very anxious to come home." She found their hotel appallingly dirty. "We would appreciate a good clean bathtub and clean plates and knives and forks much more than the attention we receive." In another letter she reported, "The waiters at the table are so dirty that I can hardly eat a mouthful of food."

She and Orville thought J. P. Morgan, his sister and daughter, "pleasant" enough, but were growing weary of the ways of the aristocracy. When word came that Victor Emmanuel would be arriving at Centocelle Field at eight in the morning to see Wilbur fly, it only went to prove that kings could be a nuisance. "They always come at such unearthly hours," wrote Katharine.

A lunch in honor of the three Wrights at the beautiful villa of the Contessa Celleri, who was providing Wilbur's living quarters, was all quite fine, as was the drive provided for their enjoyment into the countryside in a brand-new, elegant automobile, until the chauffeur, taking a curve at breakneck speed, smashed head-on into a stone wall. Fortunately no one was hurt, though the car was a total wreck.

Brother Wilbur was quite well, Katharine was pleased to report to the Bishop. Orville, too, was looking well and "improves all the time, but—like me—doesn't care much for the discomforts of Rome." They would be heading to London by way of Paris, then on to New York as soon as possible.

After two days in London, where they were feted and honored still further—a banquet at the Ritz Hotel, the first ever Gold Medal awarded by the British Aeronautical Society—the three sailed on May 5 from Southampton on the German ocean liner *Kronprinzessin Cecilie.*

For Wilbur it was the end of just over a year in Europe, much the greater part of which had been spent in France. It was there, in France, beginning at Le Mans, that he had flown as no man ever had anywhere on earth. At Le Mans and Pau he had flown far more than anyone ever had and set every record for distance, speed, altitude, time in the air, and made the first flights ever with a passenger, and all this, after so many years of the near secrecy of his and Orville's efforts, had been done for all to see. The whole world now knew.

The threesome had also become far richer financially. The time in Europe had resulted in an accumulated compensation from contracts and prizes of some $200,000.

Wilbur had also found among the French a wealth of friendship such as he had never known. As he would write much later in a letter of gratitude to Léon Bollée, "We do not forget that you expended much time and gave yourself much trouble in order to be of assistance to us and that you rejoiced with us in our successes and grieved with us in our troubles." These were not things to compensate for with money, "but we cherish them forever in our hearts."

For Orville the four-month-long Grand Tour had provided a greatly needed change of scene and the chance to recuperate at his own pace. For Katharine it was a colossal reward for all she had done for her brothers for so long in so many ways.

Further, as would become increasingly clear later, they had seen Europe at an almost perfect time, when prosperity and peace prevailed, when Americans in abundance were discovering and enjoying the experience of European travel and the changes in outlook it brought as never before, and when the horrors of modern, mechanized warfare were still to come. Travelers from all parts of America who were there then would never forget the time. Nor would the three Wrights. Nor were they ever again to enjoy such a time together.

For now, for all three, there was the overriding good feeling of being homeward bound.

Causes for Celebration

Telegram from Katharine, telling of their safe arrival in
New York, saying they will be home Thursday.

BISHOP WRIGHT'S DIARY,
TUESDAY, MAY 11, 1909

I.

After a rousing welcome at New York, with a chorus of harbor whistles blaring as their ship came in, and a swarm of reporters and photographers surrounding their every move during a one-day stopover in the city, the three Wrights went on by train to Dayton, arriving at Union Depot, Thursday, May 13, 1909, at five in the afternoon. The crowd at the station was of a size rarely seen in Dayton. Cannons were booming, factory whistles blowing across town, everyone at the station cheering.

Seeing Bishop Wright, as she and her brothers stepped from the train, Katharine shouted, "Oh, there's Daddy," and rushed to throw her arms around him. Wilbur and Orville then warmly embraced their father, but so wild was the noise no one could hear what was being said.

There were more embraces for Lorin and Netta and their children. Then, as they began inching their way through the crowd, Wilbur and Orville started shaking hands. Seeing a big, veteran member of the Dayton police force, Tom Mitchell, Wilbur said, "Hello, Tom!" "Good boy!" said Tom as he took Wilbur by the hand.

Katharine was described in one account as looking like the typical American girl at a homecoming, in a smart, gray traveling gown, with a large, broad-brimmed picture-hat of dark green. The only woman in the world who had made three flights in an airplane, she was now as much a subject of attention nearly as her brothers.

In New York she had lectured reporters on some of the "flippant" accounts that had appeared in the American press about the notable Europeans who had taken an interest in her brothers. She loved America, she said, but the American people did not always understand Europeans, who were an appreciative people. She could not listen to anyone saying unkind things about them without protesting. But here in the noise and crowds of the moment there was no call for such comment.

Wilbur looked "bronzed and hard," and Orville, too, looked well—certainly a great deal better than when he had left Dayton in January—but walked still with a limp. In the middle of all that was happening, Bishop Wright, as was noted, rarely spoke a word, but "feasted" his eyes on the two sons who had made the name Wright, as well as Dayton, known to the world.

Eleven carriages awaited at the entrance to the station to carry the family and a variety of town officials to Hawthorn Street, each of the three reserved for the Wrights pulled by four white horses. The bishop and Orville rode in the first, Wilbur and Reuchlin in the second, Katharine, Lorin, and Lorin's family in the third.

The streets were filled with more crowds the whole way. Sidewalks were packed. People were leaning from windows, children waving small flags. Hawthorn Street and the Wright homestead were bedecked with flags and flowers and Japanese lanterns. Standing at last at the railing of the front porch, Katharine called out to neighbors across the street, "I'm so glad to get home I don't know what to do."

For considerable time, she and the brothers stood in the front parlor receiving a steady procession of old friends and neighbors. Outside the crowd grew to more than ten thousand.

The day after, Mayor Edward Burkhardt, and several city officials called at 7 Hawthorn Street to discuss with the family the "real celebration" to come.

Speaking with a local reporter only shortly afterward, Orville said quite matter-of-factly that though his doctors had told him he was to do no flying in Europe and that he had obeyed them to the letter, he would soon resume his flights at Fort Myer. As he did not say, Wilbur and Katharine felt strongly that a return to the scene of the crash now would put too great a strain on him. He should wait until he was back in practice. But to Orville the matter was settled. Fort Myer it had to be. And he was ready.

The Wright workshop on West Third Street became a "beehive of industry" no less than ever, with Charlie Taylor in charge. "The most important thing we have before us at this time is to get ready for the Fort Myer tests," Wilbur told reporters, and he and Orville "personally" were constructing the plane to be used there. The old machine had been so badly broken up in the crash that all but the motor and transmission was being built anew.

On May 20 it was announced that President Taft would soon be presenting the brothers several medals at the White House.

———

Katharine was to go with them to Washington for the ceremony, of course. Bishop Wright, however, felt obliged to take part in some church work in Indiana. To attract as little attention as possible, the brothers and Katharine quietly left Dayton on an earlier train than expected and no notice was taken except for a few railroad officials at the depot.

They were to remain in Washington only the day of June 10. There was a lunch in their honor at the Cosmos Club, which for the occasion waived its long-standing policy of men only so Katharine could attend. Prominent among the more distinguished Washingtonians present was Alexander Graham Bell.

Shortly after the lunch the entire party walked the short distance to the White House, where nearly a thousand men and women stood in the East Room as President Taft formally presented two Gold Medals on behalf of the Aero Club of America. At six feet two and weighing three hundred pounds, the president loomed large as he stood beside the brothers. In addressing his two fellow Ohioans, he spoke appropriately to the point and with unmistakable warmth.

> I esteem it a great honor and an opportunity to present these medals to you as an evidence of what you have done. I am so glad—perhaps at a delayed hour—to show that in America it is not true that "a prophet is not without honor save in his own country." It is especially gratifying thus to note a great step in human discovery by paying honor to men who bear it so modestly. You made this discovery by a course that we of America like to feel is distinctly American—by keeping your noses right at the job until you had accomplished what you had determined to do.

By evening, the three Wrights were back on board the train, on their way back to Dayton. Thorough testing of new propellers had become a primary requirement. In the meantime, however, there was Dayton's "real celebration," the Great Homecoming, to be faced, like it or not.

"Gigantic" was the word used to describe the preparations. The whole story of America and Dayton from earliest times was to be portrayed with "historical exactness," in a parade of enormous floats being built at the National Cash Register plant. Indians and their canoes, the eras of the Conestoga wagon, the canal boat, the first railroad, Robert Fulton's steamboat, the evolution of the bicycle, and an up-to-date automobile, would be followed by the first American balloon and a dirigible, all this in prelude to a float titled, "All the World Paying Homage to the United States, the Wright Brothers, and the Aeroplane," and featuring a handcrafted, half-size replica of a Wright Flyer. There were to be fifteen floats and 560 people in costume ("all historically correct"), in what the newspapers promised to be the greatest parade Dayton had ever beheld.

On Main Street a "Court of Honor" was being created reaching from Third Street to the river, white columns lining both sides of the street and strung with colored lights. "Everywhere is the tri-colored bunting . . . everywhere flutters the pennants and flags and banners," the papers were saying. Soldiers, sailors, and the Fire Department would march, bands play. Some 2,500 schoolchildren dressed in red, white, and blue would be arranged as a "living-flag" on the Fair Grounds grandstand and sing "The Star-Spangled Banner."

In the nearly ten years that the Wright brothers had been working to achieve success with their invention, this was to be the first formal recognition by their hometown of their efforts and success and there was to be no mistaking the whole town's enthusiasm.

While little of such elaborate fanfare appealed to the brothers, they knew that if Dayton saw fit to celebrate, if Dayton felt that was important, then it was not for them to complain or appear in any way annoyed or disapproving. Octave Chanute wrote to Wilbur to say he knew such honors could grow "oppressive" to modest men, but then they had brought it on themselves with their ingenuity and courage. It was well-meant advice, but the brothers had no need to be reminded.

On the eve of the opening of the festivities, the *Dayton Daily News* ran an editorial expressing much that was felt by a great many:

> It is a wonderful lesson—this celebration. It comes at an auspicious time. The old world was getting tired, it seemed, and needed help to whip it into action. There was beginning a great deal of talk about man's no longer having the opportunities he once had of achieving greatness. Too many people were beginning to believe that all of the world's problems had been solved. . . . Money was beginning to tell in the affairs of men, and some were wondering whether a poor boy might work for himself a place in commerce or industry or science.
>
> This celebration throws all such idle talk to the winds. It crowns anew the efforts of mankind. It crushes for another hundred years the suspicion that all of the secrets of nature have been solved or that the avenues of hope have been closed to those who would win new worlds.

> It points out to the ambitious young man that he labors
> not in vain; that genius knows no class, no condition. . . .
> The modesty of the Wright brothers is a source of a good
> deal of comment. . . . But above all there is a sermon in their
> life of endeavor which cannot be preached too often.

The following morning, Thursday, June 17, at nine o'clock every church bell and factory whistle announced the start of what was to be a two-day celebration. Thousands of people poured into the city. Business had been suspended, except for the sale of ice cream and flags and toy airships and Wright brothers postcards. That it was raining lightly the first part of the first day seemed to matter little to anyone. And the show was all that had been expected, one spectacle following another.

There were marching bands, concerts, the presentation of medals and the keys to the city. A line of eighty automobiles—all the newest model touring cars—streamed across the Main Street Bridge and down through the "Court of Honor." The parade of historical floats, "the greatest street procession ever held in Dayton," stretched two miles.

There were laudatory speeches in abundance, and Wilbur, Orville, Katharine, and Bishop Wright were to be seen prominently present on platforms and reviewing stands. The second day, the Bishop delivered a brief but eloquent invocation in tribute to his sons.

> We have met this day to celebrate an invention—the dream of
> all ages—hitherto deemed impracticable. It suddenly breaks
> on all human vision that man, cleaving the air like a bird, can
> rise to immense heights and reach immeasurable distances.
> And we come to thee, our Father, to ask thy peace to rest on
> this occasion and thy benediction on every heart participat-
> ing in this assembly.

Amazingly, all through both days and as very few were aware, Wilbur and Orville managed to slip deftly in and out of the picture, back and forth to their West Third Street shop, one of the few buildings in town that remained undecorated and where work went on. A correspondent for the *New York Times* who kept close watch on them provided a memorable chronology of how they spent the first day:

9 A.M.—Left their work in the aeroplane shop and in their shirt sleeves went out in the street to hear every whistle and bell in town blow and ring for ten minutes.

9:10 A.M.—Returned to work.

10 A.M.—Drove in a parade to the opening ceremony of the "Homecoming Celebration."

11 A.M.—Returned to work.

Noon—Reunion at dinner with Bishop Milton Wright, the father; Miss Katharine Wright, the sister; Reuchlin Wright of Tonganoxie, Kansas, a brother; and Lorin Wright, another brother.

2:30 P.M.—Reviewed a parade given in their honor in the downtown streets.

4:00 P.M.—Worked two hours packing up parts of an aeroplane for shipment to Washington.

8:00 P.M.—Attended a public reception and shook hands with as many Daytonians as could get near them.

9:00 P.M.—Saw a pyrotechnical display on the river front in which their own portraits, 80 feet high and entwined in an American flag, were shown.

It was estimated that in the course of the fireworks, Wilbur and Orville shook hands with more than five thousand people, and according to the *Daily News,* only "the instinct of self preservation compelled them to cease."

Less than forty-eight hours later, the festivities at an end, the brothers were packed and on the train to Washington to resume the trials at Fort Myer. Shipment of the plane had been taken care of. Charlie Taylor was already on the scene.

II.

It was six-thirty the extremely warm evening of June 26, as Wilbur and Orville sat waiting on the starting rail in the parade ground at Fort Myer. Beside them their white-winged machine stood ready for flight. Farther off, behind a rope at the edge of the field, some four thousand people including men of known importance to the nation, stood, according to one account, "pawing the ground" for something to happen. Hundreds of them had been there since three o'clock.

The Senate had adjourned so its members could see the flight. Others waiting included high-ranking army officers; ambassadors; the son of the president, Charlie Taft; and Speaker of the House Joseph Cannon, whose word, as said, was "open sesame to the Treasury vaults."

Wilbur had assigned to himself full responsibility for seeing that all was in order. Given the heat, he had dispensed with his customary coat and tie. His hands and face were grimy, his work trousers grease-stained, and perspiration streamed down his face.

Orville, by contrast, was described as looking natty as the prize guest of a yachting party. "His coat was buttoned tightly about his slender form, as if it were a mistake about its being hot," wrote the *Washington Herald*. "Altogether he . . . exhaled the atmosphere of a man who finds himself on the top layer of the upper crust of the crème de la crème of all that is worthwhile."

The brothers were waiting for the wind to settle down. Again the wind would be the deciding factor, the wind would have the final say, no matter that most of the United States Senate and several thousand others were being kept waiting.

Orville got up and walked away toward the shed looking nervous. Then Wilbur walked off a while. Then both returned to sit again and chat with a small group of army officers. "She's blowing at a 16-mile clip," Wilbur told an inquiring reporter. "That's far too stiff for a first flight with a new machine." He looked windward again and sniffed the air.

"Take her back to the shed," he said.

"There is always an element of uncertainty in aviation as far as it has advanced," Wilbur explained to a writer for the *Washington Post*. "People must remember that this machine has never been flown before, and also that my brother has not been up in the air since his accident last year. They can't blame me for wanting the first flight to be made under conditions as nearly ideal as possible."

No one with a keen sense of dramatic effect, wrote the *Washington Herald*, could have created a better scene to demonstrate the "utter immunity of the two brothers from the fumes of importunity and the intoxication of an august assemblage."

Uniformed army signalmen gathered "like pallbearers" and wheeled the plane away, and four thousand spectators departed, many expressing opinions, including one senator, who was heard to say of the brothers, "I'm damned if I don't admire their independence. We don't mean anything to them, and there are a whole lot of reasons why we shouldn't."

That same day, Bishop Wright and brother Reuchlin arrived in Washington, the Bishop having acquired two new suits and two new shirts for the expedition.

Late the afternoon of June 29, Wilbur had "no quarrels" with the weather, and shortly before six o'clock Orville finally took to the air. The crowd, noticeably smaller than three days before, but still numbering several thousand, saw the plane waver, struggling, as it skimmed over the grass for no more than 75 feet, then, at a height of about 15 feet, tilt sharply to the right and its wing touch the ground, at which point Orville cut the engine and the machine came down in a cloud of dust.

A second and third flight were hardly better. Finally, on the fourth try, a flight lasting all of 40 seconds, the plane reached an altitude of 25 feet and took a turn down the field and back. Still it was enough to evoke cheers and automobile horns.

Orville and Wilbur were both in fine spirits now, perfectly confident the machine would prove a success, and that Orville would remain at the controls. He would do no flying at Fort Myer, Wilbur told reporters. That was Orville's job. But being "big brother," he would do the "bossing."

A machine was like a horse, Wilbur said. "If it's new, you have to get used to it before it will do just as you want it to. You have to learn its peculiarities." As a result of the day's test flights, it was discovered that one important "peculiarity" was that the ignition, or "sparker," was being shaken loose by vibrations, and thus the motor had too little power.

The next two days, while Wilbur, Orville, and Charlie Taylor worked on the engine, the Bishop and Reuchlin went to the Smithsonian to look at "all manner of birds, Ostrich, Emu, Condor, etc.," as the Bishop recorded in his diary.

Another day, when Orville took off again, the plane climbed only 20 feet and after a distance of 200 feet hit the ground hard enough to smash one skid.

Then, on July 2, at an elevation of 80 to 100 feet and at about the same point over the hangar where the propeller had broken the previous September and Orville's plane had plunged to the ground, the engine suddenly stopped dead. And though this time he was able to glide "nicely" down, he hit a small thorn tree, ripping open a good-sized portion of the plane's lower wing fabric. Then the machine fell heavily, breaking both skids. Fortunately, Orville was not hurt.

Again, as the previous September, reporters and some of the spectators rushed to the crash, as did Wilbur, who, seeing a photographer by the wrecked plane, lost his noted self-control, just as he had with the photographer at Le Mans, picked up a stick and threw it at the man, then demanded he turn over the exposed photographic plate, which he did.

It had not been a good day. (Wilbur would later apologize to the photographer who, it turned out, was an official with the War Department.) But the brothers had had more than a little experience with adversity and, as so often before, refused to give up.

The next day, Orville went off to Dayton to prepare a new wing covering and by July 7 was back at Fort Myer, where the work resumed. On July 21, Katharine arrived to join the brothers and that afternoon watched Orville make a short, 10-minute flight at an estimated speed of 44 miles per hour, or faster than Wilbur had ever flown in Europe, as she happily reported to those at home.

———

On July 25, a Sunday and as customary a day off for the Wright brothers, came stunning news. In a frail, under-powered monoplane, his No. XI, the French aviator Louis Blériot had flown the English Channel. He had taken off from Les Baraques, near Calais, shortly before five in the morning, and landed in the Northfield Meadow by Dover Castle, covering a distance over water of 23 miles in just under 20 minutes.

As it happened, Hart Berg and Charles de Lambert were at Dover at the same time and not far from where Blériot landed. De Lambert, too, had been planning to fly the Channel and he and Berg had come to look over possible landing places.

A porter had awakened them at quarter to five that morning to say the wireless man at the hotel had just received a message that Blériot had left France, and as Berg wrote in a long letter to Wilbur and Orville, he and de Lambert were downstairs and on the beach inside three minutes. Only minutes after that a telephone message was received that Blériot had landed on the other side of Dover Castle.

"You have had all the details from the papers," Berg continued in his letter. "I can only supplement the fact that I had a long talk with Blériot afterwards, in fact he used my room to wash up in, and the rest of the day wore my clothes.

> He told me that he had never been so thrown about in his life, as when he got into this valley. He made two complete circles, and his machine was pointing out to sea when he came to the ground. The front chassis was wrecked, the propeller blades broken, but the wings and tail of his monoplane were intact. Blériot was not hurt.

From Washington, Katharine wrote to assure the Bishop that the brothers were not at all disturbed by Blériot's flight. And, as widely reported on both sides of the Atlantic, the brothers joined in giving Blériot due credit for his performance, which they characterized as "remarkable." "I know him well," Wilbur said in an interview with the *New York Times*, "and he is just the kind of man to accomplish such an undertaking. He is apparently without fear, and what he sets out to do he generally accomplishes."

Orville noted the many accidents Blériot had had with a machine over which he had so little control and expressed amazement that he had succeeded. Wilbur was asked if he and Orville would be making any attempts to win some of the prizes to be offered at the European air meets such as that at Reims. No, they would not, said Wilbur. Their time would be put to better use, though what that was he did not say.

All the same, throughout France, indeed throughout much of the world, Blériot's flight was taken as only a prelude to the very burgeoning of French aviation that the *New York Times* had made so much of earlier in the year.

As if by magic, everything started to work at Fort Myer as it was meant to. On the evening of July 27, Orville took off with Lieutenant Frank Lahm as passenger on an official endurance trial and in an hour and 12 minutes flew around the field 79 times, at an altitude of 150 feet, not only passing the test but breaking a world record that Wilbur had set at Le Mans the year before. An estimated eight thousand spectators saw him take off and among them was President Taft.

On Friday, July 30, Orville flew what was the official cross-country speed trial required by the army. The course covered from Fort Myer to Alexandria, Virginia, a distance out and back of 10 miles. Records of the speed flown varied, from 42 to 45 miles per hour, but there was no question that Orville passed the test.

An especially smooth landing was made to the accompaniment of honking horns and cheering. Wilbur rushed to the plane, his face covered with a broad smile. Their contract with the War Department would be signed. The price to be paid by the department was $30,000—a figure that made headlines—but far more importantly their own country was at long last committed to their achievement.

"Orv finished the Fort Myer business in a blaze of glory," wrote Katharine, who ten months earlier, sitting by his bedside there at the post hospital, had wondered if he might ever have strength enough to walk again.

III.

As reported in the *Chicago Tribune,* the eager interest shown by the French people in the progress of aviation could hardly be appreciated in America, and foremost among that summer's scheduled aeronautic events was the Reims "congress of aviators where it is expected great things will be done."

It was to be the world's first international air race, and financed entirely by France's champagne industry. Its official title was "La Grande Semaine d'Aviation de la Champagne," and among the French aviation stars to take part were Henri Farman, Louis Blériot, Léon Delagrange, two of Wilbur Wright's protégés, Charles de Lambert and Paul Tissandier (flying French-built Wright planes), as well as the American Glenn Curtiss, who had been chosen to participate by the American Aero Club when the Wright brothers declined.

At age thirty-one, Curtiss was a lean, shy, intensely serious competitor who, like the Wrights, had started out as a bicycle mechanic in his hometown of Hammondsport, New York, then began building and racing motorcycles. (He became the first acclaimed American motorcycle champion, "the fastest man in the world," achieving speeds on his motorcycle as high as 130 miles an hour.)

His interest in aviation had begun when a balloonist named Tom Baldwin asked him to build a lightweight motor for a dirigible. Once, in September 1906, while in Dayton, Baldwin and Curtiss had visited Wilbur and Orville at their shop. Baldwin had thought Curtiss asked the brothers far too many questions, but, as he later said, they "had the frankness of schoolboys." The year after, Curtiss met Alexander Graham Bell, who made him "Director of Experiments" for the Aerial Experiment Association.

In 1909, with a wealthy aviation enthusiast who had worked with Oc-

tave Chanute and Samuel Langley, Augustus Herring, Curtiss formed
the Herring-Curtiss Company to build flying machines. Those they built
relied on movable flaps on the wings—ailerons, "little wings"—instead
of wing warping, to control rolling and banking. The idea had occurred
earlier to a young French engineer, Robert Esnault-Pelterie, and had been
tried by Santos-Dumont, Blériot, and others. Alexander Graham Bell, too,
had become interested, but whether on his own or having heard about
Esnault-Pelterie, is not clear. Also, it had already been described for all
to see by the Wrights as an alternative to wing warping in their patent
published in 1906.

But for Curtiss at Reims, speed would be the point and the small, new
biplane he would fly had been built strictly for that, with a powerful, lightweight engine.

Anyone wanting proof of the pace of change in the new century had
only to consider that just one year before, in August 1908, at Le Mans, all
the excitement had been about one man only, Wilbur Wright, flying one
airplane before about 150 people to start with. This August at Reims, a
total of twenty-two pilots would take off in as many planes, before colossal
grandstands accommodating fifty thousand people.

The grand opening took place Sunday, August 22, and by then Orville
and Katharine had once more sailed for Europe, heading this time for
Berlin, the brothers having concluded that demonstrations there were a
necessity. Orville, as a result of his "blaze of glory," was the one in most de-
mand. Wilbur remained in Dayton, concentrating on motors with Charlie
Taylor, and seeing to business of the kind he most disliked, including the
commencement, in mid-August, of a lawsuit against the Herring-Curtiss
Company for violation of Wright patents.

Events at Reims created an even greater sensation than promised. By
the last days the crowds numbered 200,000, four times the capacity of the
grandstands. The contestants flew higher, farther, and faster than anyone
ever had, breaking every record set by the Wright brothers in the past year,
and the biggest winner, the most celebrated of the contestants, was Glenn
Curtiss, who won the prize for speed.

Nor was the excitement limited to France and the rest of Europe, as
was clear from the American press. "The great meeting at Reims has been
an electrifying, delirious success" (New York Sun); "The scoffers scoff no

longer" (*Washington Herald*); "The aviation tournament is only a hint of what the future will soon witness when the sky shall become the common highway" (*Cincinnati Times-Star*); "This week at Reims marks a new epoch and one of the most ambitious phases of human history" (*Atlanta Constitution*).

Overnight Curtiss was the new American hero. But only a week later crowds as large as 200,000 turned out at Tempelhof Field in Berlin to see Orville fly, and in the course of his demonstration flights over the next several days, Orville, accompanied by a student pilot, flew for an hour and 35 minutes, a new world's record for a flight with a passenger. And at the same time Wilbur had signed on to make his first-ever public flight in the United States, in New York. It was to be part of a celebration commemorating the three-hundredth anniversary of Henry Hudson's ascent of the Hudson River and the hundredth anniversary of Robert Fulton's first steamboat on the Hudson. Wilbur was to be paid $15,000. Glenn Curtiss, too, was to participate in the event.

———

Writing to Orville aboard the train to New York on September 18, Wilbur reviewed some of the precautions he might take, on the chance he would be forced to land his plane in the waters off Manhattan. An idea he had of using rubber tubes no longer made sense. "So I have gone back to my old plan of mounting a canoe under the center of the machine, well forward," he wrote, adding, "Of course, I do not expect to come down, but if I do I will be reasonably safe." The canoe would be purchased in New York. The plane had already been shipped to the army base of Governors Island in New York Harbor, where Charlie Taylor would be joining him.

The great sweep of New York Harbor and the Hudson River had become a spectacle beyond anything ever seen there, with twenty American battleships at anchor, a squadron of the Royal Navy, naval vessels from France, Germany, the Netherlands, Mexico, and Argentina, in addition to ferryboats, tenders, colliers, all manner of river craft, and the giant luxury liner *Lusitania*—no fewer than 1,595 vessels.

Added to all this was the promise that for the first time New Yorkers were to witness airplane flights over their waters.

On Governors Island in Upper New York Bay, half a mile southeast of

Manhattan, two hangars had been provided, almost side by side, one for Wilbur, the other for Curtiss. When Curtiss arrived to look things over, he and Wilbur greeted each other cordially enough and talked for five minutes or so, mainly about the events at Reims. Wilbur excused himself from shaking hands, saying his hands were too greasy. At about this point Guglielmo Marconi, inventor of the wireless telegraph, appeared on the scene and was so thrilled to meet Wilbur he insisted on shaking his hand, greasy or not. It had been arranged that whenever Wilbur or Curtiss was about to take flight, Marconi would send a wireless message from Governors Island to the warships in the harbor and they in turn would raise flags as a signal to other ships and all on land.

Curtiss soon departed for Hammondsport in upstate New York, where he was to be honored with an all-out homecoming.

One day the reporters who hung about as close as permitted hoping for a chance to talk to Wilbur saw some small boys from the garrison approaching the guards and expected to see the children rebuffed as they had been. Instead they saw Wilbur, "a kindly smile" on his face, welcome them, then through the open doors watched as he "explained every detail on the machine."

"I have been here about a week and have the machine almost ready to fly," Wilbur wrote Katharine on September 26. He was staying at the stylish Park Avenue Hotel, but getting his lunches at the Officers Club on Governors Island.

> Yesterday was the big naval parade. . . . In the evening the boats were illuminated with millions of electric lights and the same was true of many of the great buildings. For ten miles the river was an almost solid mass of steamboats and but for the fact that they were nearly all outlined with electric lights, it would have been impossible to navigate.

To reporters who descended on him, Wilbur said he had not come to astonish the world but to give everybody a chance to see what the airplane was like in the air. Asked if he thought it would be perilous to fly over a harbor so filled with ships, he said an airplane ought to be able to go anywhere.

Glenn Curtiss returned from upstate late in the day on September 28, and camped that night in the hangar with his plane on Governors Island, in order to make an early test flight the next morning. As it was he made his flight shortly after six o'clock, with only a friend and one army officer as witnesses. He flew 300 yards, then went back to upstate New York.

Wilbur, who had spent the night at his hotel in the city, did not get started with his preliminary tinkering until eight o'clock then, about nine o'clock, took off on a 7-minute practice run, circling Governors Island, the white-and-silver Flyer looking much as always except for the 14-foot, canvas-wrapped, red canoe that hung beneath. Thus the newest form of transportation was making its debut over American waters with one of the oldest of all forms conspicuously in readiness, in case of trouble.

Soon after landing, Wilbur announced he would fly again. Wireless signals went out, signal flags went up, and off he went. Instead of heading toward the mouth of the Hudson, as expected, he swung to the west into the wind and, flying over two ferryboats, headed straight for the Statue of Liberty on Bedloe's Island, circled the statue, and sailed low over the *Lusitania*, which was then heading down the harbor, outward bound to Liverpool. Thousands of people were watching. Battery Park at the tip of Manhattan was thick with spectators, and passengers on deck on the *Lusitania* frantically waved hats, scarfs, handkerchiefs as Wilbur passed over their heads.

He maneuvered his plane with perfect control through a whole series of dips and turns. But it was the spectacle of Wilbur Wright and his flying machine circling the Statue of Liberty that made the most powerful impression, which would be talked about, written about, and remembered more than anything, as a writer for the *New York Evening Sun* tried to express in a front-page account:

> Once his great aeroplane, so near the horizon that it seemed one with the ocean gulls among which it flew . . . [was] just above the level of the feet of the Statue of Liberty. An instant later it appeared at the level of the statue's breast and then passed in front on an even keel.
>
> In the air Wright seemed to pause for a moment to pay the homage of an American aviator to the lady who attests his

country's destinies. Then suddenly turning eastward with the wind, he sped rapidly over the waves while the harbor craft shrieked their welcomes, and the cheering men and women ashore bore witness that our Lady of Liberty had been visited by one of her children in a vessel needing only the winds on which to sail.

Harper's Weekly, "The Journal of Civilization," would feature on its next cover a dramatic photograph of Wilbur and the plane circling the Statue of Liberty with the caption, "A New Kind of Gull in New York Harbor."

"Goes pretty well, Charlie," Wilbur was reported to have said to Charlie Taylor, when, after a smooth landing, he climbed from the plane back on Governors Island. "Looks alright to me, Will," replied Charlie.

The next day came news from Potsdam, Germany, that Orville had flown to an altitude of 984 feet, higher than anyone had yet flown in an airplane.

Stiff winds out of the north kept both Wilbur and Glenn Curtiss grounded on Governors Island for two days, Saturday and Sunday, and by then Curtiss announced he had to leave to keep a contract in St. Louis. This left only Wilbur to make the flight up the Hudson River that had been promised and all were waiting for.

The morning of Monday, October 4, though the wind out of the north had eased off to a degree, it was still blowing at 16 miles per hour, or more than Wilbur would have preferred. Sensing it was only going to increase again, he decided to fly. The plane was brought out of the hangar and he looked it over. Finding the gasoline tank not full, he took an old can and filled it himself.

At 9:53, he took off from Governors Island, the emergency canoe still hanging from beneath the plane. The one difference this time was a tiny American flag fixed to the rudder. It had been sent to him by Katharine with the request that he fly it over New York.

Again the wireless messages went off. Again signal flags were flying, and again whistles shrieked, foghorns sounded. Work came to a standstill in much of the city and there was a "stampede" to the windows and rooftops of office buildings to see the spectacle in the sky of "wonderful Wilbur Wright, the Dayton aviator," as one New York paper was calling him.

From the new skyscrapers like the Metropolitan Life Tower the view of the harbor and the Hudson River was panoramic. Most spectacular of all was the outlook from the upper floors of the forty-seven-story Singer Building on Broadway, which, once completed, would be the tallest skyscraper on earth.

When Wilbur headed across the harbor and turned northward into the wind heading for the Hudson River the excitement grew even greater. He had climbed by then to about 150 feet and was moving at a speed of about 36 miles per hour. But on reaching the river, as he later recounted, he began getting air currents such as he had never had to cope with. They were coming off the skyscrapers and so strong and dangerous he had to drop elevation "considerably" and hug the west, or New Jersey, side of the river.

"I went to a height just a little above the ferryboats until I reached the battleships, and then I skimmed over their funnels. I passed so close to the funnels that I could smell the smoke from them."

Asked later if one of the British battleships fired a salute in his honor, Wilbur said he did not know what it was, but something made an "awful noise."

Seeing the dome of Grant's Tomb on the right side of the river at West 122nd Street, he decided he had gone far enough, and after making a large 180 degree turn, he started south, back down the river, this time moving considerably faster with the wind behind him. "I think I came back in half the time. . . . I hugged the water much closer and kept further toward the Jersey shore as I passed the downtown skyscrapers."

His return trip was greeted with enthusiasm as great or greater than that upriver. Now the Jersey hills were black with people, and piers and building roofs on the Manhattan side were packed to capacity. It was estimated a million people were watching.

At precisely 10:26 A.M., Wilbur landed at Governors Island within a few feet of the spot where he had taken off. His time in the air was 33 minutes and 33 seconds. The distance traveled to Grant's Tomb and back was approximately 20 miles, his average speed 36 miles per hour.

In spite of stiff winds, skyscraper gusts, whistles, horns, shrieking crowds, and battleship salutes, he had done it. How formidable the wind problem had been could be measured by the small American flag Katharine had given him. Brand-new at the start of the flight, it had returned in shreds.

Charlie Taylor told reporters how extremely concerned he had been the whole time Wilbur was "up."

> I was staring with both eyes square at that big flag over the Singer building. Sometimes it layed down and hugged the pole, and then I knew Wilbur was having it good. And sometimes it stood out pretty near even and I knew he was having his troubles. And once it flipped right out and the tip began to point upward like it did all day Saturday. I began to tremble. For I didn't know what Wilbur could do against a gust like that.

No, he had not conquered the air, Wilbur remarked to the press as he walked away. "A man who works for the immediate present and its immediate rewards is nothing but a fool."

Shortly afterward, to much surprise, he announced he would fly again that afternoon and this time it would be much farther, an hour-long flight in which he would circle Manhattan. But about four o'clock as he and Charlie Taylor were cranking up the plane the head of one of the engine's piston rods blew off with a terrible roar, and the head, which was about six inches long and four wide, "flew like a cannon ball" no more than 20 inches from Wilbur's head.

To Charlie Taylor he said, "It's a darn good thing that didn't happen up in the air." The plane was taken away. The New York performances were over.

Talking with a correspondent for *Scientific American* magazine a little later, in the gathering dusk of the October afternoon, Wilbur was asked what the explosion of the engine indicated and what direction the development of aviation would take in the future. The broken cylinder was only "an incident," Wilbur said. As for the future, direction was the thing: "High flying."

> We must get up clear of the belt of disturbed air which re-
> sults from the irregularities of the earth's surface. From now
> on you will see a great increase in the average elevation at
> which aviators will take their flights; for not only will they
> find in the higher strata more favorable atmospheric condi-
> tions, but in case of motor trouble, they will have more time
> and distance in which to recover control or make a safe glide
> to earth.

"On Monday I made a flight up the Hudson to Grant's Tomb and back to Governor's Island," Wilbur wrote to his father three days later from College Park, Maryland. "It was an interesting trip and at times rather exciting." And that was that. He had come to College Park to begin train-ing U.S. Army pilots.

On Monday, October 18, two weeks after Wilbur's flight up the Hudson, Orville and Katharine were in Paris. Their events in Germany success-fully concluded, they had stopped for a brief stay en route home, and by all evidence were unaware that shortly before five o'clock that after-noon a Wright plane would appear in the sky causing a sensation such as Paris had never experienced. It was not only the first airplane to fly over the city, but the first to fly directly over any city. Close as he was to New York on his flight up the Hudson and back, Wilbur had flown over water only.

The Comte de Lambert, having told almost no one his plans, not even his wife, had taken off from Port-Aviation at Juvisy, fifteen miles southeast of Paris. He was spotted first in the golden afternoon sky by hundreds of visitors high up on the Eiffel Tower. Then came shouts from the streets below, *"L'Aéroplane! L'Aéroplane!"*

One of the most memorable descriptions of the spectacle was provided by the American writer Edith Wharton, who had just stepped from her chauffeur-driven limousine at the front entrance of the Hôtel de Crillon on the Place de la Concorde and noticed several people looking into the sky, as she recounted in a letter to a friend:

> And what do you think happened to me last Monday? I was getting out of the motor at the door of the H. de Crillon when I saw two or three people looking into the air. I looked also and there was an aeroplane, high up against the sky . . . and emerging on the Place de la Concorde. It sailed obliquely across the Place, incredibly high above the obelisk, against a golden sunset, with a new moon between flitting clouds, and crossing the Seine in the direction of the Pantheon, lost itself in a flight of birds that was just crossing the sky, reappeared far off, a speck against the clouds and disappeared at last into twilight. And it was the Comte de Lambert in a Wright bi-plane, who had just flown across from Juvisy—and it was the first time that an aeroplane has ever crossed the great city!! Think "what a soul was mine"—and what a setting in which to see one's first aeroplane flight!

What she had neglected to say was that the Comte de Lambert had soared over the top of the Eiffel Tower, the tallest structure in the world, and thus had been flying at an elevation of at least 1,300 to 1,400 feet, "high up" indeed.

Word of what happened had already reached Juvisy by the time de Lambert returned and landed. Thousands had gathered to welcome him. Stepping from the plane, "pale but radiant," he was instantly engulfed by reporters and an adoring crowd. There also, to his great surprise, were Orville and Katharine Wright. How they heard the news and how they got to Juvisy are not known.

De Lambert insisted he was not the hero of the hour. "Here is the real man," he said, turning to Orville. "I am only the jockey. He is the inventor," by which he meant both Orville and Wilbur. "Long live the United States! It is to that country that I owe my success."

Once Wilbur, Orville, and Katharine reached home, they hardly had time to unpack before their time and attention were taken up with business decisions and patent issues, Wilbur heading off to New York one day, Washington another, then Wilbur and Orville going together to New York, then Wilbur going alone again. And except for Christmas, so it continued on into the new year.

A Wright Company for the manufacture of airplanes was incorporated, with offices on Fifth Avenue in New York. Ground was broken for a Wright manufacturing plant in Dayton. There were more dinners in their honor, more medals and awards, including the first Langley Medal, given by the Smithsonian. And there were more patent suits.

With the increase in the number of people flying, there were increases in serious accidents and deaths. In France aviators Eugène Lefebvre, Ferdinand Ferber, and Léon Delagrange were all killed in crashes.

Extremely distressing, too, for Wilbur was an unfortunate falling-out with Octave Chanute that began in January 1910 and stretched into spring. Chanute thought the Wrights had "made a blunder" bringing suit against Glenn Curtiss and said so in a letter to the editor of *Aeronautics.* Specifically Chanute did not think that the idea of wing warping was original with the Wrights.

In a letter dated January 20, Wilbur stated clearly to Chanute, "It is our view that morally the world owes its almost universal use of our system of lateral control entirely to us." In response Chanute wrote, "I am afraid, my friend, that your usually sound judgment has been warped by the desire for great wealth."

Besides, Chanute was offended by something Wilbur had said in a speech in Boston about how he, Chanute, had "turned up" in the Wright shop in Dayton in 1901. This, Chanute felt, gave the impression that he had thrust himself upon Wilbur and omitted to say that Wilbur had been the first to write to Chanute in 1900, asking for information.

Wilbur and Orville found Chanute's letter "incredible," and in one of his longest letters ever to Chanute, Wilbur let him know. Concerning Chanute's charge that greed had taken hold of the brothers, Wilbur dismissed it saying simply, "you are the only person acquainted with us who has ever made such an accusation." He centered his considerable fury instead on the way Chanute had given the French the impression that he and Orville were "mere pupils and dependents" of his, and the fact that Chanute had never once until now expressed any question about the brothers' claim to the invention of wing warping.

> Neither in 1901, nor in the five years following, did you in any way intimate to us that our general system of lateral control had long been part of the [flying] art. . . . If the idea was really old in the art, it is somewhat remarkable that a system so important that individual ownership of it is considered to threaten strangulation of the art was not considered worth mentioning then, nor embodied in any machine built prior to ours.

Plainly wishing the dispute to be resolved, Wilbur closed on a warmer note. "If anything can be done to straighten matters out to the satisfaction of both you and us, we are not only willing but anxious to do our part. . . . We have no wish to quarrel with a man toward whom we ought to preserve a feeling for gratitude."

When nearly three months passed with no response from Chanute, Wilbur wrote again to say, "My brother and I do not form many intimate friendships, and do not lightly give them up.

> I believed that unless we could understand exactly how you felt, and you could understand how we felt, our friendship would tend to grow weaker instead of stronger. Through ignorance or thoughtlessness, each would be touching the other's sore spots and causing unnecessary pain. We prize too highly the friendship which meant so much in the years of our early struggles to willingly see it worn away by uncorrected misunderstandings, which might be corrected by a frank discussion.

This time Chanute answered in a matter of days to say Wilbur's letter had been gratifying, that he had been in bad health, and was about to sail for Europe. "I hope, upon my return from Europe, that we will be able to resume our former relations."

———

Except for one week in February, it had been an unusually mild winter in Dayton. On February 16, as Bishop Wright recorded in his diary, more than a foot of snow fell. And it snowed "very much" again on February 18. But "considerable thawing" followed the day after, and he spent time breaking icicles off the roof. But with the first week of March the snow was "passing away." One "bright, mild day" followed after another. His diary entries recorded: "Beautiful weather," "Fine weather," "Spring weather," "most beautiful weather," on into April.

Dayton's West Side, Hawthorn Street, and Wright homestead looked as they had looked so often before in springtime. Gone were the homecoming flags and bunting and Japanese lanterns of the previous fall. All was as before. The West Third Street shop and the outlook from the interurban trolley on the ride out to Simms Station and Huffman Prairie were as ever.

So, too, were the Wright brothers. For all they had seen and done, the unprecedented glory bestowed on them, it had by all signs neither changed them nor turned their heads in the least. There was no boasting, no preening, no getting too big for their britches, as said, and it was this, almost as much as their phenomenal achievements, that was so greatly admired. As one writer on the scene put it, "They are the imperturbable 'men from home,' as always." Katharine as well, for all her travels and the attention she had received, seemed no different than always.

> Pau was a mighty interesting place—Miss Wright stoutly insists on that, too, in spite of her brother Wilbur's dry smile; and there was pretty country in Germany, yes he will admit that, but if you want to see pretty country, you don't have to go any farther then their own field at Simms's. Ohio is plenty good enough for him. And Orville agrees, mildly suggesting,

however, that you really can't see it at its best till you get up about a thousand feet.

If the brothers might have had any cause for concern or annoyance, it would have been the lawsuit against the Curtiss Company over their patents. But they were confident in their case, for which there was already strong support in the press and in the country. As said in the *New York Times*, it was "a highly significant fact that, until the Wrights succeeded, all attempts at flight with heavier-than-air machines were dismal failures, but since they showed that the thing could be done everybody seems able to do it."

Nor had the argument that patents by the Wrights would retard the progress of aeronautics made much headway. "The insistence of Professor Bell upon his rights did not retard the growth in the use of the telephone," wrote the *Christian Science Monitor.* "Thomas Edison's numerous suits for protection of his inventions have not kept any of them out of the market." And as both Wilbur and Orville knew better than anyone, if ever the development of an idea had been thoroughly documented with written records and photographs nearly every step of the way, it was theirs.

———

Wednesday, May 25, 1910, was a particularly "nice day" in Dayton, noted Bishop Wright in his diary. It was also to be a very big day for the Wright family.

The brothers had invited the Aeroplane Club of Dayton, as well as friends, neighbors, anyone interested, to come to Huffman Prairie to see Orville fly, and the crowd that came numbered two or three thousand. The interurban was jammed. Automobiles lined the roadway by the field where ice cream and sandwich vendors had set up for business.

As later reported, Orville performed with his machine in such manner as to keep the spectators on tiptoe the whole time. "One minute he would be grazing the ground and the next shooting up in the air like an arrow." He did figure eights, twists and turns all in the most "remarkable manner." Most astonishing of all, he flew to an unbelievable height of 2,720 feet. And all the Wrights—the Bishop, Wilbur, Katharine, Reuchlin,

Lorin and his wife and children—were on hand to see such proof of the genius of the brothers' achievements performed there on home ground before a home crowd.

In all the years they had been working together Wilbur and Orville had never once flown together, so if something were to go wrong and one of them should be killed, the other would live to carry on with the work. But on this day at Huffman Prairie, where they had developed the first practical flying machine ever, the two of them, seated side by side, took off into the air with Orville at the controls.

To many then and later, it seemed their way of saying they had accomplished all they had set out to do and so at last saw no reason to postpone any longer enjoying together the thrill of flight.

Of the immediate family of 7 Hawthorn Street, only Bishop Wright had yet to fly. Nor had anyone of his age ever flown anywhere on earth. He had been with the brothers from the start, helping in every way he could, never losing faith in them or their aspirations. Now, at eighty-two, with the crowd cheering, he walked out to the starting point, where Orville, without hesitation, asked him to climb aboard.

They took off, soaring over Huffman Prairie at about 350 feet for a good six minutes, during which the Bishop's only words were, "Higher, Orville, higher!"

EPILOGUE

E xcept for one brief training flight he gave a German pilot in Berlin in June of 1911, Wilbur Wright was not to fly ever again, so taken up was he with business matters and acrimonious lawsuits. The Wright Company, from the start, demanded a great deal of time and attention. But it was the interminable patent infringement suits that put the most strain on both brothers. "When we think what we might have accomplished if we had been able to devote this time to experiments," Wilbur wrote to a friend in France, "we feel very sad, but it is always easier to deal with things than with men, and no one can direct his life entirely as he would choose."

Of far the greatest importance to both—more than the money at stake—was to secure just and enduring credit for having invented the airplane. It was their reputation at stake and that mattered most. Their pride of achievement, quite understandably, was great. Eventually nine suits were brought by them, three brought against them. Over time they won every case in the American courts.

Octave Chanute, who had not returned from his trip to Europe until October of 1910, died at his home on November 23, at age seventy-eight, before he and Wilbur had had an opportunity to see one another again. On hearing the news, Wilbur boarded a train to Chicago to attend the funeral and later wrote a long tribute to Chanute published in *Aeronautics*, leaving no doubt of how he felt.

> His writings were so lucid as to provide an intelligent understanding of the nature of the problems of flight to a vast

number of persons who would probably never have given the matter study otherwise. . . . In patience and goodness of heart he has rarely been surpassed. Few men were more universally respected and loved.

In 1911 Wilbur spent a full six months in Europe attending to business and legal matters. Otherwise, he was either on the move back and forth to New York or Washington, or tied down at board meetings in Dayton. And it all began to tell on him. In Orville's words, he would "come home white."

Meanwhile, the family had decided to build a new and far grander house, very like an antebellum Old South mansion in the suburb of Oakwood, just southeast of Dayton. Virtually all the planning with the architect was overseen by Orville and Katharine during Wilbur's time in Europe. Wilbur's one known expression of interest in the project was to request a room and bathroom of his own.

In the first week of May 1912, thoroughly worn down in body and spirit, Wilbur took ill, running a high fever day after day. It proved once again to be the dreaded typhoid fever. Conscious of the condition he was in, he sent for a lawyer and dictated his will.

One or another of the family were faithfully at his bedside. "Wilbur is no better," recorded Bishop Wright on May 18. Wilbur was "sinking," he wrote May 28.

Wilbur Wright died in his room at home at 7 Hawthorn Street at 3:15 in the morning, Thursday, May 30, 1912. He was forty-five years old.

A short life, full of consequences [the Bishop wrote]. An unfailing intellect, imperturbable temper, great self reliance and as great modesty, seeing the right clearly, pursuing it steadily, he lived and died.

Phone calls and telegrams of condolence poured in from friends and neighbors and all parts of the country and abroad—a thousand telegrams by that afternoon. Moving tributes were published in the days that followed. According to one Dayton paper, the quantity of flowers delivered to the house would have filled a railroad boxcar.

Though the family would have preferred a private funeral, a public viewing of Wilbur's wasted remains took place at the First Presbyterian Church during which an estimated 25,000 people passed by the coffin. At the conclusion of a brief service, burial followed at the family plot at Woodland Cemetery.

> Wilbur is dead and buried! [the Bishop wrote]. We are all stricken. It does not seem possible he is gone. Probably Orville and Katharine felt his loss most. They say little.

For the next five years Bishop Wright continued to live with Orville and Katharine. Though no longer traveling on church work, he remained remarkably active, his life, like theirs, made notably different in a variety of ways as a result of the family's greatly enhanced affluence. He delighted in long outings in Orville's new automobile with Orville at the wheel, and in the spring of 1914, after forty-two years at 7 Hawthorn Street, the three of them moved into the newly completed, white-brick, pillared mansion in Oakwood, which they had proudly named Hawthorn Hill. In 1916, Orville treated them to a summer-long vacation in Canada in a rented house on an island in Georgian Bay. So enjoyable was the time that Orville bought an island of their own for further summers.

The Bishop kept on reading, writing articles for religious publications, and enjoying his morning walks. One October Saturday he marched with Katharine and Orville in a Dayton Women's Suffrage parade. As near as he could judge he was the oldest man in the march.

Bishop Milton Wright died at age eighty-eight on April 3, 1917.

Katharine, who never went back to teaching, devoted much of her time to Oberlin College, to causes like the suffragette movement, and to providing all the help she could to Orville. In 1913, she accompanied him on still another trip to Europe, on business to London, Berlin, and Paris.

Attended by the faithful Carrie Grumbach, they lived at Hawthorn Hill, as comfortable with each other as always until 1926. It was then that

Katharine, at age fifty-eight, announced she would marry an old Oberlin classmate, Henry J. Haskell, a widower and journalist with the *Kansas City Star*. As fellow Oberlin board members they had been seeing each other for some time and though Orville knew Haskell and considered him a friend of the family, he turned furious and inconsolable. When Katharine insisted on proceeding with the wedding, held at Oberlin, Orville refused to attend or even to speak to her, feeling he had been betrayed.

Of all Orville's "peculiar spells," this was much the worst, the most regrettable, and for Katharine, painful in the extreme. She moved to Kansas City. Two years later when Orville received word she was dying of pneumonia, he refused to go see her. Only at the last did he change his mind, arriving in time to be with her at the end.

Katharine died on March 3, 1929. Her body was brought back to Dayton and buried with her father, mother, and Wilbur at Woodland Cemetery.

While Wilbur had virtually stopped flying after the flight he and Orville made together at Huffman Prairie in May of 1910, Orville continued piloting Wright planes for another seven years. In September of 1910 he flew over Dayton as no one had until then. A few weeks later, flying a new model Wright "Baby Grand," he attained a speed of 80 miles an hour. As the years passed he began experimenting with a new Wright hydroplane, then returned to Kitty Hawk to conduct gliding experiments, during which he set a soaring record of nearly 10 minutes, a record that would stand for ten years. In 1913, within two months, he made some 100 flights and tried his hand at flying a single-propeller plane. In 1914 he barely escaped being killed when his hydroplane fell into the Miami River.

Orville had hoped to fly for as long as he lived, but had to give it up in 1918 at age forty-six, due to still lingering pains and stiffness caused by the crash at Fort Myer nearly ten years before. By 1918 he had sold the Wright Company and established his own Wright Aeronautical Laboratory in a plain, one-story brick building downtown, where he intended to concentrate his energies on scientific research.

The financial rewards for their efforts and accomplishments had

RMS *Campania,* the luxury ocean liner
on which Wilbur sailed for France in 1907.

694   PARIS. — Vue sur le Jardin des Tuileries.

I am staying at point
marked X.
W. W.

The Jardin des Tuileries in the Paris postcard on which Wilbur marked
with an *X* for those at home the location of his hotel on the rue de Rivoli.

Dressed in a new, custom-tailored suit, Wilbur strikes a
handsome pose in Hart Berg's elegant Paris apartment.

Hart Berg with
his "Exhibit A."

57

58

The dirigible *La Patrie* (The Homeland), one of the
spectacular French achievements of the new air age.

A sociable crowd in the grandstand at the Hunaudières racetrack at Le Mans waits patiently for Wilbur to put on his demonstration.

Le Petit Journal

Le Petit Journal   **5** CENTIMES   SUPPLEMENT ILLUSTRE   **5** CENTIMES   ABONNEMENTS

Le Petit Journal agricole, 5 cent. — La Mode du Petit Journal, 10 cent.
Le Petit Journal illustré de la jeunesse, 10 cent.

On s'abonne sans frais dans tous les bureaux de poste

DIMANCHE 30 AOUT 1908

Dix-neuvième Année

Numéro 926

L'AEROPLANE DE WILBUR WRIGHT EN PLEIN VOL.

The response of the crowd on seeing the "miracle" with their own eyes, as featured on the cover of one of France's popular magazines.

61

Wilbur takes to the air on his triumphant, all-important first flight at Le Mans, Saturday, May 8, 1908.

Wilbur with the immensely helpful Léon Bollée.

62

Orville (in plaid cap) and Lieutenant Thomas E. Selfridge
ready for takeoff at Fort Myer, Virginia, September 17, 1908.

The close association of
Selfridge and Alexander
Graham Bell had led Orville
to distrust the young officer.

Right: Katharine's first letter
to Bishop Wright after her
arrival at Fort Myer to help
Orville in every way possible.

The disastrous crash at Fort Myer, in which Selfridge became
the first fatality in an airplane and Orville was severely injured.

Address me,
Post Hospital,
Ft. Myer, Va.
KW.

Fort Myer, Va., Sept 21, 1908.

Dear Pop,

It has been an impossible to write a line. But now I am getting settled and will write every day. At first, I was pulled and hauled a dozen ways at once for the first few days.

I am staying with Warren Shearer at 1413 Monroe St. N.W. Warren is just about as nice a man as I ever saw and his wife is very fine and interesting. I like them both immensely. They are as good to me as the day is long. It was mighty good not to have to go among strangers.

Orville's injuries are serious not dangerous. He has been fearfully restless and uncomfortable but that is better now that I am practically staying at the Hospital. They do not restrict me a bit. I never saw anything lovelier than the consideration that is shown me by everyone. Major Winter is the head surgeon but he was off on a three days' ride when the accident occurred. So Captain Bailey really has charge of the case, though technically

Wilbur and Edith Berg at Le Mans, as she was about to become the first American woman to go up in an airplane, her long skirts secured at the ankles with a rope in a way that quickly became a fashion sensation.

67

68

Katharine (far left), the Comtesse de Lambert, Orville (with cane), and Wilbur stroll the long promenade at Pau.

Katharine sits beside Wilbur ready for her first takeoff at Pont-Long, February 15, 1909.

69

70

Orville and Wilbur explain their flying machine to King Edward VII at Pont-Long, March 17, 1909.

Wilbur (left) and his best and favorite French "student," the Comte de Lambert.

72

73

A French print showing Louis Blériot setting off on his celebrated flight across the English Channel, July 25, 1909.

Glenn Curtiss, the American aviator who took first prize for speed at the world's first international air race at Reims, France in August 1909.

Wilbur, Orville, and Katharine at the White House, where
President William Howard Taft (center) presented the
brothers with gold medals from the Aero Club of America.

Right: A 1909 tribute to what the brothers meant to the nation by cartoonist Homer Davenport, autographed for Katharine: "The sister of men who have won the admiration of all of us, even to the birds of the air."

Below: With speeches, posters, flags, and bunting, a "Court of Honor" on Main Street and a parade stretching two miles, the welcome home for the Wright brothers surpassed anything ever seen in Dayton.

A Wright plane, flown by the Comte de Lambert, becomes
the first plane ever to appear in the skies over Paris.

On Governors Island in New York Harbor, Wilbur and Charlie Taylor see to
final details, emergency canoe and all, in preparation for Wilbur's flight up the
Hudson River. The American flag provided by Katharine flies at left.

HARPER'S WEEKLY

A JOURNAL OF CIVILIZATION

VOL. LIII   New York, October 9, 1909   No. 2755

A NEW KIND OF GULL IN NEW YORK HARBOR

Wilbur creates a sensation by circling the Statue of Liberty,
symbol of friendship with France and of welcome to America.
Harper's Weekly proclaims him "a new kind of gull."

"The best dividends on the labor invested have invariably
come from seeking more knowledge rather than more power."
Signed Wilbur and Orville Wright, March 12, 1906.

been considerable for the Wright brothers, though not as excessive as many imagined. In his will, Wilbur had left $50,000 each to brothers Reuchlin and Lorin, and to Katharine. The rest of his estate, an estimated $126,000, went to Orville. With the success of the Wright Company and its sale, Orville prospered far more. His total wealth at the time of his death was $1,067,105, or in present-day dollars $10,300,000. Though a fortune then, it hardly compared to that of any number of multimillionaires of the time.

If money had been his and Wilbur's main objective, Orville insisted, they would have tried something in which the chances were brighter. He thought it fair to say he was well-to-do, rather than wealthy, and loved to quote his father: "All the money anyone needs is just enough to prevent one from being a burden to others."

In the years following Wilbur's death, Orville had to face alone the burdens and tedium of continuing lawsuits. Further, he was outraged by an effort of the head of the Smithsonian Institution, Charles D. Walcott, with the help of Glenn Curtiss, to rehabilitate the reputation of Samuel P. Langley and in so doing discredit the Wrights.

Making the case that Langley's failure had been the fault of the launching device for his aerodrome, not the machine itself, the aerodrome was taken out of storage to be tested again. But as was not disclosed, Curtiss oversaw major modifications of the aerodrome, so that when tested once more in 1914 it performed with reasonable success and the Smithsonian endorsed a statement saying, "Professor Samuel P. Langley had actually designed and built the first man-carrying flying machine capable of sustained flight."

Before the aerodrome was sent back to the Smithsonian to be placed on exhibit, Walcott ordered that it be returned in its original 1903 condition.

Orville's fury on learning of what had been done was momentous and altogether justified. Earlier, when he and Wilbur had offered their 1903 Flyer to the Smithsonian, they had been turned down by Walcott. In 1928, Orville sent the 1903 Flyer to England on loan to the Science Museum in London. Only then did the Board of Regents of the Smithsonian at last pass a resolution declaring "to the Wrights belongs the credit of making the first successful flight with a power-propelled heavier-than-air machine carrying a man." But it would be another twenty years before the Wrights' 1903 Flyer was returned from London and presented to the Smithsonian for display, and by then Orville was no longer living.

Of further aggravation were stories of others who had supposedly achieved flight before the Wrights, the most annoying being that of a German American named Gustave Whitehead, who was said to have flown a plane of his own creation in Connecticut in 1901 and 1902. The story was entirely without evidence and wholly untrue, but kept drawing attention as the years passed to the point where Orville finally felt obliged to denounce it himself. In an article titled, "The Mythical Whitehead Flight," published in *U.S. Air Services* in 1945, he made plain that Whitehead was a man of delusions. Strangely, the story still draws attention, despite the fact that there is still no proof.

Advances in aviation all the while had been accelerating faster than Orville or anyone of his generation had thought possible, and starting with World War I to a form of weaponry like nothing before in human experience.

In 1927 young Charles Lindbergh flew the Atlantic to land in Paris, a feat once thought impossible by the Wrights. On his return to America, Lindbergh made a point of coming to Dayton to pay his respects to Orville at Hawthorn Hill, an event that caused excitement in Dayton of a kind not seen since the brothers had made their celebrated return from Europe eighteen years before.

Orville lived to see, too, the horrific death and destruction wrought by the giant bombers of World War II and in several interviews tried as best he could to speak both for himself and for Wilbur.

> We dared to hope we had invented something that would bring lasting peace to the earth. But we were wrong. . . . No, I don't have any regrets about my part in the invention of the airplane, though no one could deplore more than I do the destruction it has caused. I feel about the airplane much the

same as I do in regard to fire. That is I regret all the terrible damage caused by fire, but I think it is good for the human race that someone discovered how to start fires and that we have learned how to put fire to thousands of important uses.

As time went on, Orville grew increasingly inclined to withdraw from society, yet felt obliged to participate in a continuing number of public occasions in his honor, doing so in large measure out of respect for Wilbur's memory. He received honorary degrees from Harvard, the University of Cincinnati, the University of Michigan, and Oberlin College. In 1919 he received an Honorary Master of Arts degree from Yale, the university where once, nearly forty years before, Wilbur had hoped he might enroll.

Orville attended the dedication of the Wright Library in what had been named Katharine Wright Park in Oakwood, and having agreed to the removal of both the Wright bicycle shop and the family home at 7 Hawthorn Street from Dayton to the Henry Ford outdoor museum, Greenfield Village, at Dearborn, Michigan, he attended their formal opening on what would have been Wilbur's seventy-first birthday.

Of the numerous Wright monuments erected, the one dedicated to Wilbur at Le Mans in 1920 was the first. The largest, the Wright Memorial at Kitty Hawk at Kill Devil Hills, was dedicated in 1932 with Orville present to accept it on behalf of both Wilbur and himself. A Wilbur and Orville Wright memorial was created on Wright Brothers Hill overlooking Huffman Prairie, and in 1945 an aircraft carrier, the USS *Wright*, was launched.

Orville remained at Hawthorn Hill, looked after by Carrie Grumbach, and outlived Wilbur by thirty-six years. He lived to see aviation transformed by jet propulsion, the introduction of the rocket, the breaking of the sound barrier in 1947.

He died of a heart attack at age seventy-seven in Dayton's Miami Valley Hospital at ten-thirty the evening of January 30, 1948, and was laid to rest at Woodland Cemetery with his mother, father, Wilbur, and Katharine.

Ever the perfect gentleman to the end, "polite almost to a fault," as said, always neatly dressed, his shoes always shined, Orville was also known to drive his automobile at such high speed that the police of Oakwood would close their eyes and hold their breath until he passed by on the way to his laboratory downtown.

———

On July 20, 1969, when Neil Armstrong, another American born and raised in southwestern Ohio, stepped onto the moon, he carried with him, in tribute to the Wright brothers, a small swatch of the muslin from a wing of their 1903 Flyer.

ACKNOWLEDGMENTS

I t is to the incomparable Library of Congress and its staff that I wish first to express my utmost gratitude. The great body of Wilbur and Orville Wright's extensive papers—those letters, diaries, technical data books, documents, and proposals prepared by the brothers, as well as a much larger quantity of private family papers than is generally known—are all to be found there.

Rare is the collection that provides so much depth and range, and all in such detail. In a day and age when, unfortunately, so few write letters or keep a diary any longer, the Wright Papers stand as a striking reminder of a time when that was not the way and of the immense value such writings can have in bringing history to life. Seldom ever did any of the Wrights—father, sons, daughter—put anything down on paper that was dull or pointless or poorly expressed. And much that they said to each other, and only to each other, was of great importance. In all, the family letters in the Library's collection number in excess of a thousand. In addition, there are their large scrapbooks, a gold mine of insights.

Of the Library staff, I thank especially my old friend Jeff Flannery, head of the Manuscript Reading Room; Laura J. Kells, senior archives specialist; Science Manuscript Historian and Wright Brothers specialist, Len Bruno; and Michael Klein. Watching and listening to Laura Kells as she explained the actual technical diaries and data books kept by the brothers, and particularly those from the crucial weeks at Kitty Hawk, was an exciting experience.

Like so many who have taken up the study of the Wrights, I am greatly indebted as well to the landmark work of the late Marvin W. McFarland of the Library of Congress, who edited *The Papers of Wilbur and Orville Wright, 1899–1948*, in two volumes first published in 1953. His extensive footnotes alone are of matchless value.

As he has in our efforts together over many years, Mike Hill provided immense help with his expert research and particularly in his work with the Library collection. He has as well traveled with me across the whole geographical route of the Wright story, from Dayton to Kitty Hawk to the landmark flying fields at Le Mans and Pau in France. If ever there was a more skilled or good-spirited detective-on-the-case, I'm not aware of it. Again I thank him from the heart and count my lucky stars for all he does.

In addition to typing and retyping my many drafts of one chapter after another, Melissa Marchetti has been a godsend from the start in the effort she has put into a variety of research assignments, the compiling of a bibliography, and working with Mike Hill on source notes. Betsy Buddy, from her base in Paris, has provided much-needed research help there and translated a wealth of new material. I am ever thankful for her contribution.

My daughter, Dorie Lawson, has done so much and in such a variety of ways to keep the project on track that she deserves a medal.

For anyone trying to understand the immense accomplishment of the Wright brothers and its impact on history, the Smithsonian Institution must figure prominently, as it did in their own lives. There, hanging overhead at the National Air and Space Museum, is the original 1903 Flyer. There, too, can be found numerous other key elements of the story and abundant documentation on file.

In my early efforts, I was helped greatly by Tom Crouch, the Air and Space Museum's senior curator of aeronautics and author of the superb book *The Bishop's Boys: A Life of Wilbur and Orville Wright*. For the time he so generously gave me, talking about the brothers and conducting me and Mike Hill on a tour of the Wright machines exhibited at the Smithsonian's Udvar-Hazy facility at Dulles Airport, I remain highly grateful.

And for the observations and insights he offered over lunch several years afterward, I thank Peter Jakab, another of the Smithsonian's Wright brothers experts and editor with Rick Young of the excellent anthology *The Writings of Wilbur and Orville Wright*.

The extensive photographic collection at Wright State University in Dayton, Ohio, has been of exceptional value, as there is much to be found of the Wright story in the photographs of their family life and the many hundreds of their experiments, most all of which they took themselves. The time spent with the collection and its very knowledgeable archivist Dawne Dewey and her associate John Armstrong, was both helpful and highly enjoyable. I am further indebted to Dawne Dewey for her work as editor of Bishop Wright's *Diaries, 1857–1917.* The book has been for me not only a key source, but one to turn to for pure reading pleasure.

My thanks to Dean Alexander, superintendent of Aviation Heritage National Park in Dayton, a treasure house of Wright memorabilia, and Ed Roach, chief historian of the Park, who was the first to show me and Mike Hill about Dayton and Huffman Prairie and who has been most helpful answering questions over the time since.

Much appreciated, too, has been the help of Alex Heckman, director of education and museum operations, and Mary Oliver, director of collections at Dayton's Carillon Historical Park, and Nancy R. Horlacher, local history specialist at the Dayton Metropolitan Library.

The recollections and observations provided by two Wright family descendants, by Amanda Wright Lane and her brother, Stephen Wright, during the course of several evenings together in Dayton were of particular value as well as a delight. Their friendship has been one of the rewards of the work.

That such a number of people at Kitty Hawk went out of their way to give of their time and help mattered immensely. I want to thank especially Bill Harris of the First Flight Society for sharing so much that he knows about the Outer Banks at the start of the nineteenth century, as well as much of his own valuable research; Kaeli Schurr, curator, and Sarah Downing, assistant curator, and Tama Creef, archivist at the Outer Banks History Center in Manteo; and Josh Boles and Darrell Collins at the Wright Brothers National Memorial, U.S. National Park Service, at Kill Devil Hills. Both Bill Harris and Sarah Downing were also good enough to read my chapters on what happened at Kitty Hawk and offered a number of good suggestions and corrections prior to publication.

Grateful am I, too, for the friendship and hospitality provided by John Tucker and the staff of the First Colony Inn at Nags Head.

In Virginia, Paul Glenshaw and Leah Rubalcaba generously provided a day's tour of Fort Myer, answering any number of questions about the time of Orville's sensational flights and terrible crash there.

I wish to thank, too, Patricia Mooradian, Christian Overland, Marc Greuther, Terry Hoover, Matthew Anderson, and Linda Skolarus, all of the Ford Museum at Dearborn, Michigan, who did so much to make two visits of such great benefit and so enjoyable. That the home of the Wrights at 7 Hawthorn Street, along with its original furnishings, as well as the Wright bicycle shop, are there intact, exactly as they were, takes one literally into their world and way of life as nothing else could.

At Le Mans, Marc Denoueix, an authority on the importance of Wilbur Wright's performances there, and at Pau, Paul Mirat, no less an expert on that part of the story, provided tours as fine as one could wish for. I appreciated also the chance to talk with a senior member of the famous Bollée family of Le Mans, Gerard Bollée, and to have been treated to a tour of the noted Automobile Museum at Le Mans by François Piquera. And again, thanks, too, to Captain Nicole Sammels of NetJets.

I'm grateful also to the Medina County Library and the Medina County Historical Society in Ohio, and the Camden Public Library and the Owls Head Transportation Museum in Maine, Judy Schiff of the Sterling Library at Yale, and Melissa Cronyn and Miles Barger of the U.S. National Park Service.

I salute my old friend and literary agent, Mort Janklow, and sing his praises still again for providing sound advice and the kind of enthusiasm that keeps the batteries charged.

To Michael Korda, author, editor, former RAF pilot, and friend of long standing, I am indebted for much continuing interest, advice, and encouragement. As for those at Simon & Schuster—Carolyn Reidy, Jonathan Karp, Julia Prosser, Johanna Li, and my highly accomplished editor, Bob Bender—I hope you know how greatly I appreciate the role you've played and how very much, as always, I've enjoyed working with you.

My sincere thanks to Wendell Minor for his splendid design of the dust jacket and to Amy Hill, who designed the book. They are two masters of their art and it has been a privilege to work with them on this as with others of my books.

I am grateful for the close reading and improvements provided by copy editor Fred Chase, to Lisa Healy, and to Chris Carruth for such a superb index.

For the interest they have shown in my work on the book and for their many kindnesses, I thank Bob and Happy Doran, Bob and Dianthe Eisendrath, Adam van Doran, Jeff Dunn, Mike Buddy, Kenny Young, my brother George McCullough, and in particular my daughter Melissa Mc-Donald, sons David, William, and Geoffrey McCullough, and son-in-law Tim Lawson, each of whom also read and commented on the manuscript.

Then there is Tom Furrier, specialist in typewriter care, who has kept my old Royal in prime condition the whole way along.

Most helpful of all, most encouraging, inspiring, and indispensable, as always, and most deserving of my wholehearted gratitude, is my editor-in-chief and guiding star, my wife, Rosalee.

SOURCE NOTES

Prologue

1 *One savant in Spain:* Moolman, *The Road to Kitty Hawk,* 20.

1 *Others devised wings:* Gibbs-Smith, *Aviation: An Historical Survey from Its Origins to the End of the Second World War,* 6.

1 *And starting about 1490, Leonardo da Vinci:* "Leonardo da Vinci as Aviation Engineer," *Scientific American Monthly,* April 1921.

1 *"Look here, boys":* Kelly, *The Wright Brothers: A Biography,* 8.

1 *They called it the "bat":* Orville Wright, "The Wright Brothers' Aeroplane," *Century Magazine,* No. 5, September 1908; Jakab and Young, eds., *The Published Writings of Wilbur and Orville Wright,* 24.

1 *Orville's first teacher in grade school:* Crouch, *The Bishop's Boys: A Life of Wilbur and Orville Wright,* 57.

1. Beginnings

5 "If I were giving a young man advice": Remarks given by Wilbur Wright at the Twenty-fourth Annual Banquet of the Ohio Society of New York on January 10, 1910, *Reports of Proceedings, 1910,* New York: Ohio Society of New York, 1910, 93–138, as cited in Jakab and Young, eds., *The Published Writings of Wilbur and Orville Wright,* p. 35, footnote 1.

6 "Truth to tell": *The Auto: The Motorist's Pictorial,* Vol. 14, 1909, 264; H. Massac Buist, "The Human Side of Flying," *Flight Magazine,* March 6, 1909.

6 "Inseparable as twins": Bishop Milton Wright to Carl Dienstbach, December 22, 1903, McFarland, ed., *The Papers of Wilbur and Orville Wright,* Vol. 1, 400; Bishop Wright to Mrs. E. J. Wright, December 31, 1904, Papers of Wilbur and Orville Wright, Library of Congress (hereinafter referred to as LOC).

6 *even "thought together":* Wilbur Wright, April 3, 1912, McFarland, ed., *The Papers of Wilbur and Orville Wright,* Vol. 1, Preface.

7 "something terrible": Taylor, "My Story of the Wright Brothers," *Collier's Weekly,* December 25, 1948; Jakab and Young, eds., *The Published Writings of Wilbur and Orville Wright,* 290.

7 "tremendously active of movement": *Automotor Journal,* March 1909.

7 *walking always with a long, rapid stride:* Buist, "The Human Side of Flying," *Flight Magazine,* March 6, 1909.

7 *"I have no memory at all":* Washington Post, October 4, 1908.

7 *He could cut himself off from everyone:* Miller, ed., *Wright Reminiscences,* 62.

7 *"The strongest impression one gets":* Coles, "The Wright Boys as a Schoolmate Knew Them," *Out West Magazine,* January 1910.

7 *"unusual presence":* Miller, ed., *Wright Reminiscences,* 64.

7 *"never rattled":* Crouch, *The Bishop's Boys,* 15.

8 *"Will seems to enjoy writing":* Orville Wright to George A. Spratt, June 7, 1903, McFarland, ed., *The Papers of Wilbur and Orville Wright,* Vol. 1, 310.

8 *"peculiar spells":* Wilbur Wright to Bishop Wright, July 20, 1907, Papers of Wilbur and Orville Wright, LOC.

8 *"Mr. Orville Wright does not possess":* Buist, "The Human Side of Flying," *Flight Magazine,* March 13, 1909.

8 *it was up to Wilbur to marry first:* Taylor, "My Story of the Wright Brothers"; Jakab and Young, eds., *The Published Writings of Wilbur and Orville Wright,* 289.

8 *"woman-shy":* Ibid.

8 *"get awfully nervous":* Ibid.

9 *After finishing at Ohio's Oberlin College:* Kelly, ed., *Miracle at Kitty Hawk: The Letters of Wilbur and Orville Wright,* 4.

9 *"I nipped their smartness in the bud":* Katharine Wright to Bishop Wright, September 25, 1901, Papers of Wilbur and Orville Wright, LOC.

9 *gold-rimmed, pince-nez glasses:* See Bishop Wright's diary entry for June 22, 1899, Milton Wright, *Diaries, 1857–1917,* 320 and photo on 490. The original diary of Bishop Milton Wright is located at the Special Collections and Archives Department, Wright State University, Dayton, Ohio.

9 *"Of the sawed-off variety":* Katharine to Orville, July 10, 1905, Papers of Wilbur and Orville Wright, LOC.

9 *"He sits around and picks that thing":* Katharine to Bishop Wright, August 22, 1900, ibid.

9 *"You have a good mind":* Bishop Wright to Katharine, May 30, 1888, ibid.

9 *Among themselves Wilbur was Ullam:* Crouch, *The Bishop's Boys,* 50.

10 *"regular genius":* Richard Maurer, *The Wright Sister: Katharine Wright and Her Famous Brothers,* 22.

10 *"He was grave in countenance":* Crouch, *The Bishop's Boys,* 25.

12 *"a devotion to something beyond mere material splendor":* Drury, *History of the City of Dayton and Montgomery County, Ohio,* Vol. I, 181.

12 *"the courage of their dreams":* Howells, *Stories of Ohio,* 287.

12 *"Pick out a good father and mother":* Remarks given by Wilbur Wright at the Twenty-fourth Annual Banquet of the Ohio Society of New York on January 10, 1910, *Reports of Proceedings, 1910,* New York: Ohio Society of New York, 1910, 93–138, as cited in Jakab and Young, eds., *The Published Writings of Wilbur and Orville Wright,* p. 35, footnote 1.

13 *"cities of marvelous growth":* Bishop Wright to Katharine, May 30, 1888, Papers of Wilbur and Orville Wright, LOC.

13 *three locomotives were required:* Bishop Wright to Susan Wright, June 2, 1888, ibid.

13 *"Yesterday, I came down here":* Bishop Wright to Orville, July 31, 1888, ibid.

13 *"good mettle":* Bishop Wright to Wilbur Wright, September 24, 1908, ibid.

13 *"It is assumed that young folks know best":* Bishop Wright to Wilbur and Orville, October 15, 1907, ibid.

14 *"the apple of his eye":* Katharine to Wilbur, July 16, 1908, ibid.

14 *his grades were in the 90s:* See Wilbur Wright's report cards, Wright Family Papers, Wright State University, Dayton, Ohio.

14 *"man who threw the bat":* Milton Wright, *Diaries, 1857–1917,* 778.

14 *Oliver Crook Haugh:* See Dalton, *With Malice Toward All: The Lethal Life of Dr. Oliver C. Haugh.*

14 *"Oliver never was without the wish":* Dayton Journal, April 19, 1907.

14 *"Cocaine Toothache Drops":* Dalton, *With Malice Toward All,* 9–10.

15 *he had to be committed:* Ibid., 14–15.

15 *digestive complications:* Crouch, *The Bishop's Boys,* 75.

15 *"Such devotion of a son":* "Wilbur Wright, Born in Henry County," 1909, Wright Family Scrapbooks, Papers of Wilbur and Orville Wright, LOC.

15 *"What does Will do?":* Lorin Wright to Katharine, November 12, 1888, Papers of Wilbur and Orville Wright, LOC.

17 *Between formal education at school:* Author's conversation with Amanda and Steven Wright.

17 *Those works he considered "very serious":* "Books in Wright's Home Library," February 10, 1937, Benson Ford Research Library, Henry Ford Museum, Greenfield Village, Dearborn, Michigan.

17 *"He talked very freely":* Washington Post, October 4, 1908.

17 *"Every mind should be true":* Ingersoll, *The Works of Robert G. Ingersoll,* Vol. 1, 179.

18 *"But it isn't true":* Fred C. Kelly, "Interview with Orville Wright," *Today,* March 31, 1934; Jakab and Young, eds., *The Published Writings of Wilbur and Orville Wright,* 83.

18 *"My father and brother seeing my determination":* Carl J. Crane, "Interview with Orville Wright," *University of Dayton Exponent,* April 1924; Jakab and Young, eds., *The Published Writings of Wilbur and Orville Wright,* 60.

18 *offering "BIG BARGAINS":* West Side News, March 1, 1889.

19 *The editorial content for this:* Material taken from various issues of *West Side News* at the Dayton Metropolitan Library, Dayton, Ohio.

20 *"Orville Wright is out of sight":* See McFarland, ed., *The Papers of Wilbur and Orville Wright,* Vol. 2, 695–96, footnote 1.

20 *In 1893, through the influence of Bishop Wright:* Stimson, "Paul Laurence Dunbar: The Wright Brothers' Friend," *The Wright Stories,* www.wrightstories.com.

20 *"She was of retiring disposition":* Orville and Wilbur Wright, "Tribute to Our Mother," *West Side News,* July 3, 1889.

20 *"The Fourth had its Chinese firecrackers":* Bishop Wright to Wilbur, July 7, 1907, Papers of Wilbur and Orville Wright, LOC.

21 *"We've been so busy for the past few weeks":* Orville to Bishop Wright, September 27, 1892, ibid.

21 *"I've been making $2.00 to $3.25":* Ibid.

21 *"We have been living fine since you left":* Wilbur to Katharine, September 18, 1892, ibid.

21 *headed off on a "run" to the south:* Ibid.

22 *One Philadelphia physician:* Prendergast, "The Bicycle for Women," *American Journal of Obstetrics and Diseases of Women and Children,* August 1, 1896.

22 *Voices were raised in protest:* "The Bicycle and Its Riders," *Cincinnati Lancet and Clinic,* September 11, 1897.

22 *"not infrequently accompanied":* Ibid.

23 *"Cloudy day, but moderate":* Milton Wright, *Diaries, 1857–1917,* 412.

23 *"an honorable pursuit"*: Wilbur to Bishop Wright, September 12, 1894, Papers of Wilbur and Orville Wright, LOC.
23 *"I do not think I am specially fitted"*: Ibid.
24 *"In business it is the aggressive man"*: Wilbur to Lorin Wright, June 18, 1901, ibid.
24 *"I do not think a commercial life will suit you well"*: Bishop Wright to Wilbur, September 15, 1894, ibid.
25 *"It will have large tubing, high frame"*: Crouch, *The Bishop's Boys*, 113.
25 *"Van Cleves get there First"*: 1897 newspaper ad.
25 *"Through fair and liberal dealing"*: Van Cleve catalogue, Wright Cycle Company, Dayton, Ohio, 1900, 3.
26 *"If we happened to be sitting"*: Tobin, *To Conquer the Air*, 92.

2. The Dream Takes Hold

27 "I wish to avail myself of all that is already known": Wilbur to the Smithsonian Institution, May 30, 1899, Papers of Wilbur and Orville Wright, LOC.
27 *the habit of worry was strong in him:* Katharine to Wilbur and Orville, September 4, 1902, ibid.
27 *In the late summer of 1896:* See Bishop Wright's diary entries from September 4 to September 22, 1896, 458–59.
27 *"Put him in the best room for air"*: Bishop Wright to Katharine, August 31, 1896, Papers of Wilbur and Orville Wright, LOC.
28 *"prominent investigators"*: Combs and Caidin, *Kill Devil Hill: Discovering the Secrets of the Wright Brothers*, 41.
28 *"What we are seeking is the means of free motion"*: Vernon, "The Flying Man," *McClure's Magazine*, Vol. 3, 1894, 325.
28 *his* normal segel apparat: Chant, *A Century of Triumph: The History of Aviation*, 11.
28 *"stood like an athlete"*: Crouch, *The Bishop's Boys*, 144.
29 *On August 9, 1896:* Gibbs-Smith, *Aviation*, 79.
29 *"It must not remain our desire"*: Ibid., 221.
29 *"Aerial locomotion has always excited"*: Marey, *Animal Mechanism: A Treatise on Terrestrial and Aerial Locomotion*, 4.
30 *"Those authors who regard artificial flight"*: Pettigrew, *Animal Locomotion; or Walking, Swimming, and Flying, with a Dissertation on Aeronautics*, 3.
30 *"Of all animal movements"*: Ibid., 6–7.
30 They *"read up on aeronautics as a physician would read"*: Howard, *Wilbur and Orville: A Biography of the Wright Brothers*, 144.
31 *The building was a two-story, red-brick duplex:* See Keefer, *The Wright Cycle Shop Historical Report*, Benson Ford Research Library, Henry Ford Museum, Greenfield Village, Dearborn, MI, Summer 2004, 3, 5, 15.
31 *Dayton suffered the worst flood:* Orville to Bishop Wright, March 31, 1898, Papers of Wilbur and Orville Wright, LOC.
31 *"We had a very narrow escape"*: Ibid.
31 *Frank Hamberger, recalled how:* Dayton Journal, May 31, 1912.
31 *a friend of the Wrights named Cord Ruse:* Kelly, *The Wright Brothers*, 43.
32 *The Bishop and Katharine had gone to Woodland Cemetery:* Milton Wright, *Diaries, 1857–1917*, 506.
32 *"I have been interested in the problem of mechanical and human flight"*: McFarland, ed., *The Papers of Wilbur and Orville Wright*, LOC, Vol. 1, 4.

33 *Hiram Maxim had reportedly spent $100,000:* Leland D. Case, "Orville Wright: First Man to Fly," *The Rotarian,* April 1948; Jakab and Young, eds., *The Published Writings of Wilbur and Orville Wright,* 99.

33 *In the 1850s, one French inventor's ingenious idea:* New York Times, June 23, 1853.

34 *"the flying-machine crank":* San Francisco Chronicle, February 16, 1890.

34 *"The body is supported by a pair of wings":* Washington Post, June 28, 1896.

34 *"It is a fact . . . that man can't fly":* Ibid., December 24, 1897.

34 *"The birds can fly and why can't I?":* Fiske-Bates, ed., *Cambridge Book of Poetry and Song,* 788–89.

36 *"only a question of knowledge and skill":* McFarland, ed., *The Papers of Wilbur and Orville Wright,* Vol. 1, 4.

36 *"one of the most remarkable pieces of aeronautical literature":* Wilbur Wright, "What Mouillard Did," *Aero Club of America Bulletin,* April 1912; Jakab and Young, eds., *The Published Writings of Wilbur and Orville Wright,* 172.

36 *flight had become a "cause":* Ibid.

36 *"like a prophet crying in the wilderness":* Wilbur Wright quoted in *The Literary Digest,* April 27, 1912, 879.

36 *"When once this idea has invaded the brain":* Mouillard, "The Empire of the Air: An Ornithological Essay on the Flight of Birds," extracted and translated from "L'Empire de l'Air: Essai d'Ornithologie appliquee a l'Aviation."

36 *"Oh, blind humanity!":* Ibid.

37 *"He knows how to rise, how to float":* Ibid.

37 *"lead men to navigate":* Ibid.

37 *"infected us with":* Wilbur and Orville Wright, "The Wright Brothers Aeroplane," *Century Magazine,* September 1908; Jakab and Young, eds., *The Published Writings of Wilbur and Orville Wright,* 25.

38 *attaining "equilibrium" or balance in flight:* Wilbur to Octave Chanute, November 16, 1900, McFarland, ed., *The Papers of Wilbur and Orville Wright,* Vol. 1, 43.

38 *"his inability to properly balance his machine":* Orville Wright on the Wright Experiments of 1899, ibid., 7.

38 *"positive and energetic methods":* Wilbur to Octave Chanute, May 13, 1900, ibid., 17.

38 *could be twisted or "warped":* Orville Wright on the Wright Experiments of 1899, ibid., 8–9.

39 *"According to Wilbur's account of the tests":* Ibid., 11.

40 *"the boys" had given her:* Katharine to Bishop Wright, August 22, 1900, Papers of Wilbur and Orville Wright, LOC.

40 *"I guess that's about enough, Orv":* Kelly, ed., *Miracle at Kitty Hawk,* 18.

40 *"Mr. Orville would stop instantly":* Ibid.

40 *sufficient winds could be counted on:* Wilbur to Octave Chanute, May 13, 1900, McFarland, ed., *The Papers of Wilbur and Orville Wright,* Vol. 1, 18–19.

40 *"deficient in sand hills":* Octave Chanute to Wilbur, May 17, 1900, ibid., 21.

40 *In answer to an inquiry Wilbur sent:* Wilbur to Instrument Division, U.S. Weather Bureau, November 27, 1899, ibid., 12, footnote 7.

40 *extensive records of monthly wind velocities:* Ibid.

40 *the farthest the brothers had been from home:* Katharine to Bishop Wright, September 26, 1900, Papers of Wilbur and Orville Wright, LOC.

41 *"Mr. J. J. Dosher of the Weather Bureau here":* William Tate to Wilbur, August 18, 1900, ibid.

42 *The total cost of all the necessary pieces and parts:* Kelly, *The Wright Brothers,* 57.

42 *Wilbur was to go first:* Katharine to Bishop Wright, September 5, 1900, McFarland, ed., *The Papers of Wilbur and Orville Wright*, Vol. 1, 23.

42 *"I never did hear of such an out-of-the-way place":* Katharine to Bishop Wright, October 4, 1900, Papers of Wilbur and Orville Wright, LOC.

3. Where the Winds Blow

43 One ship drives east: Felleman, *The Best Loved Poems of the American People*, 364.

43 *Wilbur reached Norfolk by train on September 7, 1900:* Fragmentary Memorandum by Wilbur Wright, circa September 13, 1900, McFarland, ed., *The Papers of Wilbur and Orville Wright*, Vol. 1, 23–24.

43 *he nearly collapsed:* Ibid., 24.

44 *long spruce strips necessary for his "machine":* Wilbur to Bishop Wright, September 23, 1900, ibid., 26.

44 *a boatman on the waterfront, one Israel Perry:* Fragmentary Memorandum by Wilbur Wright, circa September 13, 1900, ibid., 24.

44 *"Oh, it's safer than the big boat":* Kelly, *The Wright Brothers*, 59.

44 *"The sails were rotten":* Fragmentary Memorandum by Wilbur Wright, circa September 13, 1900, McFarland, ed., *The Papers of Wilbur and Orville Wright*, Vol. 1, 24.

44 *"a little uneasy":* Ibid.

44 *"struck the boat from below with a heavy shock":* Ibid.

44 *"At 11 o'clock the wind had increased to a gale":* Ibid.

45 *a highly dangerous maneuver:* Ibid., 25.

45 *He would not land on sandbars:* Orville to Katharine, October 14, 1900, ibid., 33.

46 *"The community of Kitty Hawk at that time":* Captain W. J. Tate, "With the Wrights at Kitty Hawk: Anniversary of First Flight Twenty-five Years Ago," *Aeronautic Review*, December 1928; Jakab and Young, eds., *The Published Writings of Wilbur and Orville Wright*, 283.

46 *"double-barreled ISOLATION":* Ibid., 284.

46 *Houses had little in the way of furniture:* Interviews conducted by historian Bill Harris with Kitty Hawk residents who lived on the Outer Banks during the time of the Wright brothers' experiments.

46 *"proceeded to unfold a tale of hardship":* Tate, "With the Wrights at Kitty Hawk: Anniversary of First Flight Twenty-five Years Ago," *Aeronautic Review*, December 1928; Jakab and Young, eds., *The Published Writings of Wilbur and Orville Wright*, 280.

46 *"no carpets at all":* Wilbur to Bishop Wright, September 23, 1900, McFarland, ed., *The Papers of Wilbur and Orville Wright*, Vol. 1, 25–26.

47 *a beautiful white French sateen:* Wilbur to Octave Chanute, November 16, 1900, ibid., 41.

47 *"I have my machine nearly finished":* Wilbur to Bishop Wright, September 23, 1900, ibid., 26.

48 *"The man who wishes to keep at the problem":* Ibid.

48 *"every precaution" about his drinking water:* Ibid., 27.

48 *"darn fool contraption":* Tate, "With the Wrights at Kitty Hawk: Anniversary of First Flight Twenty-five Years Ago," *Aeronautic Review*, December 1928; Jakab and Young, eds., *The Published Writings of Wilbur and Orville Wright*, 281.

48 *"We believed in a good God":* Ibid., 279.

49 *"soaring machine":* Wilbur to Octave Chanute, November 16, 1900, McFarland, ed., *The Papers of Wilbur and Orville Wright,* Vol. 1, 40.

49 *With everything in place:* Wilbur to Octave Chanute, November 16, 1900, and November 26, 1900, ibid., 40–46.

49 *the "horizontal" rudder:* Wilbur to Octave Chanute, November 26, 1900, ibid., 46.

49 *With Wilbur aboard as "operator":* Wilbur to Octave Chanute, November 16, 1900, ibid., 42.

49 *"May the wind be ever at your back":* Author unknown, "An Irish Wish," *Respectfully Quoted,* 277.

49 *"We've been having a fine time":* Orville to Katharine, October 14, 1900, Papers of Wilbur and Orville Wright, LOC.

49 *"too strong and unsteady":* Ibid.

49 *"It naturally wants to go higher and higher":* Ibid.

49 *in a heap 20 feet away:* Ibid.

50 *"The site of our tent was formerly a fertile valley":* Ibid.

50 *"you see dozens of them":* Ibid.

51 *"It's just like in the north":* Ibid.

51 *"pitiable":* Ibid.

51 *bedbugs, mosquitoes, and wood ticks:* Ibid.

51 *"The vulture's needs are few":* Wilbur Wright, "What Mouillard Did," *Aero Club of America Bulletin,* April 1912; Jakab and Young, eds., *The Published Writings of Wilbur and Orville Wright,* 173.

52 *"The buzzard which uses":* Wilbur Wright's Notebook A [1900–] 1901, McFarland, ed., *The Papers of Wilbur and Orville Wright,* Vol. 1, 34.

52 *"All soarers, but especially the buzzard":* Ibid.

53 *"We couldn't help thinking":* William O. Saunders, "Then We Quit Laughing: Interview with John T. Daniels," *Collier's Weekly,* September 17, 1927; Jakab and Young, eds., *The Published Writings of Wilbur and Orville Wright,* 275.

53 *"Learning the secret of flight":* Howard, *Wilbur and Orville,* 33.

53 *a "very tame" mockingbird:* Orville to Katharine, October 14, 1900, Papers of Wilbur and Orville Wright, LOC.

53 *"When we crawl out of the tent":* Orville to Katharine, October 18, 1900, ibid.

53 *"We each have two blankets":* Ibid.

54 *"Well, part of the time we eat hot biscuits":* Orville to Katharine, October 14, 1900, ibid.

54 *words like "disremember" for "forget":* Wolfram and Schilling-Estes, *Hoi Toide on the Outer Banks: The Story of the Ocracoke Brogue,* 39–49; Discussions with historians Bill Harris and Sarah Downing at Outer Banks Historic Center, Manteo, North Carolina.

54 *"Doc" Cogswell:* Orville to Katharine, October 18, 1900, Papers of Wilbur and Orville Wright, LOC.

54 *two or three hours a day at his own work:* Orville to Katharine, October 14, 1900, ibid.

54 *"two of the workingest boys":* Saunders, "Then We Quit Laughing"; Jakab & Young, eds., *The Published Writings of Wilbur & Orville Wright,* 275.

55 *had to fire the young man:* Orville to Katharine, October 14, 1900, Papers of Wilbur and Orville Wright, LOC.

55 *"not a tree or bush anywhere":* William Tate to Wilbur, August 18, 1900, Papers of Wilbur and Orville Wright, LOC; Kelly, ed., *Miracle at Kitty Hawk,* 26.

55 *"And although in appearance":* Wilbur to Octave Chanute, November 16, 1900, McFarland, ed., *The Papers of Wilbur and Orville Wright*, Vol. 1, 43.

55 *"a pleasure trip":* Wilbur to Bishop Wright, September 23, 1900, ibid., 27.

55 *"without having our pet theories":* Wilbur Wright, "Some Aeronautical Experiments," Smithsonian Report for 1902.

56 *From the undamaged portions:* Tobin, *To Conquer the Air*, 91.

56 *"improved construction in its details":* Wilbur to Octave Chanute, May 12, 1901, McFarland, ed., *The Papers of Wilbur and Orville Wright*, Vol. 1, 54.

56 *"entirely free" on Sundays:* Wilbur to Octave Chanute, May 17, 1901, ibid., 55.

56 *He arrived at 7 Hawthorn Street on June 26:* Milton Wright, *Diaries, 1857–1917,* 551.

57 *Charles—Charlie—Taylor had been born on a farm:* Taylor, "My Story of the Wright Brothers"; Jakab and Young, eds., *The Published Writings of Wilbur and Orville Wright*, 293.

57 *just to "gas":* Ibid., 285.

58 *none was to so aggravate sister Katharine:* Katharine to Orville, October 5, 1902, Papers of Wilbur and Orville Wright, LOC.

58 *Wilbur and Orville left Dayton together:* Milton Wright, *Diaries, 1857–1917,* 551–52.

58 *winds recorded at 93 miles an hour:* Wilbur to Octave Chanute, July 26, 1901, McFarland, ed., *The Papers of Wilbur and Orville Wright*, Vol. 1, 70.

58 *sharing the most uncomfortable bed:* Orville to Katharine, July 28, 1901, Papers of Wilbur and Orville Wright, LOC.

58 *no source of fresh water within a mile:* Ibid.

58 *"grand institution with awnings at both ends":* Ibid.

58 *they built a long, solid shed:* Chanute-Huffaker diary, July 18, 1901, McFarland, ed., *The Papers of Wilbur and Orville Wright*, Vol. 1, 69.

58 *"in the form of a mighty cloud, almost darkening the sun":* Orville to Katharine, July 28, 1901, Papers of Wilbur and Orville Wright, LOC.

59 *"as nothing" by comparison:* Ibid.

59 *"Our blankets then became unbearable":* Ibid.

59 *Edward Huffaker of Chuckey City, Tennessee:* Octave Chanute to Wilbur Wright, July 3, 1901, McFarland, ed., *Papers of Wilbur and Orville Wright*, Vol. 1, 65.

60 *He arrived in the last days of the mosquito siege:* Orville to Katharine, July 28, 1901, ibid., 74–75.

60 *"mechanical facility":* Wilbur to Bishop Wright, July 26, 1901, Papers of Wilbur and Orville Wright, LOC.

60 *"character building":* Wilbur to George Spratt, September 21, 1901; George Spratt to Wilbur, November 17, 1901, and January 31, 1902, ibid.

61 *But no sooner was the machine up:* Crouch, *The Bishop's Boys*, 208–9.

61 *Something was "radically wrong":* McFarland, ed., *The Papers of Wilbur and Orville Wright*, Vol. 1, 108.

61 *"the fix" that had plunged:* Orville to Katharine, July 28, 1901, Papers of Wilbur and Orville Wright, LOC.

61 *"The adjustments of the machine are away off":* Ibid.

62 *"The machine with its new curvature":* Wilbur Wright, "Some Aeronautical Experiments," Smithsonian Report for 1902.

62 *"Mr. Huffaker remarked":* Wilbur to Bishop Wright, July 26, 1901, Papers of Wilbur and Orville Wright, LOC.

63 *helping himself to one of Wilbur's blankets:* Wilbur to George Spratt, September 21, 1901, ibid.

63 *"groping in the dark"*: Tobin, *To Conquer the Air*, 113.

63 *"not in a thousand years would man ever fly"*: Kelly, *The Wright Brothers*, 72.

63 *how disagreeable Edward Huffaker had been:* Katharine to Bishop Wright, August 26, 1901, Papers of Wilbur and Orville Wright, LOC.

4. Unyielding Resolve

PAGE

65 "We had to go ahead and discover everything ourselves": Orville Wright, "How I Learned to Fly," *Boys' Life*, September 1914; Jakab and Young, eds., *The Published Writings of Wilbur and Orville Wright*, 53.

65 *"He was at work the following day"*: *Washington Post*, October 4, 1908.

65 *"We knew that it would take considerable time"*: Jakab and Young, eds., *The Published Writings of Wilbur and Orville Wright*, 60.

65 *"boys"... "scientific" investigations:* Katharine to Bishop Wright, October 12, 1901, Papers of Wilbur and Orville Wright, LOC.

65 *"We don't hear anything but flying machine"*: Katharine to Bishop Wright, September 3, 1901, ibid.

65 *"as thrilling interest as any in the field"*: Wilbur Wright, "Some Aeronautical Experiments," Smithsonian Report for 1902.

66 *an invitation from Octave Chanute for Wilbur to address:* Octave Chanute to Wilbur Wright, August 29, 1901, McFarland, ed., *The Papers of Wilbur and Orville Wright*, Vol. 1, 91.

66 *"nagged" him into going:* Katharine to Bishop Wright, September 3, 1901, Papers of Wilbur and Orville Wright, LOC.

66 *Only days later, in the first week of September: Dayton Evening News*, September 7, 1901; Milton Wright, *Diaries, 1857–1917*, 555.

66 *"arrayed in Orv's shirt"*: Katharine to Bishop Wright, September 25, 1901, Papers of Wilbur and Orville Wright, LOC.

66 *Never had he looked "so 'swell' "*: Ibid.

66 *"Ladies' Night"*: Octave Chanute to Wilbur Wright, September 5, 1901, McFarland, ed., *The Papers of Wilbur and Orville Wright*, Vol. 1, 93.

66 *"I will already be as badly scared"*: Wilbur to Octave Chanute, September 6, 1901, ibid.

67 *"Pathetic"*: Katharine to Bishop Wright, September 11, 1901, Papers of Wilbur and Orville Wright, LOC.

67 *private study was so chock-full of models:* Wilbur to Bishop Wright, October 24, 1901, ibid.

67 *"two gentlemen from Dayton, Ohio"*: Introduction by President Chanute, "Some Aeronautical Experiments," Smithsonian Report for 1902.

67 *"the Book of Genesis of the twentieth-century"*: Howard, *Wilbur and Orville: A Biography of the Wright Brothers*, 71.

67 *"settle steadily down as a staid, sensible piece of paper"*: Wilbur Wright, "Some Aeronautical Experiments," Smithsonian Report for 1902.

68 *"Do not be afraid of making it too technical"*: Octave Chanute to Wilbur Wright, September 25, 1901, McFarland, ed., *The Papers of Wilbur and Orville Wright*, Vol. 1, 119.

68 *"somewhat in error"*: Wilbur Wright, "Some Aeronautical Experiments," Smithsonian Report for 1902.

68 *"a devilish good paper"*: Octave Chanute to Wilbur, November 27, 1901, McFarland, ed., *The Papers of Wilbur and Orville Wright*, Vol. 1, 168.

69 *Some of the letters ran:* See letters of Wilbur to Octave Chanute from October 6, 1901 to December 23, 1901, The Papers of Wilbur and Orville Wright, LOC.

69 *"The first successful flyer will be":* Newcomb, "Is the Airship Coming?" *McClure's Magazine,* September 17, 1901.

69 *"lift" and "drag" of a wing's surface:* Wilbur to Octave Chanute, August 29, 1901, McFarland, ed., *The Papers of Wilbur and Orville Wright,* Vol. 1, 86.

69 *"investigations":* Katharine to Bishop Wright, October 12, 1901, Papers of Wilbur and Orville Wright, LOC.

70 *"balances" or "airfoils":* See McFarland, ed., *The Papers of Wilbur and Orville Wright,* Vol. 1, 556–57.

70 *"those metal models told us how to build":* Orville Wright, "How I Learned to Fly," *Boys' Life,* September 1914; Jakab and Young, eds., *The Published Writings of Wilbur and Orville Wright,* 52.

70 *"It is perfectly marvelous to me":* Octave Chanute to Wilbur, November 18, 1901, McFarland, ed., *The Papers of Wilbur and Orville Wright,* Vol. 1, 156.

70 *his letters were always too brief:* Octave Chanute to Wilbur, November 27, 1901, ibid., 168.

70 *"Never in the history of the world":* *Aeronautical Journal,* Vols. 19–20, Aeronautical Society of Great Britain, 1915, 72.

70 *"A calm survey":* Crouch, *A Dream of Wings: Americans and the Airplane, 1825–1905,* 17.

71 *"Practically all the expense":* Wilbur to Octave Chanute, October 24, 1901, McFarland, *The Papers of Wilbur and Orville Wright,* Vol. 1, 142.

71 *"Would you like for me to write to him?":* Octave Chanute to Wilbur, December 19, 1901, ibid., 183.

71 *"too hardheaded a Scotchman":* Wilbur to Octave Chanute, December 23, 1901, ibid., 187.

71 *"aeronautical experts":* Wright Family Scrapbooks, Papers of Wilbur and Orville Wright, LOC.

72 *At the same time the family was facing:* Tobin, *To Conquer the Air,* 136–37, 206, 230; Crouch, *The Bishop's Boys,* 41, 43, 51–52, 63–69, 78–86, 215–18, 302; *Chicago Chronicle,* August 24, 1902; Wilbur to Octave Chanute, May 28, 1905, McFarland, ed., *The Papers of Wilbur and Orville Wright,* Vol. 1, 493.

73 *"My chief regret":* Wilbur to Bishop Wright, February 15, 1902, Papers of Wilbur and Orville Wright, LOC.

73 *"The question of whether officials shall rob":* Ibid.

73 *In mid-March, Wilbur took the train:* Milton Wright, *Diaries, 1857–1917,* 566.

73 *"very crooked":* Ibid., 567.

73 *"an exposé of Keiter's defalcations":* Ibid.

73 *an "egotist":* Crouch, *The Bishop's Boys,* 217.

73 *"absolutely inconceivable, incomprehensible":* Wilbur to Reuchlin Wright, May 20, 1902, The Papers of Wilbur and Orville Wright, LOC.

73 *"finding new instances of his stealing":* Ibid.

73 *"When my father and myself came to examine":* Wilbur Wright, "The Church Trial at Huntington," August 15, 1902, ibid.

74 *"things are moving nicely":* Wilbur to Bishop Wright, August 18, 1902, ibid.

74 *"Will is thin and nervous":* Katharine to Bishop Wright, August 20, 1902, ibid.

74 *"Some say the boys just go camping":* McMahon, *The Wright Brothers: Fathers of Flight,* 110.

74 *"Will spins the sewing machine around":* Katharine to Bishop Wright, August 20, 1902, Papers of Wilbur and Orville Wright, LOC.

74 *"He was completely unnerved"*: Katharine to Bishop Wright, August 20, 1902, ibid.

75 *"We'll never stop fighting now, Pop"*: Katharine to Bishop Wright, September 9, 1902, ibid.

75 *"too weary for words"*: Katharine to Wilbur and Orville, September 4, 1902, ibid.

75 *making an unprecedented $25 a week:* Katharine to Bishop Wright, September 27, 1902, ibid.

75 *"His former friends have become"*: Bishop Wright to Estella Petree, October 2, 1907, Milton Wright Collection, Huntington University, Huntington, Indiana.

75 *get used to some of Charlie Taylor's peculiarities:* Orville to Katharine, September 11, 1902, Papers of Wilbur and Orville Wright, LOC.

76 *"royal luxuries"*: Wilbur to Katharine, August 31, 1902, ibid.

76 *"He met with a rather warm reception"*: Orville to Katharine, September 7, 1902, ibid.

76 *"immensely improved"*: Wilbur to George Spratt, September 16, 1902, McFarland, ed., *The Papers of Wilbur and Orville Wright*, Vol. 1, 253.

76 *took only one hour, instead of three on foot:* Ibid.

77 *"learned to love 'em"*: Saunders, "Then We Quit Laughing"; Jakab and Young, eds., *The Published Writings of Wilbur and Orville Wright*, 275.

77 *"There are other improvements too numerous"*: Wilbur to George Spratt, September 16, 1902, McFarland, ed., *The Papers of Wilbur and Orville Wright*, Vol. 1, 253.

77 "Monday, September 8. *Finally began work"*: Orville Wright's diary, ibid., 249.

78 *"very satisfactory" results:* Ibid., 258.

78 *"without a bruise or a scratch"*: Ibid, 260.

78 *"My brother"*: Wilbur to Octave Chanute, September 23, 1902, McFarland, ed., *The Papers of Wilbur and Orville Wright*, Vol. 1, 261.

78 *Lorin Wright walked into camp:* Wilbur to Bishop Wright, October 2, 1902, Papers of Wilbur and Orville Wright, LOC.

78 *"We are in splendid health"*: Ibid.

79 *"always ready to oppose an idea"*: George Spratt to Octave Chanute, August 16, 1901, ibid.

79 *"a good scrap"*: Wilbur to George Spratt, April 20, 1903, ibid.

79 *"as it makes us too conservative"*: Ibid.

79 *"hip cradle"*: Kelly, *The Wright Brothers*, 79.

80 *"shell of hauteur"*: Tobin, *To Conquer the Air*, 61.

80 *wrote at once to the brothers:* See Wilbur to Octave Chanute, November 12, 1902, McFarland, ed., *The Papers of Wilbur and Orville Wright*, Vol. 1, 283.

5. December 17, 1903

PAGE

85 "When we got up a wind": Orville Wright's diary, December 17, 1903, McFarland, ed., *The Papers of Wilbur and Orville Wright*, Vol. 1, 394.

85 *"but if there is any hope for him"*: *Dayton Evening News*, January 1, 1903.

86 No new year had *"ever brought the people"*: *Albuquerque Journal-Democrat*, January 2, 1903.

86 *One of the few puzzling questions: Philadelphia Inquirer*, January 1, 1903.

86 *"Those two sure knew their physics"*: Taylor, "My Story of the Wright Brothers"; Jakab and Young, eds., *The Published Writings of Wilbur and Orville Wright*, 288.

87 *Aluminum Company of America:* Orville Wright to ALCOA, December 1939, Papers of Wilbur and Orville Wright, LOC.

87 *"The fuel system was simple":* Taylor, "My Story of the Wright Brothers"; Jakab and Young, eds., *The Published Writings of Wilbur and Orville Wright,* 288.

88 *"The spark was made by the opening":* Ibid.

88 *"little gas motor":* Milton Wright, *Diaries, 1857–1917,* 583.

88 *"I think the hardest job":* Taylor, "My Story of the Wright Brothers"; Jakab and Young, eds., *The Published Writings of Wilbur and Orville Wright,* 288.

88 *"Our minds . . . became so obsessed":* Orville Wright, "How We Made the First Flight," *Flying,* December 1913; ibid., 41.

88 *"But on further consideration":* Ibid.

89 *"discussions" became as intense:* Ibid.

89 *"If you don't stop arguing":* McMahon, *The Wright Brothers,* 129.

89 *"guessed he'd been wrong":* Taylor, "My Story of the Wright Brothers"; Jakab and Young, eds., *The Published Writings of Wilbur and Orville Wright,* 290.

89 *Each had a diameter of 8 and a half feet:* Orville Wright's Notes, The Propellers, McFarland, ed., *The Papers of Wilbur and Orville Wright,* Vol. 1, 636.

90 *Roebling wire would be used for the trusses:* Taylor, "My Story of the Wright Brothers"; Jakab and Young, eds., *The Published Writings of Wilbur and Orville Wright,* 288.

90 *"It seems very queer":* Octave Chanute to Wilbur, April 4, 1903, McFarland, ed., *The Papers of Wilbur and Orville Wright,* Vol. 1, 304.

90 *"devoted collaborators":* Howard, *Wilbur and Orville,* 98.

90 *"even a little disagreeable":* Crouch, *The Bishop's Boys,* 251–52.

91 *"A thousand glides is equivalent to":* Wilbur Wright, "Experiments and Observations in Soaring Flight," presented before the Western Society of Engineers, June 24, 1903, *Journal of the Western Society of Engineers,* August 1903; McFarland, ed., *The Papers of Wilbur and Orville Wright,* Vol. 1, 324.

92 *"The birds' wings are undoubtedly":* Ibid.

92 *"It is very bad policy to ask":* Ibid., 332.

92 *"the wind usually blows":* Ibid., 334.

92 *"As none of our experiments has been with power machines":* Ibid.

92 *"fair and mild":* Milton Wright, *Diaries, 1857–1917,* 589.

93 *From Kitty Hawk Bill Tate sent word:* Bill Tate to Wilbur Wright, June 26, 1903, Papers of Wilbur and Orville Wright, LOC.

93 *"latest contrivance":* *Chicago Tribune,* July 14, 1903.

93 *"The Great Aerodrome":* Jakab and Young, eds., *The Published Writings of Wilbur and Orville Wright,* 288.

93 *It had cost $50,000 in public money:* Howard, *Wilbur and Orville,* 125.

93 *"the ark":* *Chicago Tribune,* July 14, 1903.

93 *Langley himself arrived from Washington:* *Washington Post,* July 17, 1903.

93 *When a storm struck:* Ibid., July 20, 1903.

93 *"AIRSHIP AS A SUBMARINE":* *New York Times,* August 9, 1903.

93 *Manly went before reporters:* Ibid.

94 *"Professor Langley seems to be having":* Wilbur to Octave Chanute, July 22, 1903, Papers of Wilbur and Orville Wright, LOC.

94 *"whopper flying machine":* Wilbur to Katharine, October 18, 1903, McFarland, ed., *The Papers of Wilbur and Orville Wright,* Vol. 1, 367.

94 *"We never did assemble":* Taylor, "My Story of the Wright Brothers"; Jakab and Young, eds., *The Published Writings of Wilbur and Orville Wright,* 288.

94 *"If there was any worry":* Ibid.

95 *"Every year adds to our comprehension":* Orville to Katharine, September 26, 1903, Papers of Wilbur and Orville Wright, LOC.

95 *Ninety-mile-an-hour winds had lifted their building:* Wilbur to Bishop Wright, September 21, 1903, ibid.

95 *Mosquitoes were said to have been so thick:* Orville to Katharine, September 26, 1903, ibid.

95 *But the winds had also sculpted:* Orville to Charlie Taylor, October 4, 1903, ibid.

95 *"the finest day we ever had":* Wilbur to Octave Chanute, October 1, 1903, ibid.

95 *With the help of Dan Tate, a new 16 x 44-foot building:* Wilbur to Bishop Wright, October 4, 1903, ibid.

95 *the wind at one point blowing 75 miles per hour:* Orville Wright, "How We Made the First Flight," *Flying,* December 1913; Jakab and Young, eds., *The Published Writings of Wilbur and Orville Wright,* 43.

95 *"Worked all day in making connections":* Orville Wright's diary, October 12, 1903, McFarland, ed., *The Papers of Wilbur and Orville Wright,* Vol. 1, 362–63.

95 *"a storm hove to view":* Wilbur to Katharine, October 18, 1903; ibid., 365.

95 *"The wind suddenly whirled around":* Ibid., 365–66.

96 *"As the hammer and nails were in his pocket":* Ibid., 366–67.

96 *"but we took the advice":* Ibid., 367.

97 *"I see that Langley has had his fling":* Wilbur to Octave Chanute, October 16, 1903, Papers of Wilbur and Orville Wright, LOC.

97 *"Flying machine market has been very unsteady":* Orville to Charles Taylor, October 20, 1903, McFarland, ed., *The Papers of Wilbur and Orville Wright,* Vol. 1, 369.

97 *"Thursday, October 22: We worked all day":* Orville Wright's diary, October 22, 1903, ibid., 371.

98 *the magneto—a small generator utilizing magnets:* Orville Wright's diary, November 5, 1903, ibid., 377.

98 *"pursued by a blind fate":* Orville to Bishop Wright and Katharine, November 15, 1903, ibid., 381.

98 *"He doesn't seem to think our machines":* Ibid.

98 *"In addition to the classifications of last year":* Wilbur to Bishop Wright and Katharine, November 23, 1903, Papers of Wilbur and Orville Wright, LOC.

99 *"After a loaf of 15 days":* Orville to Charlie Taylor, November 23, 1903, McFarland, ed., *The Papers of Wilbur and Orville Wright,* Vol. 1, 385.

99 *"to keep house alone":* Wilbur to George Spratt, December 2, 1903, Papers of Wilbur and Orville Wright, LOC.

99 *In Washington, by the morning of December 8:* Gibbs-Smith, *Aviation,* 66.

99 *"now or never":* Tobin, *To Conquer the Air,* 187.

99 *The giant airship, with its wings again set:* Gibbs-Smith, *Aviation,* 66.

100 *Manly, who had disappeared into the river:* Chicago Daily News, December 9, 1903.

100 *"the most voluble":* Crouch, *The Bishop's Boys,* 263.

100 *Langley was compared to Darius Green:* Chicago Tribune, December 10, 1903.

100 *The government, said the* Washington Post: December 10, 1903.

101 *"He has constructed his aerodrome":* Chicago Tribune, December 10, 1903.

101 *"perhaps too soon":* Wilbur to Octave Chanute, November 8, 1906, McFarland, ed., *The Papers of Wilbur and Orville Wright,* Vol. 2, 737.

101 *"His work deserved neither abuse nor apology"*: Ibid.
102 *unpacking "the goods"*: Orville Wright's diary, December 11, 1903, ibid., Vol. 1, 391.
102 *On the afternoon of Monday the 14th:* Orville Wright's diary, December 14, 1903, ibid., 391–92.
102 *They simply flipped a coin:* Ibid., 392; Wilbur to Bishop Wright and Katharine, December 14, 1903, Papers of Wilbur and Orville Wright, LOC.
103 *"When we told him it was a flying machine"*: Orville Wright, "How We Made the First Flight," *Flying,* December 1913; Jakab and Young, eds., *The Published Writings of Wilbur and Orville Wright,* 45.
103 *"rigors of a cold December wind"*: Orville Wright and Wilbur Wright, "The Wright Brothers' Aeroplane," *Century Magazine,* No. 5, September 1908; Jakab and Young, eds., *The Published Writings of Wilbur and Orville Wright,* 30.
103 *"We had seen the glider fly without an engine"*: Saunders, "Then We Quit Laughing"; Jakab and Young, eds., *The Published Writings of Wilbur and Orville Wright,* 276.
103 *"a joker"*: Orville Wright, "How I Learned to Fly," *Boys' Life,* September 1914; ibid., 55.
103 *"duck-snarer"*: Ibid.
104 *"our audacity in attempting flights"*: Kelly, *The Wright Brothers,* 99.
104 *"a serious lot"*: Saunders, "Then We Quit Laughing"; Jakab and Young, eds., *The Published Writings of Wilbur and Orville Wright,* 276.
104 *"We tried," Daniels said:* Ibid.
105 *"previous acquaintance" with the conduct of the machine:* "Statement by the Wright Brothers to the Associated Press," January 5, 1904; Jakab and Young, eds., *The Published Writings of Wilbur and Orville Wright,* 15.
105 *"Were you scared?" Orville would be asked:* Leland D. Case, "Orville Wright: First Man to Fly," *The Rotarian,* April 1948; ibid., 100.
105 *"It was only a flight of twelve seconds"*: Orville Wright, "How I Learned to Fly"; ibid., 55.
105 *"went off like a bird"*: Saunders, "Then We Quit Laughing"; ibid., 276.
106 *"just like you've seen an umbrella"*: Ibid.
106 *"blowing across the beach"*: Ibid.
106 *"His escape was miraculous"*: Kelly, ed., *Miracle at Kitty Hawk,* 116.
106 *"ran up to me, pulled my legs and arms"*: Ibid., 277.
106 *Daniels could proudly claim:* John T. Daniels to Orville Wright, September 25, 1932, Papers of Wilbur and Orville Wright, LOC.
107 *"Well, they've made a flight"*: Kelly, ed., *Miracle at Kitty Hawk,* 118.
107 *"SUCCESS FOUR FLIGHTS THURSDAY MORNING"*: Orville to Bishop Wright, Telegram, December 17, 1903, McFarland, ed., *The Papers of Wilbur and Orville Wright,* Vol. 1, 397.
108 *Not incidentally, the Langley project:* Tobin, *To Conquer the Air,* 192.
108 *came to a little less than $1,000:* Kelly, *The Wright Brothers,* 112.
108 *"I like to think about it now"*: Saunders, "Then We Quit Laughing"; Jakab and Young, eds., *The Published Writings of Wilbur and Orville Wright,* 277.
108 *the two "workingest boys"*: Ibid., 275.
108 *"It wasn't luck that made them fly"*: Ibid., 278.

6. Out at Huffman Prairie

PAGE

109 "I found them in a pasture lot": Root, *Gleanings in Bee Culture,* January 1, 1905, 36–39.

109 *"Fifty-seven seconds, hey?":* Kelly, *The Wright Brothers,* 106–7.

110 *"FLYING MACHINE SOARS":* Virginian-Pilot, December 18, 1903.

110 *"POSITIVELY NO":* Tobin, *To Conquer the Air,* 194.

110 *Variations of the account appeared:* Kelly, *The Wright Brothers,* 105.

110 *In Boston, however:* Ibid., 115.

110 *"It seems to me":* Kelly, ed., *Miracle at Kitty Hawk,* 122.

111 *no "jig steps":* Taylor, "My Story of the Wright Brothers"; Jakab and Young, eds., *The Published Writings of Wilbur and Orville Wright,* 289.

111 *"There wasn't any other money":* Ibid., 288.

111 *great variety of bicycle "sundries":* Wright brothers' ledger books, Papers of Wilbur and Orville Wright, LOC.

111 *Charlie Taylor's $18 a week:* Taylor, "My Story of the Wright Brothers"; Jakab and Young, eds., *The Published Writings of Wilbur and Orville Wright,* 285.

112 *a popular science teacher:* Crouch, *The Bishop's Boys,* 279.

113 *The pasture belonged to Torrence Huffman:* Kelly, *The Wright Brothers,* 122.

113 *"They're fools":* Crouch, *The Bishop's Boys,* 279.

113 *"History was being made":* Miller, *Wright Reminiscences,* 68.

113 *could be seen out in the grass:* Kelly, *The Wright Brothers,* 206.

113 *When it came to building a shed:* There is a replica of the Wright brothers' shed at Huffman Prairie in Dayton, Ohio.

113 *On May 23, a Monday:* Kelly, *The Wright Brothers,* 123.

113 *On Wednesday, when the crowd gathered again:* Dayton Press, May 26, 1904.

113 *The morning after, May 26:* Ibid.; Wilbur to Octave Chanute, May 27, 1904, McFarland, ed., *The Papers of Wilbur and Orville Wright,* Vol. 1, 437–38.

114 *Bishop Wright, who had been watching:* Milton Wright, *Diaries, 1857–1917,* 608.

114 *"Tail stick broken in starting":* Wilbur Wright's diary, August 2, 1904, McFarland, ed., *The Papers of Wilbur and Orville Wright,* Vol. 1, 447.

114 *"disarranged":* Ibid., 448.

114 *"struck ground at start":* Wilbur Wright's diary, August 5, 1904, ibid.

114 *"a little rusty":* Wilbur to Octave Chanute, June 21, 1904, ibid., 442.

114 *"There was nothing spectacular":* Aero Club of America News, June 1912.

115 *An exception was Luther Beard:* Kelly, *The Wright Brothers,* 139.

115 *"render us independent of wind":* Wilbur to Octave Chanute, August 8, 1904, McFarland, ed., *The Papers of Wilbur and Orville Wright,* Vol. 1, 449.

115 *"starting apparatus":* Wilbur to Octave Chanute, August 28, 1904, ibid., 453. A replica of the Wright brothers' catapult can be seen at Huffman Prairie, Dayton, Ohio.

116 *reports coming "to our office":* Cox, *Journey Through My Years,* 83.

116 *"I guess the truth is that we were just plain dumb":* Kelly, *The Wright Brothers,* 135.

117 *He was Amos Ives Root:* Ibid., 142–43.

117 *Born in a log cabin:* Medina County Gazette, December 22, 1911; Root, *An Eyewitness Account of Early American Beekeeping: The Autobiography of A. I. Root,* 1.

117 *"the bee man":* Medina County Gazette, December 29, 1922, and March 9, 1923.

117 *He loved clocks, windmills, bicycles:* Ibid., May 1, 1923; Root, *An Eyewitness Account of Early American Beekeeping,* 18, 33, 146, 149.

117 *"While I like horses in a certain way"*: Root, *Gleanings in Bee Culture*, January 15, 1904, 85.

117 *at $350 it cost less than a horse and carriage:* Ibid., August 1, 1904.

118 *"I hope you will excuse me, friends"*: A. I. Root to Wilbur and Orville, February 16, 1904, Papers of Wilbur and Orville Wright, LOC.

118 *"Please excuse me, friends, but I am so anxious"*: A. I. Root to Wilbur and Orville, July 26, 1904, ibid.

118 *"one of the bright spots in my life"*: A. I. Root to Wilbur and Orville, August 23, 1904, ibid.

118 *He had promised he would say nothing:* Ibid.; Root, *Gleanings in Bee Culture*, January 1, 1905, 48.

118 *"In a recent trip of 400 miles through Ohio"*: Ibid., September 1, 1904.

119 *In the second week of September came word from the Wrights:* A. I. Root to Wilbur, September 12, 1904, Papers of Wilbur and Orville Wright, LOC.

119 *He reached Dayton on Tuesday, September 20:* Root, *Gleanings in Bee Culture*, January 1, 1905.

119 *"God in his great mercy"*: Ibid., 37.

120 *"when we shall not need to fuss"*: Ibid., 38.

121 *had been taken for a "nut"*: *Medina County Gazette*, May 1, 1923; *New York Times*, April 4, 1971.

121 *he was a man of strong religious convictions:* Root, *Gleanings in Bee Culture*, September 1, 1904.

121 *"Mr. Root seems to be a fine gentleman"*: Milton Wright, *Diaries, 1857–1917*, 618.

121 *"If such sensational and tremendously important experiments"*: *Scientific American*, January 1906.

122 *"If they will not take our word"*: Tobin, *To Conquer the Air*, 263.

122 *An officer of the British Army's Balloon Section:* Wilbur to Octave Chanute, November 15, 1904, McFarland, ed., *The Papers of Wilbur and Orville Wright*, Vol. 1, 465.

122 *"not ready to begin considering"*: Kelly, ed., *Miracle at Kitty Hawk*, 133.

122 *Wilbur flew almost four circles:* Milton Wright, *Diaries, 1857–1917*, 616.

123 *Nevin suggested that Wilbur write a proposal:* Wilbur to Octave Chanute, January 1, 1905, McFarland, ed., *The Papers of Wilbur and Orville Wright*, Vol. 1, 494–95.

123 *The letter, dated January 18:* Kelly, *The Wright Brothers*, 149.

123 *Congressman Nevin forwarded the letter:* Ibid., 150.

123 *"practical operation"*: Crouch, *The Bishop's Boys*, 292.

123 *"flat turn down"*: Wilbur to Octave Chanute, June 1, 1905, McFarland, ed., *The Papers of Wilbur and Orville Wright*, Vol. 1, 495.

124 *"The power consumed by any bird"*: Wilbur to Octave Chanute, March 11, 1905, ibid., 480–81.

125 *"The best dividends on the labor invested"*: Grimes, "Man May Now Fly at Will," *Technical World Magazine*, Vol. 5, June 1906, 33.

125 *"The operator, not relishing the idea of landing"*: Orville Wright, *Selections from the Writings of the Wright Brothers*, privately printed for the Orville Wright Dinner, 1918, 11; Orville Wright, "The Wright Brothers' Aeroplane," *Century Magazine*, No. 5, September 1908; Jakab and Young, eds., *The Published Writings of Wilbur and Orville Wright*, 31.

125 *Orville was able to nose the plane upward again:* Wilbur Wright's Summary of the Experiments of 1905, McFarland, ed., *The Papers of Wilbur and Orville Wright*, Vol. 1., 520.

126 *"When you know, after the first few minutes"*: New York Herald, November 25, 1906.

126 *"a perfect blur"*: Wright, "The Wright Brothers' Aeroplane," Century Magazine, September 1908; Jakab and Young, eds., The Published Writings of Wilbur and Orville Wright, 32.

126 *"At a height of one hundred feet"*: Ibid.

127 *On the afternoon of October 5, 1905*: Dayton Daily News, October 6, 1905.

127 *"I saw Wilbur fly twenty-four miles"*: Milton Wright, Diaries, 1857–1917, 633.

128 *"When I went out to Huffman Prairie"*: Dayton Daily News, January 5, 1906.

128 *"scant consideration"*: Wilbur and Orville to the Secretary of War, October 9, 1905, McFarland, ed., The Papers of Wilbur and Orville Wright, Vol. 1, 515.

128 *"the same thing that they had before"*: Katharine to Bishop Wright, October 18, 1905, Papers of Wilbur and Orville Wright, LOC.

128 *"such drawings and descriptions"*: Kelly, ed., Miracle at Kitty Hawk, 149.

128 *"horizontal flight and to carry an operator"*: McFarland, ed., The Papers of Wilbur and Orville Wright, Vol. 1, 518, footnote 1; Kelly, ed., Miracle at Kitty Hawk, 152.

128 *"Those fellows are a bunch of asses"*: Thomas P. Hughes, American Genesis: A Century of Invention and Technological Enthusiasm, 1870–1970, Chicago: University of Chicago Press, 2004, 102.

128 *In the last week of 1905*: Milton Wright, Diaries, 1857–1917, 636.

129 *"Saturday, December 30 In the afternoon"*: Ibid.

7. A Capital Exhibit A

PAGE

131 "He inspires great confidence": Memorandum of Hart O. Berg to Charles Flint on first meeting Wilbur Wright in London, May 26, 1907, Papers of Wilbur and Orville Wright, LOC.

131 "You people at home must stop worrying!": Wilbur to Katharine, July 17, 1907, ibid.

131 *"merely to see the sights"*: Dayton Herald, March 26, 1906.

132 *The one American, Walter Berry*: Milton Wright, Diaries, 1857–1917, 643; McFarland, ed., The Papers of Wilbur and Orville Wright, Vol. 2, 705, footnote 2.

132 *"The Wrights have flown or they have not flown"*: Kelly, The Wright Brothers, 192–93.

132 *On the evening of March 24*: Milton Wright, Diaries, 1857–1917, March 24, 1905, 643.

133 *"Notwithstanding the failure"*: Wilbur to Commandant Henri Bonel, April 6, 1906, McFarland, ed., The Papers of Wilbur and Orville Wright, Vol. 2, 708–9.

133 *Charles Webbert, from whom the Wrights rented the bicycle shop*: Jakab and Young, eds., The Published Writings of Wilbur and Orville Wright, 18, footnote 5.

133 *"absolutely free from the time it left the rail"*: Scientific American, April 7, 1906.

133 *In France, Alberto Santos-Dumont*: McFarland, ed., The Papers of Wilbur and Orville Wright, Vol. 2, 734–35.

133 *"gained the greatest glory"*: Crouch, The Bishop's Boys, 326.

134 *"I fancy that he is now very nearly where you were"*: Octave Chanute to Wilbur, November 1, 1906, McFarland, ed., The Papers of Wilbur and Orville Wright, Vol. 2, 733.

134 *"Fear that others will produce a machine"*: Wilbur to Octave Chanute, April 22, 1907, ibid., 756.

134 *Flint & Company was offering the Wrights $500,000:* Wilbur to Octave Chanute, December 20, 1906, ibid., 743.

134 *In February, Germany offered $500,000:* Wilbur to Orville, February 8, 1907, ibid., 751.

134 *"I am more careful than he is":* Wilbur to Bishop Wright, July 20, 1907, Papers of Wilbur and Orville Wright, LOC.

135 *"grabbed a few things":* Wilbur to Octave Chanute, May 16, 1907, McFarland, ed., *The Papers of Wilbur and Orville Wright,* Vol. 2, 760.

135 *By Saturday, May 18:* Wilbur to Katharine, May 18, 1907, Papers of Wilbur and Orville Wright, LOC.

135 *"I sailed this morning about 9 o'clock":* Ibid.

135 *The weather was "splendid":* Ibid.

135 *"We made 466 miles the first day":* Ibid.

135 *The third day out he took a tour:* Wilbur to Katharine, May 20, 1907, ibid.

135 *He kept note of the miles made day by day:* Wilbur to Katharine, May 21, 1907, ibid.

136 *"The waves are probably 10 feet high":* Wilbur to Katharine, May 23, 1907, ibid.

136 *"a little sick":* Ibid.

136 *"and how they could skim within a foot":* Wilbur to Katharine, May 24, 1907, ibid.

136 *"I have never seen a picture of him":* Memorandum of Hart O. Berg to Charles Flint on first meeting Wilbur Wright in London, May 26, 1907, ibid.

136 *At a tailor shop in the Strand:* Ibid.

136 *"Orv had marched off to Perry Meredith's":* Katharine to Wilbur, June 8, 1907, ibid.

137 *"He inspires great confidence":* Memorandum of Hart O. Berg to Charles Flint on first meeting Wilbur Wright in London, May 26, 1907, ibid.

137 *Berg and his wife, Edith:* Milwaukee Journal, December 18, 1928.

137 *"The Tuileries Palace and the Louvre":* Wilbur to Katharine, May 27, 1907, Papers of Wilbur and Orville Wright, LOC.

137 *The "New Hotel Meurice":* New York Tribune, March 23, 1907.

138 *"rendezvous of fashion":* Ibid., April 18, 1908.

139 *"Paris is the most prodigal of land":* Wilbur to Bishop Wright, June 4, 1907, Papers of Wilbur and Orville Wright, LOC.

139 *"There is always an open space":* Ibid.

139 *"a little shabby":* Wilbur to Bishop Wright, June 7, 1907, ibid.

139 *He spent considerable time at the Panthéon:* Wilbur to Katharine, June 5, 1907, ibid.

139 *"My imagination pictures things":* Wilbur to Katharine, June 8, 1907, ibid.

140 *"right on the sidewalks":* Wilbur to Bishop Wright, June 4, 1907, ibid.

140 *He preferred the Rembrandts:* Wilbur to Orville, May 30, 1907, ibid.

140 *"While I do not pretend to be much of a judge":* Wilbur to Katharine, June 5, 1907, ibid.

141 *"entirely another thing from flying":* Washington Post, June 30, 1907.

141 *"You are over here on pleasure":* Paris Herald, June 14, 1907.

142 *"the Standard Oil King of France":* Crouch, The Bishop's Boys, 335.

142 *"pretty slick hand":* Wilbur to Orville, May 31, 1907, Papers of Wilbur and Orville Wright, LOC.

142 *Berg was "very practical":* Wilbur to Orville, May 28, 1907, ibid.

142 *"about as enthusiastic now":* Wilbur to Orville, June 7, 1907, ibid.

142 *"The pot is beginning to boil":* Ibid.

142 *"bluffers like all Americans":* M. Lazare Weiller, "De Montgolfier a Wilbur

Wright." From a report of the 52nd meeting of La Societe Archeologique le Vieux Papier, December 22, 1908.

143 *One Monday morning, while Wilbur was lying in bed:* Wilbur Wright's diary, July 8, 1907, McFarland, ed., *The Papers of Wilbur and Orville Wright*, Vol. 2, 790.

143 *"very successful trial":* Ibid., 791.

143 *"Don't worry over Flint's commission":* Wilbur to Orville, June 12, 1907, Papers of Wilbur and Orville Wright, LOC.

144 *"distributed among persons who had the power":* Wilbur to Orville, July 12, 1907, ibid.

144 *"I presume you will have everything packed":* Wilbur to Orville, June 28, 1907, ibid.

144 *"Orv can't work any":* Katharine to Wilbur, June 30, 1907, ibid.

144 *"I can't stand Berg's looks":* Ibid.

144 *"What on earth is happening to your letters?":* Katharine to Wilbur, July 5, 1907, ibid.

144 *"We are all so nervous":* Ibid.

145 *"Why couldn't you tell us sooner":* Katharine to Wilbur, July 16, 1907, ibid.

145 *"in one of his peculiar spells":* Wilbur to Bishop Wright, July 20, 1907, McFarland, ed., *The Papers of Wilbur and Orville Wright*, Vol. 2, 804–5.

145 *"In view of the fact that I have written":* Wilbur to Katharine, July 17, 1907, Papers of Wilbur and Orville Wright, LOC.

146 *"I have done what I know he would have done":* Ibid.

146 *"It is not my custom to voice my complaints":* Ibid.

146 *"merely sort of an exhibit":* Ibid.

146 *They took off from the Aéro-Club grounds:* Wilbur to Bishop Wright, July 18, 1907, ibid.

146 *"The alterations of rich brown newly plowed soil":* Ibid.

147 *"What we are seeking is the means":* Vernon, "The Flying Man," *McClure's Magazine*, Vol. 3, 1894.

147 *"pretty well fizzled out":* Katharine to Wilbur, August 1, 1907, Papers of Wilbur and Orville Wright, LOC.

147 *Early on a Sunday morning in late July: New York Herald*, July 29, 1907; *L'Aérophile*, June 1907; London *Daily Mail*, September 2, 1907.

147 *"a rather warm heart-to-heart talk":* Wilbur Wright's diary, July 29, 1907, McFarland, ed., *The Papers of Wilbur and Orville Wright*, Vol. 2, 809.

147 *"We are, and intend to be":* Notes of Conversation between Wilbur and Orville Wright and Hart O. Berg, Paris, November 6, 1907, ibid., 827, 830.

148 *"Our friends F":* Orville to Katharine, June 28, 1907, Papers of Wilbur and Orville Wright, LOC.

148 *Wilbur led Orville on a first stroll:* Wilbur to Bishop Wright, August 2, 1907, ibid.

148 *Frank Cordley hosted an evening at the . . . Tour d'Argent:* Orville to Katharine, August 2, 1907, ibid.

148 *"The legs, wings, etc.":* Ibid.

148 *"We have been real good over here":* Orville to Bishop Wright, August 23, 1907, ibid.

149 *On the way to Berlin:* Kelly, *The Wright Brothers*, 204.

149 *"We do not want the papers":* Orville to Katharine, August 14, 1907, Papers of Wilbur and Orville Wright, LOC.

149 *occupied primarily with sitting in the park: Paris Herald*, September 29, 1907.

149 *"You need not worry about me":* Orville to Katharine, September 9, 1907, Papers of Wilbur and Orville Wright, LOC.

150 *"They jump on and off the horses":* Ibid.

150 *Greatest by far was the spectacle:* Ibid.

151 *The "mystery" of the Wrights: Paris Herald,* September 29, 1907.

151 *Apparently the brothers caught on quickly to the diabolo art:* Wilbur to Katharine, August 27, 1907, Papers of Wilbur and Orville Wright, LOC.

151 *"You never told me whether you learned to talk":* Katharine to Orville, September 22, 1907, ibid.

151 *His sense of humor plainly in play again:* Orville to Katharine, September 26, 1907, ibid.

151 *"getting along famously":* Katharine to Wilbur, August 25, 1907, ibid.

151 *He had bought a new typewriter:* Bishop Wright to Wilbur, September 5, 1907, ibid.

151 *She had ordered a new stove:* Katharine to Wilbur and Orville, October 13, 1907, ibid.

152 *"What plans do you suggest?":* Wilbur to Orville, September 29, 1907, ibid.

152 *"Aren't you getting worried over 'Farman's flights'?":* Katharine to Wilbur, November 21, 1907, ibid.

153 *"It seems that to the genius of France":* John Sweetman, *Cavalry of the Clouds: Air War Over Europe, 1914–1918* (Gloucestershire, UK: History Press, 2010), 15.

153 *"We will spend the winter":* Wilbur to Bishop Wright, November 22, 1907, ibid.

8. Triumph at Le Mans

155 "Gentlemen, I'm going to fly": Tobin, *To Conquer the Air,* 306.

155 *"I am on my way to Kitty Hawk":* Wilbur to Octave Chanute, April 8, 1908, McFarland, ed., *The Papers of Wilbur and Orville Wright,* Vol. 2, 861.

155 *Though he had been forewarned:* Wilbur Wright's diary, April 10, 1908, ibid., 862.

155 *Walking among the ruins:* Wilbur to Orville, April 11, 1908, ibid.

156 *"Conditions are almost intolerable":* Wilbur Wright's diary, April 18, 1908, ibid., 866.

156 *Nor did the fact that so many of those:* Wilbur to Bishop Wright, April 28, 1908, Papers of Wilbur and Orville Wright, LOC.

156 *A Dayton mechanic the brothers had hired:* Wilbur to Bishop Wright, April 16, 1908, ibid.

156 *"Spent afternoon cleaning out trash":* Wilbur Wright's diary, April 25, 1908, McFarland, ed., *The Papers of Wilbur and Orville Wright,* Vol. 2, 869.

156 *The morning of Monday, April 27:* Wilbur Wright's diary, April 27, 1908, ibid.; Wilbur to Bishop Wright, April 28, 1908, Papers of Wilbur and Orville Wright, LOC.

156 Virginian-Pilot: Howard, *Wilbur and Orville,* 241.

157 *Test flights got started on May 6:* Renstrom, *Wilbur and Orville Wright: A Re-Issue of a Chronology Commemorating the Hundredth Anniversary of the Birth of Orville Wright, August 19, 1871,* 85.

157 *Once he left, Wilbur took off again:* Ibid.

157 *"The Wrights we found were some twelve or fourteen miles":* "Journal of Byron Newton," Byron Newton Papers, Oberlin College, Oberlin, Ohio.

157 *"the end of the world"*: Ruhl, "History at Kill Devil Hills," *Collier's Weekly*, May 30, 1908.

158 *"There was something weird"*: Walsh, *One Day at Kitty Hawk: The Untold Story of the Wright Brothers and the Airplane*, 215.

158 *"We couldn't have delayed"*: Kelly, *The Wright Brothers*, 224.

158 *"dazzling white sand dunes"*: Ruhl, "History at Kill Devil Hills."

158 *"[We were] all seasoned campaigners"*: "Journal of Byron Newton," Byron Newton Papers, Oberlin College, Oberlin, Ohio.

158 *A photographer for* Collier's Weekly: Renstrom, *Wilbur and Orville Wright*, 85.

158 *Early the morning of May 14*: Ibid., 86; *Chicago Examiner*, May 15, 1908; *Philadelphia Press*, May 17, 1908.

159 *"I was watching with the field glass"*: Tise, *Conquering the Sky: The Secret Flights of the Wright Brothers at Kitty Hawk*, 115.

159 *He had been violently thrown*: Renstrom, *Wilbur and Orville Wright*, 86.

159 *"I hate like anything to go away"*: Wilbur to Katharine, May 19, 1908, Papers of Wilbur and Orville Wright, LOC.

159 *"Write often"*: Katharine to Wilbur, May 31, 1908, ibid.

160 *"smooth but foggy much of the time"*: Wilbur Wright's diary, May 29, 1908, McFarland, ed., *The Papers of Wilbur and Orville Wright*, Vol. 2, 883.

160 *He reached Paris on May 29*: *Dayton Daily News*, May 29, 1908.

160 *a "tendency" to be hostile*: Wilbur to Orville, June 3, 1908, McFarland, ed., *The Papers of Wilbur and Orville Wright*, Vol. 2, 806.

160 *"The first thing is to get some practice"*: Tise, *Conquering the Sky*, 178.

160 *Hart Berg assured a correspondent*: *L'Auto*, June 3, 1908 and June 14, 1908.

160 *Bollée met Wilbur and Berg*: Wilbur Wright's diary, June 8, 1909, McFarland, ed., *The Papers of Wilbur and Orville Wright*, Vol. 2, 895.

161 *Short and dark bearded*: Kelly, *The Wright Brothers*, 236; Howard, *Wilbur and Orville*, 249; Wilbur to Orville, October 4, 1908, Papers of Wilbur and Orville Wright, LOC.

161 *"Léon Bollée automobiles"*: Le Figaro, March 22, 1908.

161 *Wilbur received word from Bollée*: Wilbur Wright's diary, June 11, 1908, McFarland, ed., *The Papers of Wilbur and Orville Wright*, Vol. 2, 896.

161 *a young French aviation journalist*: L'Auto, June 14, 1908; see also Peyrey, *Premiers Les Hommes-Oiseaux*.

162 *Wilbur arrived back in Le Mans*: Wilbur Wright's diary, June 16, 1908, McFarland, ed., *The Papers of Wilbur and Orville Wright*, Vol. 2, 899.

162 *overlooking the main square, the Place de la République*: Wilbur to Bishop Wright, June 21, 1908, Papers of Wilbur and Orville Wright, LOC.

162 *he began opening the crates*: Wilbur Wright's diary, June 17, 1908, McFarland, ed., *The Papers of Wilbur and Orville Wright*, Vol. 2, 899.

162 *"I am sure that with a scoop shovel"*: Wilbur to Orville, June 17, 1908, ibid., 900.

162 *"Worked all today and a few hours yesterday"*: Wilbur Wright's diary, June 18, 1908, ibid., 901.

162 *"I have had an awful job sewing the section together"*: Wilbur to Orville, June 20, 1908, Papers of Wilbur and Orville Wright, LOC.

163 *"I have to do practically all the work"*: Ibid.

163 *Hôtel du Dauphin*: *Motor Car Journal*, December 7, 1907; *Autocar*, February 1906.

163 *He loved the sound of the chimes*: Wilbur to Katharine, June 28, 1908, Papers of Wilbur and Orville Wright, LOC.

163 *"The arches forming the openings"*: Wilbur to Katharine, June 23, 1908, ibid.

164 *"impresses me more and more":* Wilbur to Katharine, June 28, 1908, ibid.

164 *He wrote of the comforts of the hotel:* Wilbur to Katharine, June 23, 1908, ibid.

164 *"some sort of cake":* Ibid.

164 *"I was a little astonished":* Wilbur to Katharine, June 28, 1908, ibid.

165 *"I have to do all the work myself":* Wilbur to Orville, June 28, 1908, ibid.

165 *On the evening of July 4:* Wilbur to Katharine, July 7, 1908, ibid.

165 *"Fortunately we had picric acid":* Léon Bollée to Hart Berg, June 4, 1908, ibid.

167 *"We voted him 'mule-headed' ":* London *Daily Mail,* August 17, 1908.

167 *"I did not ask you to come here":* Ibid.

167 *Their nickname for him was* Vieille Burette: Combs and Caidin, *Kill Devil Hill,* 284.

167 *"In a corner of the shed was his 'room' ":* London *Daily Mail,* August 17, 1908.

167 *The sky overhead was a great blue vault:* Cleveland *Plain Dealer,* August 9, 1908.

168 *"The famous Wright brothers may today claim":* Crouch, *The Bishop's Boys,* 345.

169 *Such "quiet self-confidence":* Kelly, *The Wright Brothers,* 236.

169 *"Neither the impatience of waiting crowds":* Sproul, *The Wright Brothers: The Birth of Modern Aviation,* 52.

169 *After much show of despair: Paris Herald,* August 9, 1908.

171 *"C'est l'homme qui a conquis l'air!":* Kelly, *The Wright Brothers,* 238.

171 *"I would have waited ten times as long": Paris Herald,* August 9, 1908.

171 *"C'est merveilleux!":* Ibid.; Tobin, *To Conquer the Air,* 309.

171 *"very calmly":* London *Daily Mail,* August 8, 1908.

171 *headline news everywhere:* Le Matin, August 9, 1908, *Paris Herald,* August 9, 1908, London *Daily Mail,* August 9, 1908, *Echo de Paris,* August 9, 1908, *Chicago Tribune,* August 9, 1908, *Dayton Journal,* August 9, 1908.

172 *"The mystery":* Le Matin, August 9, 1908.

172 *"the most marvelous aeroplane flight":* London *Daily Mail,* August 8, 1908.

172 *"Not one of the former detractors":* Crouch, *The Bishop's Boys,* 368.

172 *"For a long time, for too long a time":* Ibid.

172 *"Today, because it is Sunday":* Le Petit Journal, August 10, 1908.

172 *"a harvest of money":* New York Times, August 12, 1908.

173 *"ablaze with anger":* Walsh, *One Day at Kitty Hawk,* 228.

173 *"In a flight lasting":* London *Daily Mail,* August 11, 1908.

173 *"Well, we are beaten!":* Gibbs-Smith, *Aviation,* 131; Howard, *Wilbur and Orville,* 259.

173 *"Now all have seen":* New York Herald, August 10, 1908.

174 *"and the features, dominated by a long prominent nose":* London *Daily Mail,* August 17, 1908.

174 *"The flecks of gold":* Le Figaro, August 11, 1908.

174 *"Even if this man sometimes deigns to smile":* Léon Delagrange, "Impressions sur L'Aéroplane Wright," *L'Illustration,* August 15, 1908.

174 *"Wilbur Wright is the best example of strength of character":* Ibid.

175 *"un timide": L'Auto,* August 8, 1908.

175 *On Thursday, August 13:* Renstrom, *Wilbur and Orville Wright,* 87.

176 *"a pretty bad smash-up":* Wilbur to Orville, August 15, 1908, McFarland, ed., *The Papers of Wilbur and Orville Wright,* Vol. 2, 912.

176 *"Mr. Wright is as superb":* Howard, *Wilbur and Orville,* 260.

176 *"All question as to who originated the flying machine":* Wilbur to Katharine, August 22, 1908, Papers of Wilbur and Orville Wright, LOC.

176 *"I cannot even take a bath":* Ibid.

176 *A new song, "Il Vole":* Ibid.

176 *because of "their grit":* Dayton Herald, August 18, 1908.

176 *"How many, many times have we wished":* Katharine to Wilbur, August 9, 1908, ibid.

176 *a big "welcome home":* Katharine to Wilbur, August 18, 1908, ibid.

177 *"all kinds of the finest sardines":* Wilbur to Bishop Wright, August 15, 1908, ibid.

177 *"The new grounds are much larger":* Ibid.

177 *"excitement almost beyond":* Wilbur to Orville, August 25, 1908, Papers of Wilbur and Orville Wright, LOC.

177 *"They flock from miles":* Le Figaro, August 25, 1908.

177 *The public is:* Ibid.

178 *Orville had gone to Washington:* Dayton Journal, September 3, 1908.

178 *"avoid all unnecessary personal risk":* Bishop Wright to Wilbur, August 2, 1908, Papers of Wilbur and Orville Wright, LOC.

178 *"I tell them plainly that I intend":* Wilbur to Orville, August 25, 1908, Papers of Wilbur and Orville Wright, LOC.

178 *"I can only say":* Ibid.

178 *On the evening of August 25:* Paris Herald, August 26, 1908.

9. The Crash

PAGE

181 [He] rode the air as deliberately: Crouch, *Wings: A History of Aviation from Kites to the Space Age,* Prologue.

181 *Orville was in Washington:* Orville to Katharine, August 27, 1908, Papers of Wilbur and Orville Wright, LOC.

181 *"stacks of prominent people":* Orville to Katharine, August 29, 1908, ibid.

181 *"Suppose you tell me about a few things":* Katharine to Wilbur, August 27, 1908, ibid.

181 *"very smart" and "charming woman, like yourself":* Wilbur to Katharine, August 13, 1908, ibid.

182 *"answering the ten thousand fool questions":* Orville to Katharine, August 27, 1908, ibid.

182 *"Mr. Wright stood and talked":* Washington Post, September 2, 1908.

182 *"I am meeting some very handsome young ladies!":* Orville to Katharine, August 31, 1908, Papers of Wilbur and Orville Wright, LOC.

182 *"I don't know when Pop":* Katharine to Wilbur, August 27, 1908, ibid.

182 *"Now, if you and Orville don't":* Katharine to Wilbur, August 30, 1908, ibid.

182 *It was a space smaller even:* Orville to Bishop Wright, September 7, 1908, ibid.

182 *After several days of trouble:* Washington Post, September 1, 1908.

182 *the first full-scale public performance of a Wright plane:* New York Times, September 4, 1908.

182 *Not until late in the afternoon of September 3:* New York Times, September 4, 1908; Washington Evening Star, September 4, 1908; Dayton Journal, September 4, 1908.

182 *"For the first time since his arrival":* New York Times, September 4, 1908.

183 *"That man's nerves":* Washington Post, September 18, 1908.

183 *At last, at about six o'clock:* New York Times, September 4, 1908.

183 *"frenzy of enthusiasm":* Ibid.

183 *"It shows I need a great deal of practice":* Ibid.

183 *By his estimate he had flown:* Atlanta Constitution, September 4, 1908.

183 *The day after, Friday, September 4: New York Times*, September 5, 1908; *Paris Daily Mail*, September 5, 1908.

183 *thought the flight "splendid": New York Times*, September 5, 1908.

183 *"seemed to respond perfectly":* Ibid.

183 *Orville provided one sensational performance: Dayton Journal*, September 9, 1908.

183 *Early the morning of Wednesday, September 9:* Ibid.; *Washington Times*, September 9, 1908.

184 *"At 5:15": Dayton Journal*, September 9, 1909.

184 *The next day, September 10: Paris Herald*, September 11, 1908.

184 *Worried that Orville might be losing count:* Ibid., September 12, 1908; *Dayton Herald*, September 12, 1908.

184 *with a pot of white paint: New York Times*, September 11, 1908.

184 *One of those watching that day:* Crouch, *Wings*, Prologue.

185 *"the coolest man around": Dayton Journal*, September 10, 1908.

185 *Indeed, seeing Lieutenant Frank Lahm: Paris Herald*, September 11, 1908.

186 *"Good for you, my boy!": New York Times*, September 12, 1908.

186 *"Pretty good," Orville said: Dayton Herald*, September 12, 1908.

186 *"Everyone here is very enthusiastic":* Orville to Wilbur, September 13, 1908, Papers of Wilbur and Orville Wright, LOC.

186 *"No place is safe":* Wells, *The War in the Air*, 123.

187 *"Orv telegraphed after he made his long flight":* Katharine to Wilbur, September 13, 1908, Papers of Wilbur and Orville Wright, LOC.

188 *"Do you suppose we could scratch up the cash?":* Katharine to Orville, September 12, 1908, ibid.

188 *"Enjoy fame ere its decadence":* Bishop Wright to Wilbur, September 9, 1908, ibid.

188 *"He wants to go alright":* Katharine to Wilbur, September 13, 1908, ibid.

188 *"The newspapers for several days":* Wilbur to Orville, September 13, 1908, ibid.

188 *He was having motor troubles:* Ibid.

188 *To Katharine he reported:* Wilbur to Katharine, September 13, 1908, ibid.

189 *"The excitement and the worry":* Wilbur to Bishop Wright, September 13, 1908, ibid.

189 *he carried on his correspondence sitting in his shed:* Wilbur to Katharine, September 15, 1908, ibid.

189 *another few days to "quiet down":* Orville to Katharine, September 15, 1908, ibid.

189 *Rumors in Washington and in an article in the* New York Times: *Dayton Herald*, September 15, 1908; *New York Times*, September 15, 1908.

189 *"given to the espousal of the unusual": New York Times*, ibid.

189 *Two years before he had startled the country: Dayton Herald*, September 15, 1908.

189 *"Of course, if the President asks me": New York Times*, September 15, 1908.

190 *On Thursday, September 17: Paris Herald*, September 18, 1908; *New York Journal*, September 18, 1908; *Washington Evening Star*, September 18, 1908; *Washington Post*, September 18, 1908.

190 *Lieutenant Thomas Selfridge was a twenty-six-year-old: Washington Evening Star*, September 18, 1908; *Washington Post*, September 18, 1908.

190 *"I don't trust him an inch":* Crouch, *The Bishop's Boys*, 375.

190 *"Selfridge is endeavoring":* Orville to Bishop Wright, September 7, 1908, Papers of Wilbur and Orville Wright, LOC.

190 *Selfridge also weighed 175 pounds: Washington Evening Star*, September 18, 1908.

190 *Selfridge removed his coat and campaign hat:* Ibid.; *Washington Post*, September 18, 1908.

191 *"It was noticed that Lieutenant Selfridge was apparently":* Ibid.

191 *passing over the "aerial garage":* Ibid.

191 *"That's a piece of the propeller":* Ibid.

191 *"Quick as a flash, the machine turned down":* Orville to Wilbur, November 14, 1908, McFarland, ed., *The Papers of Wilbur and Orville Wright*, Vol. 2, 937.

191 *"Oh! Oh!":* Ibid.

191 *"like a bird shot dead in full flight":* New York Times, September 18, 1908.

192 *Orville and the lieutenant lay pinned: Washington Post*, September 18, 1908.

192 *"If they won't stand back, ride them down":* Roseberry, *Glenn Curtiss: Pioneer of Flight*, 128.

192 *Several army surgeons: Washington Evening Star*, September 18, 1908.

192 *A reporter wrote of having seen Charlie Taylor: Washington Post*, September 18, 1908.

192 *Not until well after dark: Washington Evening Star*, September 18, 1908.

192 *"If Mr. Wright should never again":* Ibid.

193 *"I am afflicted with the pain you feel":* Bishop Wright to Orville, September 20, 1908, Papers of Wilbur and Orville Wright, LOC.

193 *It was eight o'clock at Camp d'Auvours: Washington Evening Star*, September 18, 1908; *New York Times*, September 18, 1908.

193 *Wilbur postponed all flights:* Wilbur to Bishop Wright, September 22, 1908, Papers of Wilbur and Orville Wright, LOC.

193 *"Now you understand why":* New York Times, September 18, 1908; *Washington Evening Star*, September 18, 1908.

193 *Left alone, he sat with head in hands: Washington Post*, September 19, 1908.

194 *Others present saw him struggle: Washington Evening Star*, September 18, 1908.

194 *He felt very bad about "this business": Paris Herald*, September 19, 1908.

194 *"I do not mean that Orville was incompetent":* Wilbur to Katharine, September 20, 1908, McFarland, ed., *The Papers of Wilbur and Orville Wright*, Vol. 2, 926.

195 *It is sad that Orville is hurt:* Bishop Wright to Wilbur, September 19, 1908, Papers of Wilbur and Orville Wright, LOC.

195 *"the bull by the horns":* Wilbur to Orville, September 23, 1908, ibid.

195 *Among the enormous crowd: Paris Herald*, September 22, 1908.

195 *"I found Orville looking pretty badly":* Katharine to Lorin Wright, September 19, 1908, Papers of Wilbur and Orville Wright, LOC.

196 *"in a sort of cradle":* Katharine to Wilbur, September 24, 1908, ibid.

196 *"When I went in his chin quivered":* Ibid.

196 *"The thousand proud":* Katharine to Lorin Wright, September 19, 1908, ibid.

196 *At first she lived with a couple named Shearer:* Katharine to Bishop Wright, September 21, 1908, ibid.

196 *To get to the hospital from their home:* Katharine to Bishop Wright, October 1, 1908, ibid.

196 *"Last night was a rather bad time":* Katharine to Bishop Wright, September 21, 1908, ibid.

196 *"Tonight I am staying all night":* Ibid.

197 *"Will had his nerve with him":* Ibid.

197 *"Orville thinks that the propeller":* Ibid.

197 *"the only time anything has broken"*: Wilbur to Bishop Wright, September 22, 1908, ibid.

198 *On September 23, Alexander Graham Bell:* Octave Chanute to Katharine Wright, September 29, 1908, McFarland, ed., *The Papers of Wilbur and Orville Wright*, Vol. 2, 929, footnote 1.

198 *"very cheeky"*: Bishop Wright to Katharine, October 3, 1908, Papers of Wilbur and Orville Wright, LOC.

198 *The doctors and the day nurse were "splendid"*: Katharine to Bishop Wright, October 1, 1908, ibid.

199 *"Brother has been suffering so much"*: Katharine to Bishop Wright, September 24, 1908, ibid.

199 *it was she who represented Orville at the funeral ceremony: New York Times*, September 26, 1908.

199 *"Your sister has been devotion itself"*: Octave Chanute to Wilbur Wright, October 7, 1908, McFarland, ed., *The Papers of Wilbur and Orville Wright*, Vol. 2, 930.

199 *Most important by far:* Katharine to Bishop Wright, October 2, 1908, Papers of Wilbur and Orville Wright, LOC.

199 *"Have lost eighty-two and a half dollars"*: Katharine to Wilbur, October 2, 1908, Papers of Wilbur and Orville Wright, LOC.

199 *his temperature jumped to 101 degrees:* Katharine to Bishop Wright, October 4, 1908, ibid.

199 *"I took Bollée (240 pounds)"*: Wilbur to Orville, October 4, 1908, ibid.

200 *"We are both fairly wild to get home"*: Katharine to Wilbur, October 19, 1908, ibid.

200 *"I think I will have to stay"*: Katharine to Bishop Wright, October 17, 1908, ibid.

200 *Orville continued having his "ups and downs"*: Katharine to Wilbur, October 19, 1908, ibid.

200 *So she began cooking for him:* Katharine to Bishop Wright, October 19, 1908, ibid.

200 *"too tired to talk!"*: Katharine to Bishop Wright, October 22, 1908, ibid.

200 *Three days before he was to leave: New York Times*, October 31, 1908, November 1, 1908.

200 *But on October 31, after five weeks:* Bishop Wright to Wilbur, November 2, 1908, Papers of Wilbur and Orville Wright, LOC.

200 *A good-sized crowd stood waiting: Dayton News*, November 2, 1908; *Dayton Journal*, November 2, 1908.

200 *"Many had come there to cheer"*: *Dayton Journal*, November 2, 1908.

200 *Brother Lorin had come to the station:* Ibid.

201 *Orville's mind was "good as ever"*: Milton Wright, *Diaries, 1857–1917*, 684.

201 *"tired to death"*: Katharine to Wilbur, November 13, 1908, Papers of Wilbur and Orville Wright, LOC.

201 *"a good deal of attention"*: Ibid.

201 *A local surgeon who looked him over:* Ibid.

201 *Charlie Taylor was pushing him in the wheelchair:* Ibid.

201 *"I have an awful accumulation of work"*: McFarland, ed., *The Papers of Wilbur and Orville Wright*, Vol. 2, 939.

10. A Time Like No Other

203 "Every time we make a move": Katharine to Lorin Wright, January 24, 1909, Papers of Wilbur and Orville Wright, LOC.

203 *Wilbur's days at Le Mans:* See *Paris Herald,* September 22, 1908, September 26, 1908; *La Vie Au Grand Air,* Summer 1908.

203 *"individuality":* *Washington Post,* October 10, 1908.

203 *"Every day there is a crowd":* Kelly, ed., *Miracle at Kitty Hawk,* 323.

204 *To avoid the embarrassment of having her long skirts: Dayton Journal,* November 1, 1908.

204 *"Mr. Wright, with both hands grasping the levers":* Crouch, *The Bishop's Boys,* 382.

205 *"Queen Margherita of Italy was in the crowd":* Wilbur to Orville, October 9, 1908, Papers of Wilbur and Orville Wright, LOC.

205 *"M. Wright appeared a bit too rough":* See Peyrey, *Premiers Les Hommes-Oiseaux.*

206 *"How I long for Kitty Hawk!":* Wilbur to Octave Chanute, November 10, 1908, McFarland, ed., *The Papers of Wilbur and Orville Wright,* Vol. 2, 935.

206 *In his honor the Aéro-Club de France: New York Times,* November 6, 1908.

206 *"I will have quite a collection":* Wilbur to Reuchlin Wright, October 26, 1908, Papers of Wilbur and Orville Wright, LOC.

206 *"They are really almost the only ones":* Wilbur to Reuchlin Wright, October 26, 1908, Papers of Wilbur and Orville Wright, LOC.

206 *The Aéro-Club de France's banquet took place: New York Times,* November 6, 1908; *Paris Herald,* November 6, 1908; *L'Aérophile,* November 6, 1908.

206 *menus at each of their places:* Wright Family Scrapbooks, Papers of Wilbur and Orville Wright, LOC.

207 *"hearty speech of congratulation": New York Times,* November 6, 1908.

207 *"For myself and my brother":* Wilbur Wright to Aéro Club de France, November 5, 1908, McFarland, ed., *The Papers of Wilbur and Orville Wright,* Vol. 2, 934.

208 *"He knows the little chores": L'Aérophile,* November 15, 1908.

209 *"I know that you love 'Old Steele' ":* Wilbur to Katharine, December 7, 1908, Papers of Wilbur and Orville Wright, LOC.

209 *"Brother and I are coming over":* Katharine to Wilbur, December 10, 1908, ibid.

210 *"It is quite a wonderful toy": Chicago Tribune,* January 10, 1909.

210 *On the day of the event, December 31:* Renstrom, *Wilbur and Orville Wright,* 20.

210 *"But I could not afford to lose the Michelin Prize":* Wilbur to Bishop Wright, January 1, 1909, McFarland, ed., *The Papers of Wilbur and Orville Wright,* Vol. 2, 948.

211 *"He informed me that the government had decided":* Ibid.

211 *On January 5, 1909, in New York:* Katharine to Bishop Wright, January 5, 1909, Papers of Wilbur and Orville Wright, LOC; *New York Herald,* January 6, 1909.

211 *"a sort of family reunion": New York Herald,* January 6, 1909.

211 *In their absence, Bishop Wright would be looked after:* Katharine to Bishop Wright, January 8, 1909, Papers of Wilbur and Orville Wright, LOC.

211 *Except for one rough day at sea:* Ibid.

211 *"pleasant company":* Ibid.

211 *"in silk hat and evening clothes":* Katharine to Bishop Wright, January 13, 1909, ibid.

212 *large bouquet of American Beauty roses:* Ibid.

212 *the three Wrights sat up talking:* Ibid.
212 *The following day the brothers met for lunch:* Ibid.
212 *"a pretty woman and very stylish":* Ibid.
212 *Orville asked her also to tell:* Ibid.
212 *En route, at about seven A.M., the train crashed:* Katharine to Bishop Wright, January 17, 1909, ibid.
212 *"not even scratched":* Ibid.
212 *Grand Hôtel Gassion:* Ibid.
213 *"I never saw anything":* Ibid.
213 *Wilbur would not be staying at the hotel:* Katharine to Bishop Wright, January 20, 1909; Wilbur to Bishop Wright, March 1, 1909, ibid.
213 *The chef did not last long:* Katharine to Bishop Wright, February 1, 1909, ibid.
213 *"simply gone mad about aviation":* Paris Herald, January 19, 1909.
213 *"the whole show":* Katharine to Lorin Wright, January 24, 1909, Papers of Wilbur and Orville Wright, LOC.
213 *"Every time we make a move":* Ibid.
214 *At a luncheon at their hotel, their host:* Katharine to Bishop Wright, February 8, 1909, ibid.
214 *"We all liked them very much":* Ibid.
214 *"rousing good time":* Katharine to Bishop Wright, February 11, 1909, ibid.
214 *Arthur Balfour, former prime minister of England:* Paris Herald, February 12, 1909.
214 *"I'm so glad that young man":* Kelly, The Wright Brothers, 253.
215 *One of those helping her with her French:* Katharine to Bishop Wright, February 22, 1909, Papers of Wilbur and Orville Wright, LOC.
215 *On those days when there was no sun:* Katharine to Bishop Wright, January 20, 1909; Katharine to Lorin Wright, January 24, 1909, ibid.
215 *French army lieutenant had charged Wilbur in a divorce case:* Dayton Herald, January 8, 1909; Lorin Wright to Katharine and Orville, January 10, 1909, Papers of Wilbur and Orville Wright, LOC; Wilbur to Lorin Wright, January 24, 1909, Wright Family Papers, Wright State University, Dayton, Ohio.
215 *"Well, if I talked":* H. Massac, Flying, March 6, 1909.
216 *"The masters of the aeroplane":* "The American Girl Whom All Europe Is Watching," World Magazine, no date, Wright Family Scrapbooks, Papers of Wilbur and Orville Wright, LOC.
216 *"Who was it who gave them new hope":* Ibid.
216 *"Like most American girls":* Dayton Journal, April 13, 1909.
216 *all Pau was "AGOG":* Paris Herald, February 3, 1909.
216 *Virtually every day but Sunday:* Ibid., February 4, 1909.
217 *"If we have to alter":* Motor News, June 8, 1912.
217 *devoted to training the Comte de Lambert:* Ibid., February 19, 1909; Katharine to Bishop Wright, February 1, 1909, Papers of Wilbur and Orville Wright, LOC.
217 *"Southern sunny France is a delusion":* Katharine to Bishop Wright, February 16, 1909, ibid.
217 *She was most happily surprised:* Paris Herald, February 16, 1909; Washington Post, February 16, 1909; Cincinnati Enquirer, March 14, 1909; ibid.
217 *"I don't know exactly how a bird feels":* Dayton Daily News, May 13, 1909.
218 *"Oh, I dare say that can be arranged":* Kelly, The Wright Brothers, 252.
218 *"I understand a great deal now":* Katharine to Bishop Wright, February 22, 1909, Papers of Wilbur and Orville Wright, LOC.

218 *"A year in France and not understand"*: Bishop Wright to Katharine, February 19, 1909, ibid.

218 *"not entirely himself"*: Wilbur to Bishop Wright, March 1, 1909, ibid.

218 *"not a bit lonely"*: Bishop Wright to Katharine, February 22, 1909, ibid.

218 *He had begun work on an autobiography:* Ibid.

219 *"place of pilgrimage"*: *Paris Herald*, February 23, 1909.

219 *Afterward, as his entourage:* Ibid.; Katharine to Bishop Wright, February 22, 1909, Papers of Wilbur and Orville Wright, LOC.

219 *"I have seen what you can do"*: *Paris Herald*, February 21, 1909.

219 *Wilbur at once consented:* Ibid.

219 *"It was great"*: Katharine to Bishop Wright, February 25, 1909, Papers of Wilbur and Orville Wright, LOC.

219 *Not long after that she would take off:* Ibid., February 28, 1909.

219 *"too much excitement"*: Katharine to Bishop Wright, March 14, 1909, ibid.

219 *"royal weather"*: *Paris Herald*, March 19, 1909.

220 *a small bunch of shamrock:* Ibid.

220 *He was taken first to see the Flyer:* Ibid.

220 *"bated breath"*: *World Magazine*, no date, Wright Family Scrapbook, Papers of Wilbur and Orville Wright, LOC.

221 *"Most of us can remember when the automobile"*: Waco, Texas, *Times-Herald*, April 25, 1909.

222 *"Scores of inventors"*: *New York Times*, April 25, 1909.

222 *A few days later the three Wrights went to Le Mans:* Katharine to Bishop Wright, March 28, 1909, Papers of Wilbur and Orville Wright, LOC.

222 *she was the only woman ever invited:* Katharine to Bishop Wright, April 2, 1909, ibid.

222 *"You ought to seen it"*: Katharine to Wilbur, April 3, 1909, ibid.

222 *"They drank a champagne in your honor!"*: Katharine to Bishop Wright, April 2, 1909, ibid.

222 *Katharine and Orville left for Rome:* Katharine to Bishop Wright, April 11, 1909, ibid.

223 *Hart Berg had found rooms:* Ibid.

223 *"I was homesick for the first time"*: Ibid.

223 *"very anxious to come home"*: Katharine to Bishop Wright, April 14, 1909, ibid.

223 *"We would appreciate a good clean bathtub"*: Katharine to Bishop Wright, April 11, 1909, ibid.

223 *"The waiters at the table are so dirty"*: Katharine to Bishop Wright, April 14, 1909, ibid.

224 *"They always come at such unearthly hours"*: Katharine to Bishop Wright, April 20, 1909, ibid.

224 *A lunch in honor of the three Wrights:* Ibid.

224 *"improves all the time"*: Katharine to Bishop Wright, April 14, 1909, ibid.

224 *They would be heading to London:* *New York Times*, May 2, 1909.

224 *After two days in London:* *Paris Herald*, May 4, 1909, May 5, 1909.

224 *"We do not forget"*: Wilbur Wright to Léon Bollée, February 11, 1909, Papers of Wilbur and Orville Wright, LOC.

11. Causes for Celebration

PAGE

227 *After a rousing welcome at New York: New York Times,* May 9, 1909, May 12, 1909; *Paris Herald,* May 12, 1909.

227 *"Oh, there's Daddy":* "Bishop Wright Kisses Sons as They Arrive," *Dayton News,* no date, Wright Family Scrapbooks, Papers of Wilbur and Orville Wright, LOC.

228 *"Hello, Tom!":* "Strewn Carnations in Aviators' Path," ibid.

228 *"bronzed and hard":* *Paris Herald,* May 12, 1909.

228 *"I'm so glad to get home":* *Dayton Journal,* May 14, 1909.

228 *Outside the crowd grew to more than ten thousand:* Milton Wright, *Diaries, 1857–1917,* 693.

229 *"real celebration":* *Dayton Daily News,* June 16, 1909.

229 *"beehive of industry":* *Dayton Herald,* May 13, 1909.

229 *Shortly after the lunch the entire party: New York Times,* June 11, 1909; *Washington Post,* June 11, 1909; *Paris Herald,* June 11, 1909.

230 *"I esteem it a great honor": New York Times,* June 11, 1909.

230 *The whole story of America:* Ibid., June 19, 1909.

230 *On Main Street a "Court of Honor": Dayton Daily News,* June 16, 1909.

231 *"Everywhere is the tri-colored bunting":* Ibid.

231 *"It is a wonderful lesson":* Ibid.

232 *The following morning, Thursday, June 17:* Ibid., June 17, 1909, June 18, 1909.

232 *A line of eighty automobiles: Dayton Journal,* June 19, 1909.

232 *There were laudatory speeches:* Ibid., June 18, 1909, June 19, 1909.

232 *"We have met this day":* Ibid., June 19, 1909.

233 *"9 A.M.—Left their work in the aeroplane shop": New York Times,* June 18, 1909.

233 *Less than forty-eight hours later: Dayton Journal,* June 21, 1909.

234 *It was six-thirty the extremely warm evening of June 26: Washington Herald,* June 29, 1909; *Chicago Inter-Ocean,* June 19, 1909; *Washington Evening Star,* June 29, 1909; *Dayton Herald,* July 8, 1909.

234 *"pawing the ground": Washington Herald,* June 29, 1909.

234 *The Senate had adjourned:* Ibid.

234 *"open sesame to the Treasury vaults":* Ibid.

234 *His hands and face were grimy: Washington Post,* June 29, 1909.

234 *"His coat was buttoned tightly": Washington Herald,* June 29, 1909.

234 *The brothers were waiting:* Ibid.

234 *"She's blowing at a 16-mile clip": Washington Post,* June 29, 1909.

235 *"Take her back to the shed": Washington Herald,* June 29, 1909.

235 *"There is always an element": Washington Post,* June 29, 1909.

235 *"utter immunity of the two brothers": Washington Herald,* June 29, 1909.

235 *"like pallbearers":* Ibid.

235 *"I'm damned if I don't admire": Washington Post,* June 29, 1909.

235 *Wilbur had "no quarrels": Washington Herald,* June 30, 1909.

235 *The crowd, noticeably smaller:* Ibid.

236 *"If it's new, you have to get used to it": Chicago Inter-Ocean,* June 30, 1909.

236 *"all manner of birds":* Bishop Wright's diary, June 30, 1909, Milton Wright, *Diaries, 1857–1917,* 696.

236 *Another day, when Orville took off again: New York Times,* July 1, 1909; *Washington Evening Star,* July 1, 1909; *Dayton Journal,* July 1, 1909.

236 *Then, on July 2:* Undated, unsourced news article in Wright Family Scrapbooks, circa July 1909, Papers of Wilbur and Orville Wright, LOC; *Washington Herald,* July 3, 1909.

236 *Wilbur, who, seeing a photographer:* Ibid.

237 *faster than Wilbur had ever flown:* Katharine to Bishop Wright, July 22, 1909, Papers of Wilbur and Orville Wright, LOC.

237 *"You have had all the details from the papers":* Hart O. Berg to Wilbur and Orville Wright, July 26, 1909, ibid.

237 *"He told me that he had never been so thrown about":* Ibid.

237 *From Washington, Katharine wrote:* Katharine to Bishop Wright, July 27, 1909, ibid.

238 *"I know him well":* New York Times, July 26, 1909.

238 *All the same, throughout France:* Ibid., July 27, 1909.

238 *An estimated eight thousand spectators:* Katharine Wright postcard to Bishop Wright, July 19, 1909, ibid.

238 *On Friday, July 30: Paris Herald,* July 31, 1909.

238 *The price to be paid by the department was $30,000: New York Times,* August 1, 1909.

239 *"Orv finished the Fort Myer business":* Katharine Wright to Agnes Beck, August 5, 1909, Papers of Wilbur and Orville Wright, LOC.

239 *"congress of aviators":* Chicago Tribune, July 4, 1909.

239 *they "had the frankness of schoolboys":* Roseberry, *Glenn Curtiss,* 354; Kelly, *The Wright Brothers,* 289.

241 *"So I have gone back to my old plan":* Wilbur to Orville, September 18, 1909, Papers of Wilbur and Orville Wright, LOC.

242 *"I have been here about a week":* Wilbur to Katharine, September 26, 1909, ibid.

243 *Battery Park at the tip of Manhattan was thick: New York Evening Telegram,* September 29, 1909.

243 *"Once his great aeroplane, so near the horizon": New York Evening Sun,* September 29, 1909.

244 Harper's Weekly: *Harper's Weekly,* October 9, 1909.

244 *"Goes pretty well, Charlie": New York Herald,* September 30, 1909.

244 *The morning of Monday, October 4: New York Journal,* October 4, 1909; *New York Evening Sun,* October 4, 1909.

244 *a tiny American flag fixed to the rudder: New York Journal,* October 4, 1909.

245 *"wonderful Wilbur Wright": New York Evening Telegram,* September 29, 1909.

245 *"I went to a height just a little above the ferryboats": New York Journal,* October 4, 1909.

245 *"awful noise": New York Evening Telegram,* September 29, 1909.

245 *"I think I came back":* Ibid.

246 *"I was staring with both eyes":* Ibid.

246 *"A man who works":* Ibid.

246 *"flew like a cannon ball":* Ibid.

246 *"It's a darn good thing":* "Bird Men Thrill Gotham," uncited news article dated September 30, 1909, Wright Family Scrapbooks, Papers of Wilbur and Orville Wright, LOC.

247 *"We must get up clear of the belt of disturbed air": Scientific American,* October 23, 1909.

247 *"On Monday I made a flight up the Hudson":* Wilbur to Bishop Wright, October 7, 1909, Papers of Wilbur and Orville Wright, LOC.

247 *The Comte de Lambert, having told almost no one:* London *Times,* October 19, 1909; *New York Times,* October 19, 1909.

248 *"And what do you think happened":* Edith Wharton to Sara Norton, October 20, 1909, Wharton, *Letters of Edith Wharton,* 192.

248 *What she had neglected to say:* London *Times*, October 19, 1909.

248 *There also, to his great surprise, were Orville and Katharine:* Ibid.

248 *"I am only the jockey":* New York Herald, October 19, 1909.

249 *"It is our view that morally":* Wilbur to Octave Chanute, January 20, 1910, McFarland, ed., *The Papers of Wilbur and Orville Wright*, Vol. 2, 979.

249 *"I am afraid, my friend":* Octave Chanute to Wilbur, January 23, 1910, ibid., 981.

249 *Chanute, had "turned up":* Ibid.

249 *found Chanute's letter "incredible":* Wilbur to Octave Chanute, January 29, 1910, ibid., 982.

250 *"you are the only person":* Ibid., 983.

250 *"mere pupils and dependents":* Ibid., 984.

250 *"Neither in 1901":* Ibid., 982–83.

250 *"If anything can be done":* Ibid., 986.

250 *"My brother and I do not form":* Wilbur to Octave Chanute, April 28, 1910, ibid., 991.

251 *"I hope, upon my return":* Octave Chanute to Wilbur Wright, May 14, 1910, ibid., 995.

251 *"They are the imperturbable":* Ruhl, "Up in the Air with Orville," *Collier's Weekly*, July 2, 1910.

251 *"Pau was a mighty interesting place":* Ibid.

252 *"a highly significant fact":* New York Times, April 8, 1910.

252 *"The insistence of Professor Bell":* Christian Science Monitor, April 8, 1910.

252 *Wednesday, May 25, 1910:* Bishop Wright's diary, 1910, McFarland ed., *The Papers of Wilbur and Orville Wright*, Vol. 2, 996; Milton Wright, *Diaries, 1857–1917*, 714; Dayton Daily News, May 26, 1910.

252 *"One minute he would be grazing":* Dayton Daily News, May 26, 1910.

253 *"Higher, Orville, higher!":* See McFarland, ed., *The Papers of Wilbur and Orville Wright*, Vol. 2, 996, footnote 5.

Epilogue

PAGE

255 *"When we think what we might have accomplished":* Crouch, *The Bishop's Boys*, 447.

255 *His writings:* Wilbur Wright, *Aeronautics*, January 1911, 3–4, 35, as cited in Jakab and Young, eds., *The Published Writings of Wilbur and Orville Wright*, 169.

256 *"come home white":* McMahon, *The Wright Brothers*, 266.

256 *Wilbur's one known expression:* Ibid.

256 *dictated his will:* A copy of Wilbur Wright's will is on deposit in the Papers of Wilbur and Orville Wright at the LOC.

256 *"Wilbur is no better":* Milton Wright, *Diaries, 1857–1917*, 748.

256 *"sinking":* Ibid., 749.

256 *"A short life, full of consequences":* Ibid.

256 *a thousand telegrams:* Crouch, *The Bishop's Boys*, 449.

256 *According to one Dayton paper:* Ibid.

257 *"Wilbur is dead and buried!":* Milton Wright, *Diaries, 1857–1917*, 750.

257 *the three of them moved:* Ibid., 784.

257 *Orville treated them to a summer-long vacation:* Ibid., 810–13.

257 *bought an island:* Miller, ed., *Wright Reminiscences*, 137; Crouch, *The Bishop's Boys*, 478.

257 *One October Saturday he marched:* Milton Wright, *Diaries, 1857–1917,* October 24, 1914, 792.
258 *In September of 1910:* Renstrom, *Wilbur and Orville Wright,* 29.
258 *A few weeks later:* Ibid.
258 *experimenting with a new Wright hydroplane:* May–June 1914, ibid., 34.
258 *In 1913, within two months:* June–July 1913, ibid., 119.
258 *he barely escaped being killed:* August 20, 1914, ibid., 120.
258 *Orville had hoped:* Jakab and Young, eds., *The Published Writings of Wilbur and Orville Wright,* 218–19.
259 *In his will, Wilbur had left:* Miller, ed., *Wright Reminiscences,* 63; Crouch, *The Bishop's Boys,* 450.
259 *His total wealth at the time of his death:* Roach, *The Wright Company: From Invention to Industry,* 202, footnote 161, quoting an article in the *Dayton Herald,* "Inventory Puts Wright Estate at $1,067,105.73," March 18, 1948; Crouch, *The Bishop's Boys,* 525.
259 *"All the money anyone needs":* Kelly, *The Wright Brothers,* 5.
259 *"Professor Samuel P. Langley":* Crouch, *The Bishop's Boys,* 487; Kelly, *The Wright Brothers,* 311.
259 *Before the aerodrome was sent back:* Kelly, *The Wright Brothers,* 311–15.
259 *Earlier, when he and Wilbur:* Ibid., 307.
259 *In 1928, Orville sent the 1903 Flyer:* Ibid., 308.
259 *"to the Wrights belongs the credit":* Ibid.
260 *In an article titled:* Orville Wright, "The Mythical Whitehead Flight," *U.S. Air Services,* August 1945, 9, as cited in Jakab and Young, eds., *The Published Writings of Wilbur and Orville Wright,* 187–88.
260 *Lindbergh made a point of coming to Dayton: New York Times,* June 23, 1927; *Chicago Tribune,* June 23, 1927; see also telegram from Orville Wright congratulating Lindbergh on his flight and extending invitation to visit Dayton, June 10, 1927, Papers of Wilbur and Orville Wright, LOC.
260 *"We dared to hope we had invented":* Kelly, "Orville Wright Takes Look Back on 40 Years Since First Flight; Despite Air War, Has No Regrets," *St. Louis Post-Dispatch,* November 7, 1943; Jakab and Young, eds., *The Published Writings of Wilbur and Orville Wright,* 261–62; Miller, *Wright Reminiscences,* 65–66.
261 *"polite almost to a fault":* Crouch, *The Bishop's Boys,* 196.
262 *Orville was also known to drive:* Miller, ed., *Wright Reminiscences,* 16–17; Crouch, *The Bishop's Boys,* 513.
262 *On July 20, 1969, when Neil Armstrong:* Hansen, *First Man: The Life of Neil A. Armstrong,* 527.

BIBLIOGRAPHY

Manuscript and Archival Sources

Collections of the Dayton Aviation Heritage National Historical Park, Dayton, Ohio.

Local History Division, Dayton Metropolitan Library, Dayton, Ohio.

Benson Ford Research Library, Henry Ford Museum, Greenfield Village, Dearborn, Michigan.

Fred C. Kelly Papers, Special Collections Research Center, Syracuse University Libraries, Syracuse, New York.

Byron Newton Papers, Oberlin College, Oberlin, Ohio.

Outer Banks Historical Center, Manteo, North Carolina.

Wright Family Papers, Special Collections and Archives Department, Wright State University, Dayton, Ohio.

Milton Wright Collection, United Brethren Historical Center, Huntington University, Huntington, Indiana.

Papers of Wilbur and Orville Wright, including family correspondence of Bishop Milton and Katharine Wright, Library of Congress (LOC), Washington, DC.

Books

Barfield, Rodney. *Seasoned by Salt: A Historical Album of the Outer Banks.* Chapel Hill: University of North Carolina Press, 1995.

Bernstein, Mark. *Grand Eccentrics, Turning the Century: Dayton and the Invention of America.* Wilmington, OH: Orange Frazer Press, 1996.

———. *Wright Brothers' Home Days Celebration 1909: Dayton Salutes Wilbur, Orville, and Itself.* Dayton, Ohio: Carillon Historical Park, 2003.

Chant, Christopher. *A Century of Triumph: The History of Aviation.* New York: Free Press, 2002.

Combs, Harry, and Martin Caidin. *Kill Devil Hill: Discovering the Secrets of the Wright Brothers.* Boston: Houghton Mifflin, 1979.

Cox, James Middleton. *Journey Through My Years.* Macon, GA: Mercer University Press, 2004.

Crouch, Tom D. *The Bishop's Boys: A Life of Wilbur and Orville Wright.* New York: W. W. Norton, 1989.

——. *A Dream of Wings: Americans and the Airplane, 1825–1905*. New York: W. W. Norton, 2002.

——. *Wings: A History of Aviation from Kites to the Space Age*. Washington, DC: Smithsonian Institution, 2003.

Dalton, Curt. *Dayton*. Charleston, SC: Arcadia, 2006.

——. *With Malice Toward All: The Lethal Life of Dr. Oliver C. Haugh*. Dayton, OH: Create Space, 2013.

DeBlieu, Jan. *Wind: How the Flow of Air Has Shaped Life, Myth, and the Land*. Berkeley, CA, Counterpoint, 1998.

Deines, Ann, ed. *Wilbur and Orville Wright: A Handbook of Facts*. Fort Washington, PA: Eastern National, 2001.

Downing, Sarah. *Hidden History of the Outer Banks*. Charleston, SC: History Press, 2013.

Drury, Augustus. *History of the City of Dayton and Montgomery County, Ohio*. Vol. I. Dayton, OH: S. J. Clarke, 1909.

DuFour, H. R. *Charles D. Taylor: 1868–1956: The Wright Brothers Mechanician*. Dayton, OH: Prime Digital Printing, 1997.

Felleman, Hazel, ed. *The Best Loved Poems of the American People*. New York: Doubleday, 1936.

Fiske-Bates, Charlotte, ed. *Cambridge Book of Poetry and Song*. New York: Thomas Y. Crowell, 1882.

Gibbs-Smith, Charles Harvard. *Aviation: An Historical Survey from Its Origins to the End of the Second World War*. London: Her Majesty's Stationery Office, 1970.

——. *The Rebirth of European Aviation*. London: Her Majesty's Stationery Office, 1974.

——. *The Wright Brothers: A Brief Account of Their Work, 1899–1911*. London: Her Majesty's Stationery Office, 1963.

Hansen, James R. *First Man: The Life of Neil A. Armstrong*. New York: Simon & Schuster, 2012.

Heppenheimer, T. A. *First Flight: The Wright Brothers and the Invention of the Airplane*. Hoboken, NJ: Wiley, 2003.

Herlihy, David V. *Bicycle: The History*. New Haven: Yale University Press, 2004.

History of Medina County of Ohio. Chicago: Baskin & Battey, 1881.

Honious, Ann. *What Dreams We Have: The Wright Brothers and Their Hometown of Dayton, Ohio*. Fort Washington, PA: Eastern National, 2003.

Howard, Fred. *Wilbur and Orville: A Biography of the Wright Brothers*. New York: Alfred A. Knopf, 1987.

Howells, William Dean. *Stories of Ohio*. New York: American Book Company, 1897.

Hughes, Thomas P. *American Genesis: A Century of Invention and Technological Enthusiasm, 1870–1970*. Chicago: University of Chicago Press, 2004.

Ingersoll, Robert G. *The Works of Robert G. Ingersoll*. Vol. 1. New York: Dresden Publishing Company, 1901.

Jakab, Peter L. *Visions of a Flying Machine: The Wright Brothers and the Process of Invention*. Washington, DC: Smithsonian Books, 1990.

Jakab, Peter L., and Rick Young, eds. *The Published Writings of Wilbur and Orville Wright*. Washington, DC: Smithsonian Books, 2000.

Keefer, Kathryn. *The Wright Cycle Shop Historical Report*. Benson Ford Research Library, Henry Ford Museum, Greenfield Village, Dearborn, MI: Henry Ford Library, Summer 2004.

Keenan, Jack. *The Uncertain Trolley: A History of the Dayton, Springfield and Urbana Electric Railway.* Fletcher, OH: Cam-Tech Publishing, 1992.

Kelly, Fred C. *The Wright Brothers: A Biography.* New York: Dover, 1989.

———, ed. *How We Invented the Airplane: An Illustrated History by Orville Wright.* New York: Dover, 1953.

———, ed. *Miracle at Kitty Hawk: The Letters of Wilbur and Orville Wright.* New York: Da Capo, 2002.

Kinnane, Adrian. "The Crucible of Flight." Diss., Wright State University, 1982.

Lilienthal, Otto. *The Problem of Flying.* Washington, DC: U.S. Government Printing Office, 1894.

Loening, Grover. *Our Wings Grow Faster.* Garden City, NY: Doubleday, Doran, 1935.

Mackersey, Ian. *The Wright Brothers: The Remarkable Story of the Aviation Pioneers Who Changed the World.* London: Time Warner, 2003.

Marey, Etienne Jules. *Animal Mechanism: A Treatise on Terrestrial and Aerial Locomotion.* New York: D. Appleton, 1874.

Maurer, Richard. *The Wright Sister: Katharine Wright and Her Famous Brothers.* Brookfield, CT: Roaring Brook Press, 2003.

McFarland, Marvin W., ed. *The Papers of Wilbur and Orville Wright: Including the Chanute-Wright Letters and Other Papers of Octave Chanute.* Vol. 1, 1899–1905, and Vol. 2, 1906–1948. New York: McGraw-Hill, 1953.

McMahon, Robert. *The Wright Brothers: Fathers of Flight.* Boston: Little, Brown, 1930.

Miller, Ivonette Wright, ed. *Wright Reminiscences.* Wright-Patterson Air Force Base, OH: U.S. Air Force Museum, 1978.

Moolman, Valerie. *The Road to Kitty Hawk.* Alexandria, VA: Time-Life Books, 1980.

The Ohio Guide. Columbus, OH: Ohio State Archaeological and Historical Society, 1940.

Parramore, Thomas C. *Triumph at Kitty Hawk: The Wright Brothers and Powered Flight.* Raleigh: North Carolina Division of Archives and History, 1993.

Pettigrew, J. Bell. *Animal Locomotion; or Walking, Swimming, and Flying, with a Dissertation on Aeronautics.* London: Henry S. King, 1874.

Peyrey, François. *Premiers Les Hommes-Oiseaux.* Paris: H. Guiton, 1908.

Renstrom, Arthur George. *Wilbur and Orville Wright: A Re-Issue of a Chronology Commemorating the Hundredth Anniversary of the Birth of Orville Wright, August 19, 1871.* Washington, DC: NASA, 2003.

Roach, Edward J. *The Wright Company: From Invention to Industry.* Athens: Ohio University Press, 2014.

Root, A. I. *An Eyewitness Account of Early American Beekeeping: The Autobiography of A. I. Root.* Medina, OH: A. I. Root Company, 1984.

Roseberry, C. R. *Glenn Curtiss: Pioneer of Flight.* Syracuse: Syracuse University Press, 1991.

Selections from the Writings of the Wright Brothers. Privately printed for the Orville Wright Dinner, 1918.

Short, Simine. *Locomotive to Aeromotive: Octave Chanute and the Transportation Revolution.* Urbana: University of Illinois Press, 2011.

Sproul, Anna. *The Wright Brothers: The Birth of Modern Aviation.* Woodbridge, CT: Blackbirch Press, 1999.

Stick, David. *An Outer Banks Reader.* Chapel Hill: University of North Carolina Press, 1998.

———. *The Outer Banks of North Carolina, 1594–1958.* Chapel Hill: University of North Carolina Press, 1958.

Sweetman, John. *Cavalry of the Clouds: Air War Over Europe, 1914–1918.* Gloucestershire, UK: History Press, 2010.

Tise, Larry E. *Conquering the Sky: The Secret Flights of the Wright Brothers at Kitty Hawk.* New York: Palgrave Macmillan, 2009.

———. *Hidden Images: Discovering Details in the Wright Brothers Kitty Hawk Photographs.* Charleston, SC: History Press, 2005.

Tobin, James. *To Conquer the Air: The Wright Brothers and the Great Race for Flight.* New York: Free Press, 2003.

Walsh, John Evangelist. *One Day at Kitty Hawk: The Untold Story of the Wright Brothers and the Airplane.* New York: Thomas Y. Crowell, 1975.

Wells, H. G. *The War in the Air.* New York: Penguin, 2007.

Wharton, Edith. *Letters of Edith Wharton.* Edited by R. W. B. Lewis and Nancy Lewis. New York: Charles Scribner's Sons, 1988.

Wohl, Robert. *A Passion for Wings: Aviation and the Western Imagination, 1908–1918.* New Haven: Yale University Press, 1994.

Wolfram, Walt, and Natalie Schilling-Estes. *Hoi Toide on the Outer Banks: The Story of the Ocracoke Brogue.* Chapel Hill: University of North Carolina Press, 1997.

Wright, Milton. *Diaries, 1857–1917.* Dayton, OH: Wright State University Libraries, 1999.

Articles

Buist, H. Massac. "The Human Side of Flying." *Flight Magazine,* March 6, 1909, and March 13, 1909.

Coles, Thomas R. "The Wright Boys as a Schoolmate Knew Them." *Out West Magazine,* January 1910.

Delagrange, Léon. "Impressions sur L'Aéroplane Wright," *L'Illustration,* August 15, 1908.

Grimes, E. B. "Man May Now Fly at Will." *Technical World Magazine,* Vol. 5, June 1906.

Kelly, Fred C. "Orville Wright Takes Look Back on 40 Years Since First Flight; Despite Air War, Has No Regrets." *St. Louis Post-Dispatch,* November 7, 1943.

"Leonardo da Vinci as Aviation Engineer." *Scientific American Monthly,* April 1921.

Meader, J. R. "Miss Katharine Wright." *Human Life,* June 1909.

Mouillard, Louis Pierre. "The Empire of the Air: An Ornithological Essay on the Flight of Birds," extracted and translated from *L'Empire de l'Air: Essai d'Ornithologie appliquee a l'Aviation.* G. Masson: Paris, 1881.

Newcomb, Simon. "Is the Airship Coming?" *McClure's Magazine,* September 17, 1901.

Prendergast, James. "The Bicycle for Women." *American Journal of Obstetrics and Diseases of Women and Children,* August 1, 1896.

Root, A. I. "Our Homes." *Gleanings in Bee Culture,* September 1, 1904, and January 1, 1905.

Ruhl, Arthur. "History at Kill Devil Hill." *Collier's Weekly,* May 30, 1908.

———. "Up in the Air with Orville." *Collier's Weekly,* July 2, 1910.

Saunders, William O. "Then We Quit Laughing: Interview with John T. Daniels." *Collier's Weekly,* September 17, 1927.

Stimson, Dr. Richard. "Paul Laurence Dunbar: The Wright Brothers' Friend." *The Wright Stories,* www.wrightstories.com.

Taylor, Charles E., as told to Robert S. Ball. "My Story of the Wright Brothers." *Collier's Weekly*, December 25, 1948.

Tobin, James. "The First Witness: Amos Root at Huffman Prairie." Presentation at Ann Arbor, Michigan, September 28, 2001.

Vernon. "The Flying Man." *McClure's Magazine*, Vol. 3, 1894.

Weiller, M. Lazare. "De Montgolfier a Wilbur Wright," from a report of the 52nd meeting of La Societe Archeologique le Vieux Papier. December 22, 1908.

Wright, Orville, as told to Leslie Quick. "How I Learned to Fly." *Boys' Life*, September 1914.

Wright, Orville, and Wilbur Wright. "Tribute to Our Mother." *West Side News*, July 3, 1889.

———. "The Wright Brothers' Aeroplane." *Century Magazine*, No. 5, September 1908.

Wright, Wilbur. "Experiments and Observations in Soaring Flight." Presented before the Western Society of Engineers, June 24, 1903, *Journal of the Western Society of Engineers*, August 1903.

———. "Remarks given by Wilbur Wright." Twenty-fourth Annual Banquet of the Ohio Society of New York, January 10, 1910, *Reports of Proceedings, 1910*, New York: Ohio Society of New York, 1910.

Newspapers and Journals

Aero Club of America Bulletin

Aero Club of America News

Aeronautical Journal

Aeronautics

L'Aérophile

Albuquerque Journal-Democrat

Atlanta Constitution

L'Auto

The Auto: The Motorist's Pictorial

Autocar

Automotor Journal

Chicago Chronicle

Chicago Daily News

Chicago Examiner

Chicago Inter-Ocean

Chicago Tribune

Christian Science Monitor

Cincinnati Enquirer

Cleveland *Plain Dealer*

Collier's Weekly

Dayton Daily News

Dayton Evening News

Dayton Herald

Dayton Journal

Dayton Press

Echo de Paris
Evening Item
Flight Magazine
Flyer
Gleanings in Bee Culture
Harper's Weekly
L'Illustration
London *Daily Mail*
London *Daily Mirror*
London *Times*
Le Matin
Medina County Gazette
Milwaukee Journal
Motor Car Journal
New York Evening Sun
New York Evening Telegram
New York Journal
New York Sun
New York Times
New York World
Paris Daily Mail
Paris Herald
Le Petit Journal
Philadelphia Inquirer
San Francisco Chronicle
Scientific American
St. Louis Post-Dispatch
U.S. Air Services
La Vie Au Grand Air
Waco, Texas, *Times-Herald*
Washington Evening Star
Washington Herald
Washington Post
Washington Times
West Side News
World Magazine

ILLUSTRATION CREDITS

Part title images: *L'Empire du L'Aire* by Louis-Pierre Mouillard.

Frontis, 1–4, 7, 8, 10–12, 14, 17, 20, 22, 35, 39, 41, 49, 56, 57, 59, 61, 62, 68–71, 74, 75, 77, 81: Courtesy of Special Collections and Archives, Wright State University.

5, 6, 18, 24, 27, 31, 33, 34, 36, 38, 44, 48, 54, 63–65, 72, 73, 78: Prints and Photographs Division, Library of Congress.

9: Map Division, Library of Congress.

13: Courtesy Curt Dalton, Dayton, Ohio.

15, 21, 32, 47, 52, 53, 55, 60, 66, 67: Papers of Wilbur and Orville Wright, Library of Congress.

16: From the NCR Archive Dayton History, Dayton, Ohio.

19, 40: Courtesy, Nick Engler, Wright Brothers Aeroplane Company.

23: Local History Room, Dayton Metropolitan Library, Dayton, Ohio.

25, 26, 37, 42, 45, 79, 80: National Air and Space Museum, Smithsonian Institution, Washington, D.C.

28: NASA Langley Research Center.

29: Smithsonian Institution Archives, Washington, D.C.

30: Courtesy Division of Publications, Harpers Ferry Center, National Park Service, U.S. Department of the Interior.

43: Courtesy London Science Museum, London, England.

50: Illustration by Michael Gellatly.

51: Manatee County Public Library Digital Collection, Bradenton, Florida.

58: Author's Collection.

76: Courtesy Edward Roach, Chief Historian, Dayton Aviation Heritage, National Historic Park, Dayton, Ohio.

INDEX

311